The English language
a historical introduction

CHARLES BARBER

Formerly Reader in English language and literature,
School of English, University of Leeds

CAMBRIDGE
UNIVERSITY PRESS

PUBLISHED BY THE PRESS SYNDICATE OF THE UNIVERSITY OF CAMBRIDGE
The Pitt Building, Trumpington Street, Cambridge, United Kingdom

CAMBRIDGE UNIVERSITY PRESS
The Edinburgh Building, Cambridge CB2 2RU, UK   www.cup.cam.ac.uk
40 West 20th Street, New York, NY 10011–4211, USA   www.cup.org
10 Stamford Road, Oakleigh, Melbourne 3166, Australia
Ruiz de Alarcón 13, 28014 Madrid, Spain

First published 1993
Reprinted 1994 (twice), 1995
Canto edition 2000

Printed in the United Kingdom at the University Press, Cambridge

Set in Photina 10/12pt

A catalogue record for this book is available from the British Library

Library of Congress Cataloguing in Publication data
Barber, Charles Laurence.
The English language : a historical introduction / Charles Barber.
    p.   cm. – (Cambridge approaches to linguistics)
Includes bibliographical references and index.
ISBN 0 521 78570 7 (paperback)
1. English language–History.   2. Historical linguistics.
I. Title.   II. Series
PE1075.B265   1993
420–dc20   92–18555   CIP

ISBN 0 521 78570 7 paperback

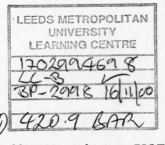
Cover illustration: 'A poor old MAN was driving a PIG TOE mARKet with a STRING tEYE-d TOE its LEG WHEN by SUM accident the PIG got loose. The MAN ran after him BUTT PIGgy 'sCAPEd...' now read on. Popular sheet, sold for sixpence (early nineteenth century). Mary Evans Picture Library.

The *English language: a historical introduction* is the ideal introductory textbook for all students of the English language, and essential reading also for students of linguistics and social studies. In a thoroughly updated version of his universally acclaimed *The story of language*, Charles Barber covers the history of the English language from its remote Indo-European origins to the present day. He provides substantial information about the English language at different periods, and introduces the main theoretical and technical concepts of historical linguistics, taking into account recent work in sociolinguistics and historical linguistics generally. Chapters on the nature of language and on language change are followed by a chronological survey, beginning in the Prehistoric age and working down from Anglo-Saxon times to the twentieth century. Topics covered include vocabulary, grammar, pronunciation, semantics, dialect, attitudes to language and English as a world language. Short passages of English are used to illustrate the state of the language in different periods and all over the world, in a range of contexts.

CHARLES BARBER was formerly Reader in English language and literature at the University of Leeds.

Canto is a paperback imprint which offers a broad range of titles, both classic and more recent, representing some of the best and most enjoyable of Cambridge publishing.

Contents

List of figures   *page*   vii
Preface to the Canto edition   viii
Preface to the first edition   x
Map   xii

 1 What is language?   1
 2 The flux of language   32
 3 The Indo-European languages   58
 4 The Germanic languages   81
 5 Old English   100
 6 Norsemen and Normans   127
 7 Middle English   151
 8 Early Modern English   175
 9 English in the scientific age   199
10 English as a world language   234
11 English today and tomorrow   262

Notes and suggestions for further reading   279
Bibliography   283
Index   292

Figures

1	Main speech-organs	*page*	3
2	Vowel diagram. Typical tongue positions for twelve vowels of present-day English (RP)		5
3	Vowel diagram. Six diphthongs of present-day English (RP)		7
4	Vowel diagram for the pure vowels of present-day English (RP)		14
5	British traffic signs		25
6	Two intersecting isoglosses		73
7	Britain before the Vikings		103
8	The main dialect-areas of Old English		105
9	The division of England between King Alfred and the Danes		129
10	The main dialect areas of Middle English		137
11	The Great Vowel Shift		192
12	Vowel diagram. The pure vowels of Standard English, c.1700		210

Preface to the Canto edition

I am delighted that this book now appears in the Canto series: these editions introduce ideas to a wider general public, and this has always been one of the aims of my book. Enormous numbers of ordinary people are fascinated by language, and have views about it, often strong. This book aims to provide material which will interest these general readers, and give them things to think about. Its central theme is the history of the English language, beginning with our remote Indo-European ancestors and working its way from Anglo-Saxon times down to the present day. Use is made of numerous short passages of English, to illustrate the varieties of the language in different times and places.

Many other languages are also given some attention. In the course of its history, English has been influenced by numerous languages, especially by Latin, by French, and by the Scandinavian languages. In more recent times, colonization and world-wide trade have led to contributions to its vocabulary by the speech of many countries – from Greenland to South Africa, from India to Mexico. Something is therefore said about such languages, but nevertheless the main theme of the book is the English language.

But while there is widespread interest in language, there is also a good deal of prejudice and ignorance about it. Much of the ignorance is due to an absence of technical knowledge about such things as phonology and grammar: it is difficult, for example, to write coherently about pronunciation without some grasp of phonetics. I try to overcome this difficulty by giving a clear and simple introduction to the basic concepts of linguistics, which are not really difficult to grasp. Books written for specialists in the field are often obscure to the general reader. On the other hand, many popular books about language avoid technicalities, thus limiting their range and usefulness. This book tries to bridge the gap, by building on a basic theoretical structure while remaining easily accessible to the ordinary reader. As for prejudices about language, many of these arise from an absence of historical knowledge, and I hope that this history of English will help to clear some of them away.

But at the same time, you should try to *enjoy* language. English is extremely rich and varied, and it can be great fun just to listen to the speech of different groups and different individuals – to the speech of Australians, Scots, Irishmen, West Indians, to the speech of different social classes and different occupations, and to the latest modish inventions of the young. I hope that this book will help you to have fun!

Leeds, 2000

Preface

This is a book about the history of the English language, from its remote Indo-European origins down to the present day. It is a complete revision and rewriting of an earlier work, *The Story of Language*, published in 1964 and now considerably out of date.

In carrying out this revision, I have been fortunate to have the constant help and advice of Dr Jean Aitchison, the General Editor of the series. Without her penetrating and invariably constructive suggestions it would have been a much poorer work. Other friends and colleagues who have given valuable help include Karin Barber, David Denison, Stanley Ellis, Joyce Hill, Colin Johnson, Göran Kjellmer, Rory McTurk, Peter Meredith, Karl Inge Sandred, and Loreto Todd. To all, my grateful thanks. For the errors and shortcomings which remain, I alone am to be held responsible.

I am also grateful to the publishers concerned for permission to quote the following copyright material: a passage of Nigerian pidgin from Loreto Todd's *Modern Englishes* (1990), by permission of Blackwell Publishers; two passages from G. N. Garmonsway's edition of Ælfric's *Colloquy* (1947), by permission of Methuen & Co.; a passage from the translation by B. Colgrave and R. A. B. Mynors of Bede's *Ecclesiastical History* (1969), two passages from Trevisa's translation of Higden's *Polychronicon* as reproduced in Kenneth Sisam's *Fourteenth Century Verse and Prose* (1921), and a passage from D. F. Bond's edition of *The Spectator* (1965), all by permission of Oxford University Press; and a passage from *The New English Bible* ©1970 by permission of Oxford and Cambridge

University Presses. In some cases the version given in the text differs in small ways from that of the source, for example by the insertion of length-marks over vowels or the adoption of emendations.

Throughout the work, use is made of the traditional division of England into counties, before the local government changes of the 1970s (see the map at the beginning of the book). This can hardly be avoided, since the traditional county framework has been used by the majority of earlier works, including such major ones as the Survey of English Dialects and the publications of the English Place Name Society.

Leeds, 1992
Amended 2000

The counties of England before 1974

Bedfordshire 25, Berkshire 34, Buckinghamshire 24, Cambridgeshire 20, Cheshire 7, Cornwall 30, Cumberland 2, Derbyshire 8, Devon 31, Dorset 35, Durham 3, Essex 28, Gloucestershire 22, Hampshire 36, Herefordshire 15, Hertfordshire 27, Huntingdonshire 19, Kent 39, Lancashire 5, Leicestershire 13, Lincolnshire 10, Middlesex 29, Norfolk 21, Northamptonshire 18, Northumberland 1, Nottinghamshire 9, Oxfordshire 23, Rutland 14, Shropshire 11, Somerset 32, Staffordshire 12, Suffolk 26, Surrey 37, Sussex 38, Warwickshire 17, Westmorland 4, Wiltshire 33, Worcestershire 16, Yorkshire 6

1 What is language?

It is language, more obviously than anything else, that distinguishes humankind from the rest of the animal world. At one time it was common to define a human as a thinking animal, but we can hardly imagine thought without words – not thought that is at all precise, anyway. More recently, humans have often been described as tool-making animals; but language itself is the most remarkable tool that they have invented, and is the one that makes most of the others possible. The most primitive tools, admittedly, may have come earlier than language: the higher apes sometimes use sticks as elementary tools, and even break them for this purpose. But tools of any greater sophistication demand the kind of human co-operation and division of labour which is hardly possible without language. Language, in fact, is the great machine-tool which makes human culture possible.

Other animals, it is true, communicate with one another, or at any rate stimulate one another to action, by means of cries. Many birds utter warning calls at the approach of danger; some animals have mating-calls; apes utter different cries to express anger, fear or pleasure. Some animals use other modes of communication: many have postures that signify submission, to prevent an attack by a rival; hive-bees indicate the direction and distance of honey from the hive by means of the famous bee-dance; dolphins seem to have a communication system which uses both sounds and bodily posture. But these various means of communication differ in important ways from human language. Animals' cries are not *articulate*. This means, basically, that they lack structure. They lack, for example, the kind of structure given by the contrast between vowels and consonants. And they lack the kind of structure that enables us to divide a human utterance into **words**. We can change an utterance by replacing one word by another: a sentry can say 'Tanks approaching from the North', or he can change one word and say 'Aircraft approaching from the North' or 'Tanks approaching from the West'; but a bird has a single indivisible alarm-cry, which means 'Danger!'. This is why the number of signals that an animal can make is very limited: the Great Tit has about thirty different calls, whereas in human language the number of possible utterances is infinite. It also explains why animal cries are very *general* in meaning. These differences will become clearer if we consider some of the characteristics of human language.

What is language?

A human language is a signalling system. As its material, it uses vocal sounds. Basically, a language is something which is *spoken*: the written language is secondary and derivative. In the history of each individual, speech is learned before writing, and there is good reason for believing that the same was true in the history of the species. There are primitive communities that have speech without writing, but we know of no human community which has a written language without a spoken one. Gestures and facial expression also play a part in linguistic communication: we all know that talking on the telephone is much less satisfactory than face-to-face conversation. It is also true that a remarkable sign-language has been developed for use by the deaf. But the fact remains that speech is the primary form of language.

Vocal sounds

The vocal sounds which provide the materials for a language are produced by the various *speech organs* (see Figure 1). The production of sounds requires energy, and this is usually supplied by the diaphragm and the chest muscles, which enable us to send a flow of breath up from the lungs. Some languages use additional sources of energy: it is possible to make clicking noises by

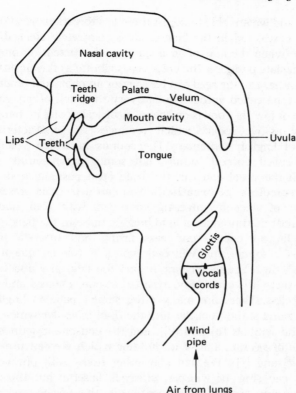

Figure 1   Main speech-organs. The tongue is usually divided (1. to r.) into tip, blade, front, back, and root. The glottis is the opening between the vocal cords. Alternative names: *soft palate (velum)* and *alveolar ridge (teeth-ridge)*

muscular movements of the tongue, and popping noises by movements of the cheeks and lips, and such sounds are found in some of the African languages. It is also possible to use air flowing *into* the lungs, i.e. to utilize indrawn breath for the production of speech-sounds in very short utterances. In English, however, we rely on the *outflow* of air from the lungs, which is modified in various ways by the 'set' of the organs that it passes through before finally emerging at the mouth or nose.

First the air from the lungs passes through the vocal cords, in the larynx. These are rather like a small pair of lips in the windpipe, and we are able to adjust these lips to various positions, from fully closed (when the flow of air is completely blocked) to wide open (when the flow of air is quite unobstructed). In one of the intermediate positions, the vocal cords vibrate as the air passes through, rather like the reed of a bassoon or an oboe, and produce a musical tone called **voice**. We can vary the pitch of our voice (how high or low the tone is on the musical scale), and it changes constantly as we speak, which produces the characteristic melodies of English sentences. The sounds in which voice is used are called **voiced** sounds, but some speech-sounds are made with the vocal cords in the wide open position, and are therefore **voiceless** (or **breathed**). You can detect the presence or absence of voice by covering your ears with your hands: voiced sounds then produce a loud buzzing noise in the head. For example, if you cover your ears firmly and utter a long continuous *v* sound, you will hear voice; if you change it to an *f* sound, the voice disappears. In fact the English *v* and *f* are made in exactly the same way, except that one is voiced and the other voiceless. There are many other similar pairs in English, including *z* and *s*, the *th* of *this* and the *th* of *thing* (for which we can use the symbols [ð] and [θ]), and the consonant sounds in the middle of *pleasure* and of *washer* (for which we can use the symbols [ʒ] and [ʃ]). We can play other tricks with our vocal cords: we can sing, or whisper, or speak falsetto: but the two most important positions for speech are the voiced and the voiceless.

After passing through the vocal cords, the stream of air continues upwards, and passes out through the mouth, or the nose, or both. The most backward part of the roof of the mouth, called the *velum* or the soft palate, can be moved up and down to close or open the entrance to the nasal cavity, while the mouth passage can be blocked by means of the lips or the tongue.

In a **vowel** sound, voice is switched on, and the mouth cavity is left unobstructed, so that the air passes out freely. If the nasal passage is also opened, we get a nasal vowel, like those of French *bon* 'good' or *brun* 'brown', but for the English vowels the nasal passage is normally closed (though some American speakers habitually leave the door ajar and speak with a nasal 'twang').

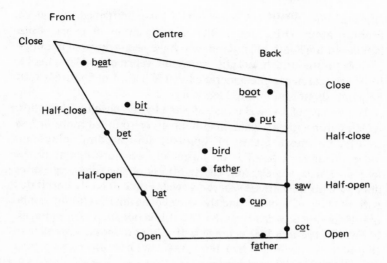

Figure 2   Vowel diagram. Typical tongue positions for twelve vowels of present-day English (RP)

The quality of a vowel is determined by the position of the tongue, lower jaw, and lips, because these can change the shape of the cavity that the air passes through, and different shapes give different resonances. The tongue is the most important. If we raise part of our tongue, we divide the mouth passage into two cavities of different sizes, one at the back and one at the front; the quality of the vowel is, to a great extent, determined by the relative sizes of these two cavities. To describe any vowel sound, therefore, we specify the position of the highest part of the tongue: we can do this in terms of its height (open, half-open, half-close, close) and of its retraction (front, central, or back). A little experimentation with your finger in your mouth, or with a torch and a mirror, will show you the way your tongue changes position for different vowels. The different positions of the tongue to create different vowel sounds can be shown by means of a *vowel diagram*. This is a conventionalized cross-section of the mouth cavity seen from the left-hand side, on which a vowel is marked as a dot, representing the position of the highest point of the tongue. Figure 2 shows a vowel diagram for twelve English vowels in standard British

English. The accent in question is usually called 'Received Pronunciation' (RP), and is the pronunciation of people from families in the South of England who have been educated at public schools (in the British, not the American, sense of 'public school'). RP is very similar to the general educated accent of South-Eastern England, though not quite identical to it.

The quality of a vowel is also affected by the position of the lips, which can be spread wide, held neutral, or rounded more or less tightly. In most forms of English, lip-rounding plays no independent part, for it is an automatic accompaniment of the four backmost vowels, and the tightness of the rounding varies directly with the closeness of the vowel. You can easily check this with the help of a mirror and the vowel diagram (but it may not be true if you are Scottish or Irish). But this is not so in all languages: in French, the *u* of *lune* is made with a tongue-position similar to that of the *ea* of English *lean*, but is made with rounded lips, which gives it quite a different sound.

Vowels can also differ in length. In fact, the English vowels all have different lengths, but they fall into two broad groups, the long and the short. The short vowels are those heard in *pick*, *peck*, *pack*, *put*, *cut*, and *cot*, together with [ə], the short central vowel which is heard in the *er* of *father* and the *a* of *about*.

The vowel diagram in Figure 2 assumes that the vocal organs remain stationary while the vowel is uttered, but this is not always the case, for there are vowels in which the speech organs change their positions in the course of the sound. These are called **glides** or **diphthongs**. An example is the vowel heard in the word *boy*. Here the speech organs begin quite near the position they have for the vowel of *saw*, but almost immediately move towards the position they have for the vowel of *bit*, though they may not go all the way there. During most of the sound, the speech organs are moving, though they may remain in the initial position for a short time before the gliding movement begins. Other English diphthongs are heard in the words *hide*, *house*, *make*, *home*, *hare*, *here*, and *poor* (though if you are from the United States, Scotland or Northern England you may use a pure vowel in some of these, especially in *home*). On the vowel diagram, diphthongs are represented by arrows, and examples are given in Figure 3.

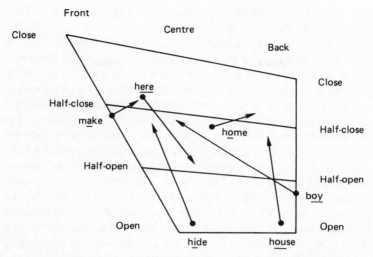

Figure 3   Vowel diagram. Six diphthongs of present-day English (RP)

Notice that our definition of a diphthong is concerned with *sound*, not with spelling. In popular usage, the *au* of *cause* and the æ of *mediæval* are often referred to as diphthongs, but these are not diphthongs in our sense of the word: they are pure vowels which happen to be represented in spelling by two letters (the digraph *au* and the ligature æ). Conversely, a diphthong may be represented in spelling by a single letter, like the *y* of *fly*.

I have spoken of diphthongs as single vowel sounds, not as combinations of two vowel sounds. One good reason for doing so is that a diphthong forms only one syllable, not two. A syllable is a peak of prominence in the chain of utterance. If you could measure the acoustic power output of a speaker as it varies with time, you would find that it goes continually up and down, forming little peaks and valleys: the peaks are syllables. The words *lair* and *here* form only one peak each, and so only one syllable, whereas the words *player* and *newer* are usually pronounced with two peaks and so contain two syllables. It is thus desirable to distinguish between a diphthong (which is one syllable) and a sequence of two vowels (which is two syllables). Alternatively, a diphthong can be analysed as the combination of a vowel with a semivowel (a non-syllabic glide, like the *y* in *yes*), and this analysis is adopted by many linguists, especially Americans.

In all vowels, the mouth passage is unobstructed. If it is obstructed at any time during the production of a speech-sound, the resulting sound will be a **consonant**. In English, there are three main types of consonant: **fricatives**, **stops**, and **sonorants**.

Fricatives are made by narrowing the air passage so much that the stream of air produces audible friction. In *f* and *v*, the constriction is made by pressing the lower lip against the top teeth, while in *th* ([θ] and [ð]) the tip of the tongue is pressed against the upper teeth. In *s* and *z*, the front of the tongue is pressed against the teeth-ridge, and the air allowed to flow down a narrow channel in the middle of the tongue, while for [ʃ] and [ʒ] the passage is made wider and flatter. The English *h* consonant can perhaps also be classed as a fricative, but in this case the friction occurs in the glottis, and the mouth passage is completely unobstructed.

In stop consonants, the flow of air from the lungs is completely blocked at some point, and pressure built up behind the blockage; then the blockage is suddenly removed, and there is an outrush of air. The exact sound produced will depend on where and how the blockage is made, and on the speed of the release. In *p* and *b*, the blockage is made by pressing the two lips together. In *t* and *d*, the tip of the tongue is pressed against the teeth-ridge, that is, the convex part of the roof of the mouth immediately behind the upper teeth (not against the teeth themselves, as in many other languages). In *k* and *g*, the back part of the tongue is lifted and pressed against the soft palate. In these six sounds, the release is very sudden. In *ch* (as in *church*) and *j* (as in *judge*), which are made in much the same position as *t* and *d*, the release of the blockage is slower, and this gives a different effect, so that *ch* sounds something like a *t* followed very rapidly by a *sh*. Stops with rapid release are called **plosives**, and those with slow release **affricates**. In some varieties of English, notably Cockney, there is a plosive called the **glottal stop**, in which the blockage is made by complete closure of the vocal cords.

In the sonorant consonants, use is made of resonant cavities, as in the vowels, but there is some kind of obstruction in the mouth passage. The English sonorants are the nasals, *m*, *n*, and *ng* (as in *sing*), the lateral consonant *l*, and the approximant *r*. In the nasals, the nasal passage is open but the mouth passage is blocked, the blockages being similar to those made for the plosives *b*, *d*, and *g* respectively. In the lateral, the centre of the mouth is blocked by the tongue, while the air is allowed to escape down one side, or down both. In English these are all normally voiced, though they may become voiceless or partially voiceless under certain conditions, for example when they follow an *s*. In Welsh, you will hear an *l* sound (spelt *ll*, as in *Llanelli*) which is regularly voiceless, but this is a fricative consonant rather than a sonorant.

The *r* consonant has various realizations in different varieties of English, but in Received Pronunciation, and in much American English, it is an **approximant**. This is a consonant in which the articulators approach one another, but not closely enough to produce a fricative or a stop. In *r*, the tip of the tongue approaches the teeth-ridge, as if for *d*, but does not make contact, and the tongue is usually curled slightly backward, with the tip raised. In some varieties of English *r* is a trill, in which the tip of the tongue vibrates rapidly, or a flap, in which the tip of the tongue makes a single tap against the teeth-ridge. In some languages, the consonant written as *r* is a different sort of sound: in the best known varieties of French and German, it is not made with the tip of the tongue, but with the uvula (the small fleshy appendage to the soft palate, which can be seen hanging at the back of the mouth), and in many Indian languages there is a retroflex *r* made by curling the tongue right back and articulating against the roof of the mouth.

In English, sonorant consonants can form syllables. It is sometimes asserted that every syllable must contain a vowel, but this is not so, as can be seen from words like *table* and *button*: in normal pronunciation, each of these has two syllables, the second of which contains no vowel. Syllabic *r* is very common in American speech, in positions where RP instead has the vowel [ə], in words like *perceive*.

With the sonorant consonants we can also group the English semivowels, heard in the *y* of *yes* and the *w* of *wet*. A semivowel is a glide, like a diphthong; but, unlike a diphthong, it does not constitute a syllable. To make the *y* of *yes*, we put our tongue in the position for a short *i* (as in *pin*), and then glide to the position for the following *e*. Similarly, to make *w*, we put our tongue in the position for short *u* (as in *put*), and again glide to the following vowel.

Phonetic symbols

Even in this short account of the English speech-sounds, it has already become apparent that it is difficult to discuss the subject without making use of special symbols. We have in English no single unambiguous spelling to represent the consonant-sound in the middle of the word *pleasure* or the first vowel of the word *about*, or to distinguish between the voiced and voiceless *th* of *this* and *thing*, and for this reason I have already introduced the phonetic symbols [ʒ], [ə], [ð], and [θ] to represent these sounds. In the course of this book, I shall use phonetic symbols when they make things simpler and clearer, but shall often use ordinary letter-symbols in cases where no ambiguity can arise. When I introduce a new phonetic symbol, I shall of course indicate what it stands for, but for convenience of reference I give below two tables in which all the symbols used are gathered together. In Table 1.1, I give a list of symbols which can be used for the transcription of present-day English (Received Pronunciation), together with illustrative examples.

Table 1.1 *Phonetic symbols for the transcription of present-day English (Received Pronunciation)*

I. VOWELS

Pure Vowels

ɪ as in *sit* /sɪt/
e as in *pen* /pen/
æ as in *hat* /hæt/
ʌ as in *cup* /kʌp/
ɒ as in *hot* /hɒt/
ʊ as in *put* /pʊt/
ə as in *admit* /əd'mɪt/, *father* /'fɑ:ðə/

i: as in *tree* /tri:/
ɑ: as in *far* /fɑ:/, *father* /'fɑ:ðə/
ɔ: as in *saw* /sɔ:/, *short* /ʃɔ:t/
u: as in *goose* /gu:s/, *few* /fju:/
ɜ: as in *bird* /bɜ:d/

Diphthongs

eɪ as in *make* /meɪk/
aɪ as in *time* /taɪm/
ɔɪ as in *boy* /bɔɪ/
əʊ as in *go* /gəʊ/
aʊ as in *loud* /laʊd/

ɪə as in *here* /hɪə/
ɛə as in *air* /ɛə/
ʊə as in *poor* /pʊə/ (but many speakers say /pɔ:/)

II. CONSONANTS

Fricatives

f as in *far* /fɑ:/
θ as in *thin* /θɪn/
s as in *sit* /sɪt/
ʃ as in *shoe* /ʃu:/
h as in *hit* /hɪt/

v as in *voice* /vɔɪs/
ð as in *this* /ðɪs/
z as in *zoo* /zu:/
ʒ as in *pleasure* /'pleʒə/

Stops

p as in *peel* /pi:l/
t as in *took* /tʊk/
k as in *come* /kʌm/
tʃ as in *church* /tʃɜ:tʃ/

b as in *bee* /bi:/
d as in *deed* /di:d/
g as in *geese* /gi:s/
dʒ as in *judge* /dʒʌdʒ/

Sonorants

m as in *make* /meɪk/
n as in *not* /nɒt/
ŋ as in *sing* /sɪŋ/
      finger /'fɪŋgə/

l as in *leak* /li:k/
j as in *yes* /jes/
w as in *wait* /weɪt/
r as in *red* /red/

The examples assume Received Pronunciation. Speakers of General American (the most widespread accent in the United States) use the same vowel in *hot* as in *father*, pronounce the /r/ in *air* and *bird*, and lack the centring diphthongs /ɪə/, /ɛə/ and /ʊə/ (the word *here*, for example, being /hɪr/). The symbol [:] is used to denote vowel-length, so that [ə] is short and [ɜ:] long. In General American, however, vowel-length is less significant than in RP, and it is usual to transcribe it without using length-marks, so that for example *tree* is transcribed /tri/.

Similarly, the examples will not fit all speakers in Britain. If you are a northerner, you may well use the same vowel in *put* as in *cut*, where RP makes a distinction. If you are a Scot, you may use the same vowel in *put* as in *goose*. If you come from the West Midlands, or South Lancashire, or the Sheffield area, you may pronounce *sing* as /sɪŋg/, with a [g] after the [ŋ].

Diphthongs are represented by two symbols, the first showing the vowel-position in which the diphthong starts, and the second showing the position towards which it glides. So the diphthong in the word *here* begins in about the same position of the [ɪ] of *pin*, and glides towards the central vowel [ə]. We therefore represent it by the notation [ɪə]. The symbol ['] is used to mark stress, and is placed before the syllable that is stressed, so that *admit* is transcribed [əd'mɪt].

We can now redraw the vowel diagram of Figure 2, using phonetic symbols. Figure 4 shows typical tongue-positions for the pure vowels of Received Pronunciation in present-day English.

Table 1.2 gives a list of other phonetic symbols which will occur in the course of the book, again with illustrative examples. The table does not include diphthongs, since the pronunciation of these can be deduced from the two phonetic symbols used in their transcription.

Table 1.2 *Other phonetic symbols used*

ɑ like the *a* of *father*, but short; often heard in American pronunciation of words like *hot*.

a as in French *la*, German *Mann*, Northern English *hat*.

a: as in French *tard*, Australian English *park*.

æ: the long vowel often heard in the London pronunciation of words like *bad*, *man*.

ɛ as in French *même*, German *Bett*; the starting position of the English diphthong heard in *air*.

ɛ: as in French *faire*, German *fährt*.

e: as in German *zehn*; like the vowel of French *été* but lengthened.

ɔ as in French *donne*, German *von*; like the vowel of English *law*, but short.

o: as in French *chose*, German *wo*.

o the corresponding short vowel, as in French *dos*.

ø: as in French *feu*, German *schön* (a long [e:] produced with rounded lips).

y as in French *cru*, German *Hütte* (a short [i] produced with rounded lips).

y: as in French *sûr*, German *führen* (a long [i:] produced with rounded lips).

x as in *ch* of Scots *loch*, German *ach*.

ç as in *gh* of Scots *night*, *ch* of German *ich*.

ɤ a voiced velar fricative: like [g], but a fricative instead of a stop.

ʔ the glottal stop: a plosive in which the blockage is made by complete closure of the vocal cords.

This brief account has perhaps given some idea of the kind of vocal material used in the human signalling system. Let us now turn to the word *system*, which is crucial.

System in language

A language consists of a number of linked systems, and structure can be seen in it at all levels. For a start, any language selects a small number of vocal sounds out of all those which human beings are able to make, and uses them as its building bricks, and the selection is different for every language. The number of vocal sounds that a human being can learn to make (and to distinguish between) is quite large – certainly running into hundreds – and if you know a foreign language you will also be

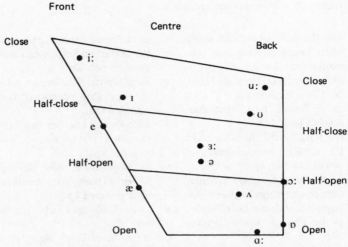

Figure 4   Vowel diagram. Typical tongue position for the pure vowels of present-day English (RP). Examples: *tree*/tri:/, *sit*/sɪt/, *pen*/pen/, *hat*/hæt/, *bird* /bɜːd/, *father*/ˈfɑːðə/, *boot*/buːt/, *put*/pʊt/, *saw*/sɔː/, *cup*/kʌp/, *hot*/hɒt/, *far*/fɑː/

familiar with speech-sounds which do not occur in English, like the vowel of the French word *feu* or the consonant of the German *ich*. But out of all these possible sounds, most languages are content with a mere twenty or thirty as their basic material. In English, if you treat the diphthongs as independent sounds, the number is about forty-five; if you treat the diphthongs and the long vowels as combinations of a vowel and a semivowel, the number comes down to about thirty-five. Some languages are more modest in their demands: Italian uses only seven different vowels, and manages with twenty-seven basic sounds altogether; Hawaiian is said to manage with only thirteen. Some languages, on the other hand, use sixty or more.

You may have thought of an objection to my suggestion that English makes use of no more than forty-five basic sounds: pronunciation varies from speaker to speaker. Speakers from Texas, from Manchester, from Edinburgh, from New York use different sounds. Doesn't this mean, therefore, that there are hundreds of different sounds in English? This is obviously true. These variations, moreover, occur between different social groups as well as between different regions, for there are class accents as well as regional accents. Observe, however, that all these speakers use what is essentially the same *system* of sounds. When they pronounce the word *man*, they may all use rather different vowel-sounds, but all these sounds occupy the same place in the system: they all contrast, for example, with a different vowel-sound in *men*, but fail to contrast with the vowel-sound heard in a whole number of other words, like *fan* and *mad*. Consequently, these different speakers can understand one another without too much difficulty. This assumes, of course, that many sounds will not vary greatly from one speaker to another, and this is in fact true: the *m* and the *n* of the word *man* are pronounced in pretty well the same way by native speakers of English all over the world, and it is only the vowel in the word that varies.

The phoneme

Not only do the forty-five basic sounds of English vary from region to region, from class to class, and even from speaker to speaker within a class or region: they also vary in a systematic way within the speech of each individual. These variations depend on the position of the sound – the other sounds that are adjacent to it, the part of the word that it occurs in. Take the English /p/-sound. This is a **voiceless stop**, made by blocking the flow of air through the mouth by pressing the two lips together, and then suddenly releasing the blockage by opening the lips. In the speech of most English people, the release of the /p/ is normally followed by a little rush of air, which makes a kind of *h* sound between the stop and the sound that comes next in the word; but when the /p/ follows an /s/ which belongs to the same syllable, this rush of air is missing, so that we use slightly different variants of the /p/-sound in the words *park* and *spark*. You can test this by holding the palm of your hand about an inch in front of your mouth and speaking the two words aloud; in *park* you will feel a strong puff of breath on your hand, but in *spark* the puff is much reduced. If you listen carefully you can also *hear* the difference between these two different /p/-sounds, but you don't usually notice it in speech because it has no significance for the meaning of what is said: the difference between the two sounds is determined automatically by the neighbouring sounds, and is not used to distinguish between different words.

Another variant of the /p/-sound is heard before /m/, as in *topmost*: in this case the stop is released, not by opening the lips, but by letting the air flow out of the nose in an /m/ sound, and the lips are not opened until the end of the /m/. Yet another variant is often heard when /p/ comes at the end of a sentence, as when you say 'Can I take your cup?'; here it is common not to release the blockage at all, but just to leave the lips together at the end of the sentence. We see, then, that what I have called the English /p/-sound in fact consists of a whole group of sounds, slightly different variants being used according to the phonetic context.

This is true of the English speech-sounds generally. If you listen carefully to your pronunciation of the initial /k/ in the words *keep* and *cool*, you will realize that they differ a good deal; and if you concentrate on the position of your tongue, you will find that the blockage is made much further forward in the former word than in the latter. Or listen to your pronunciation of the /i:/ sound in *bead* and in *beat*: in the first word the vowel is noticeably longer than in the second. Similarly you will probably find that you use different kinds of /m/ in the words *come*, *triumph*, and *smooth*; different kinds of /l/ in the words *old*, *leak*, and *sleek*; and different kinds of /u:/ in the words *do*, *cool*, and *few*.

You may now feel inclined to ask what has happened to my forty-five basic sounds of English, the building bricks that the language is made up from. It has become clear, at any rate, that the word 'sounds' is hardly suitable: let us say instead that the sound-system of English has forty-five basic terms or positions, each of which is represented by a whole group of related sounds. The sounds of any one group have a good deal in common, but there are small variations which depend on the context; these variations are normally unnoticed by the native speaker, because they are produced automatically, but they may be very obvious to a foreigner, whose language has a different sound-system. Such groups of related and non-contrasting sounds are called **phonemes**, and we can now amend my earlier statement and say that the English language has about forty-five phonemes: the exact number depends on how you decide to treat diphthongs, and also varies slightly between different varieties of English. The variant forms of any phoneme are called the **allophones** of that phoneme.

In Table 1.1, I have given only one phonetic symbol for each phoneme of present-day English, so that the same /p/ symbol would be used in transcribing *park* /pɑːk/ and *spark* /spɑːk/. A transcription of this kind is called a **phonemic** transcription, and is usually placed between oblique lines. But of course it is also possible to use a larger number of symbols, in order to show finer distinctions: so one could distinguish between the /p/ of *park* and that of *spark*, by transcribing [pʰɑːk] and [spɑːk]. If the transcription shows such finer distinctions, or if the transcriber does not wish to make a firm decision about the analysis of the language into phonemes, the transcription is usually placed within square brackets, and is called an **allophonic** or a **phonetic** transcription. Notice carefully the difference between *phonemic* (with an *m*) and *phonetic* (with a *t*): in a phonemic transcription there is one symbol, and only one, for each phoneme of the language; in a phonetic transcription there is no such limitation.

System can also be seen in the ways in which the phonemes can be combined into words. As far as I know, there is no English word *grust* or *blomby*, but there is no reason why there shouldn't be; whereas the groups *ngust* and *glbombr* (although perfectly pronounceable if you care to try) will immediately be rejected by a native speaker as not conforming to the pattern of English words. There are restrictions on the combinations in which English phonemes can occur. The /ŋ/ phoneme (as in *sing*) cannot occur at the beginning of a word, nor can the /ʒ/ phoneme (though in French a similar phoneme can, as in the word *je*, 'I'). Some of the short vowels, such as /æ/ (as in *man*) never occur as the last sound in a word, nor does /h/. (Don't be misled by the *spelling*, and say that there's an *h*-sound in *oh*, or an *a*-sound in *China*.) Again, at the beginning of a word we can have the cluster of consonants /spl-/, but not the cluster /stl-/; and you may care to amuse yourself by trying to work out which clusters of three consonants can in fact occur at the beginning of an English word.

At the end of a word, we can have the cluster /-ðmz/ (as in *rhythms*) but not the cluster /-gbz/. And so on. These rules, of course, apply only to the English language; other languages have their own systems, and combinations that are impossible in English, and which may even seem quite jaw-breaking to us, may be perfectly normal in another language, and will not seem at all difficult or surprising to the speakers of that language, who are used to them.

Stress and rhythm

When we consider, not isolated words, but whole utterances, we notice such things as stress, pitch, and rhythm, which are also systematic. We have already spoken of the small peaks of loudness which form syllables, but syllables themselves vary in loudness, and in any English utterance of any length there are syllables of many different degrees of loudness. They fall, however, into two main groups, those that are relatively prominent and those that are not; we can call these **stressed** and **unstressed syllables** respectively.

In English, stress is closely linked with rhythm. Large numbers of languages, including French and many of the languages of India, have a rhythm in which the syllables are evenly spaced: if a Frenchman speaks a sentence containing twenty syllables, and takes five seconds to speak it, then the syllables will follow one another pretty regularly at quarter-second intervals. But this is not true of English. Try speaking the following two sentences as naturally as you can, stressing in each the four syllables marked:

> There's a new mánager at the works todáy.
> There's a new bóss there nów.

Although the first has eleven syllables, and the second only six, you will find that the two sentences take about the same time to speak. The reason for this is not hard to see: a speaker of English tries to space the *stressed* syllables evenly, so that both sentences contain four time-units. In the first sentence, the interval between *new* and *man-* is about the same as that between *man-* and *works*, so that the sequence *manager at the works* has to be taken very quickly. This characteristic of the English language plays a large part in the rhythm of English poetry, since a sequence of stressed syllables makes the verse move slowly, whereas a sequence of unstressed syllables makes it move fast.

Intonation

I have already mentioned the way in which the musical pitch of the voice changes during an utterance, giving the characteristic melodies of English. These melodies are called **intonation**. The use of intonation for conveying meaning can be shown very simply by speaking the two sentences:

(a)   He's going to be there?
(b)   He's going to be there.

In (a) we have a rising tone on the final stressed syllable, and in (b) a falling tone, and this makes the difference between a question and a statement. These two are very common intonation patterns in English: (b) is used in statements and in '*wh-* questions' (ones beginning with words like *which*, *where*, and *who*), while (a) is used in questions which can be answered 'Yes' or 'No'. It is also possible to use a tone that falls and then rises: if you speak the word 'No' with falling-rising tone, you communicate doubt or encouragement (depending on the context); this is an example of the common use of intonation to communicate a mood or an attitude. Intonation can also be used to single out the part of the sentence that we want to emphasize. Take the sentence 'Is John going to wear those trousers?'. We can select for special emphasis any word in this sentence except *to* (*Is* John going to wear those trousers?', 'Is *John* going to wear those trousers?', etc.). If you examine what is going on when you speak the sentence with these various emphases, you will see that it is not just a matter of stressing the chosen word more strongly: you also begin it on a higher pitch than the other words, and use a falling tone on it.

In English, we only use musical pitch as a feature of a whole phrase: we use intonation to distinguish between different sentences, but not between different words. But in some languages, like Chinese, Thai, and Yoruba, musical pitch is a distinguishing feature of the single word: if you change the intonation it becomes a different word. Such languages are called *tone languages*.

Morphology: words and morphemes

System is also found in the way words are constructed from smaller parts. Words are often defined as minimum free forms, i.e. the smallest pieces of language which can by themselves constitute a complete utterance. But they are not the smallest *meaningful* pieces of language: in the words *refill* and *slowly* we know perfectly well what *re-* and *-ly* mean, but these do not constitute words. The smallest meaningful element in a language is called a **morpheme**. So *re-* and *fill* are both morphemes. The former cannot exist except when joined to other morphemes, and so is a **bound morpheme**; but *fill* is also a word, and is therefore a **free morpheme**. A word may consist of one morpheme or of many: the word *unthoughtful* consists of three morphemes, whereas the word *molecule* is only one; and the word *I* is a single morpheme which is itself composed of a single phoneme.

Bound morphemes are used extensively in English for the formation of new words. Especially productive are prefixes (*un-*, *re-*, *de-*, etc.) and suffixes (*-ly*, *-ness*, *-ize*, etc.). We also make extensive use of bound morphemes when words change their form for grammatical purposes, as in *boy/boys* or *talk/talks/talking/talked*.

Lexical words and grammatical words

English words fall into a number of different grammatical categories – what were traditionally called 'the parts of speech', but which are now usually called word-classes. Obvious examples of word-classes are nouns (such as *brother*, *idea*, *library*), adjectives (such as *new*, *beautiful*, *young*), verbs (such as *come*, *annihilate*, *fraternize*), and pronouns (such as *you*, *I*, *who*, *anybody*).

Suppose now that I asked you to give me a complete list of the personal pronouns of present-day English (*I*, *he*, etc.). Would that be possible? Given a little time, you should be able to give me a list:

I, he, she, it, we, you, and *they,* together with their accusative forms
me, him, her, it, us, you, and *them.* You might too have noticed that
there are also seven corresponding forms which are used before
nouns (*my, his, her,* etc.), and seven corresponding possessive
pronouns (*mine, his, hers,* etc.). But suppose I next asked you to
give me a similar list of the nouns of present-day English. Would
that be possible? I'm afraid that, even given plenty of time and
secretarial assistance, you would never finish the job. The moment
you thought you had finished, you would discover that somebody
had just invented a new word, for words are being coined all the
time. You would have no idea whether a particular word would
catch on, or whether it would disappear after a single use. Nor
indeed could you be certain whether some old-fashioned words
were dead or not: you might think a word was obsolete, but then
hear somebody use it.

Nouns and personal pronouns, therefore, are quite different
kinds of word-class. The personal pronouns form a closed system,
whose members can be listed exhaustively. The nouns form an
open-ended system, blurred at the edges, constantly changing. Of
course, the system of pronouns changes with time: four hundred
years ago there were the forms *thou, thee, thy,* and *thine,* and there
was no form *its.* But this is a long-term process: individuals cannot
just invent a new pronoun, in the way they can invent a noun.
These two different types are often called **lexical words** (open-
ended class) and **grammatical words** (closed class). In the lexical
class are nouns, verbs, and adjectives. In the grammatical class
are pronouns (*he, who, somebody,* etc.), conjunctions (*and, but,
although,* etc.), auxiliaries (*must, might, would,* etc.), and
determiners (words that go before nouns, like *the, a, this, every*).
Prepositions (*on, by, in, in spite of,* etc.) are rather numerous, but
still belong to the grammatical class. What were traditionally
called adverbs fulfil different functions: some are verb-modifiers
('to run *quickly*'), some are sentence-modifiers ('Undoubtedly,
. . .'), and some modify adjectives or adverbs ('*extremely* happy',
'*very* quickly'). And some are grammatical, others lexical: those
formed from adjectives (*quickly, beautifully, contrariwise*) are lexical,
but there is a group which is probably to be classed as
grammatical (e.g. *then, there, very,* and ones identical in form

with prepositions, like *by*, *in*, etc.). This is by no means an exhaustive account of the word-classes of present-day English, but will give you a starting-point.

Syntax

System is also found in the rules for combining words into utterances. We say 'the good old times', not 'the old good times', and 'a beautiful young American girl', not 'an American young beautiful girl'; and there is a complicated set of rules regulating the way a phrase of this kind is put together in English (rules which English speakers have obviously internalized). Again, we say 'The dog bit John', and it seems almost like part of the order of nature that this shall mean that it was the dog that did the biting and John that suffered it. But it is not at all part of the order of nature: it is just one of the conventions of our language. In normal English sentences, the Subject ('The dog') comes before the Verb ('bit'), which itself comes before the Direct Object ('John'), and it is this word-order which tells us which is the biter and which the bitten. But this S-V-O word-order is not found in all languages: many languages, like Turkish and classical Latin, have the equivalent of 'The dog John bit' (S-O-V); some, like Welsh, have the equivalent of 'Bit the dog John' (V-S-O). In some languages, for example Russian, the word-order is very free, and it is word-endings alone which show which is the Subject ('biter') and which the Object ('bitten'). Nor is the word-order of 'The dog' universal: the order here is Determiner-Noun, which is obligatory in English, but some languages have the order Noun-Determiner. In Swedish, for example, 'dog' is *hund*, but 'the dog' is *hunden*, the definite article being attached to the end of the noun. In fact the permissible arrangements of words, and the meanings of particular arrangements, vary from language to language.

Lexical sets

System is also found in the realm of meaning. Words tend to form sets, and the meaning of a word depends on the other words in the set, with which it can be contrasted. This is very clear in sets of words denoting such things as military ranks (*captain, major, colonel,* etc.), where the meaning of each term depends on its position in the hierarchy. In Shakespeare's time, there were far fewer military ranks (usually about eight) than in the modern British army; an Elizabethan corporal or colonel, therefore, cannot be equated directly with a present-day one. In the sets of words for family relationships, the categories are different in different languages: Swedish has no word exactly corresponding to our *uncle,* but has *farbror* (paternal uncle) and *morbror* (maternal uncle). Another obvious set is formed by words for colours, where different languages divide up the spectrum differently: for example, in Russian there is no single word corresponding to our *blue,* but two words, (a) *síniy* (roughly 'dark blue') and (b) *golubóy* (roughly 'light blue'). The sky can be either, but the sea can only be (a), while eyes are usually (b), though exceptionally dark-blue eyes can be (a). Other clear sets are series of words corresponding to degrees of intensity of some kind, like *hot, warm, tepid, cool, cold:* if any one of these terms were missing from the language, the meanings of the others would be different, since they would have to cover the same range of intensity in a smaller number of divisions.

Hierarchy

In these various intertwined systems that constitute a language, a large part is played by hierarchy. There is a hierarchy of units: phoneme, morpheme, word, phrase, clause, sentence. Within the sentence itself, there is a hierarchical structure. Take a simple sentence:

(a)   The women were wearing white clothes.

This can be divided into two parts, Subject and Predicate, in each of which there is a main part and a subordinate part. The Subject consists of a Noun Phrase ('The women'), in which a noun ('women') is the head, and a determiner ('The') is a modifier. The Predicate has as its head a Verb Phrase ('were wearing') which governs a Noun Phrase ('white clothes') as its Object. The Verb Phrase has a main verb ('wear') + -ing as its head, and an auxiliary ('were') as a subordinate part, while the Noun Phrase has as its head a noun ('clothes'), and an adjective ('white') as a modifier.

Now let us expand the sentence a little:

(b)   The women in the house were wearing white clothes.

We have now added another modifier to the head 'women', namely the Preposition Phrase 'in the house'. This has a head, the preposition 'in', which governs the Noun Phrase 'the house', which itself has a head (the noun 'house') and a modifier (the determiner 'the'). The hierarchy of constituents thus extends downwards.

Let us try another expansion of our original sentence:

(c)   The women who lived in the house were wearing white clothes.

We have now added a different modifier to the noun 'women', and this time it is a relative clause, 'who lived in the house'. This resembles a sentence, having a Noun Phrase as Subject (the relative pronoun 'who') and a Predicate consisting of a verb ('lived') as its head and a Preposition Phrase as modifier. This relative clause is an example of what is often called *embedding*: one sentence ('The women lived in the house') is embedded in another sentence ('The women were wearing white clothes'), of which it becomes a subordinate part. In traditional terminology, the embedded sentence is a *subordinate clause*. This explains why my hierarchy of constituents contained 'clause' as well as 'sentence'. Our original sentence (a) was also a clause, but an independent one, and we can say that Sentence (c) consists of a main clause and a subordinate clause.

This notion of hierarchy in sentence-structure is of first-class importance. For example, if we wish to change a sentence (for example, from a statement to a question, or from an affirmative to a negative form), we cannot do it by rules which just shuffle individual words around: the rules have to recognize the various units of the sentence and the ways in which they are subordinated to one another.

Language is symbolic

In all these ways a language shows system, and it is now perhaps clear, at any rate in a general way, what we mean when we say that a language is a system of vocal sounds. These sounds are *symbolic*. That is, they stand for something other than themselves, and their relationship to the thing that they stand for is not a necessary one, but arbitrary. A symbol is a kind of sign, but not all signs are symbols. This is illustrated in Figure 5, which shows two British traffic signs, both of which were in use at different times during the twentieth century. The first shows two children running into the road: this is not symbolic, but representational, for it gives an actual picture of the hazard ahead, and the motorist does not need to be initiated into its meaning. The second shows a blazing torch. This stands for learning, and indicates that there is a school ahead, but the relationship between a blazing torch and learning is an arbitrary one, and the motorist needs to have its meaning explained to him. The blazing torch is a symbol.

The same kind of distinction applies to gestures: when a chimpanzee shows a companion that it is hungry by pretending to eat, it is using a representational gesture, but when a man nods his head to indicate assent (or, in some cultures, refusal) the gesture is arbitrary and therefore symbolic. Weeping is a sign of sorrow, blushing a sign of shame, and paleness a sign of fear, but these signs are *caused* by the emotional states in question, and so

Figure 5   British traffic signs (a) representational (b) symbolic

are not arbitrary or symbolic. When a man shakes his fist in anger, he is delivering a blow in pantomime, and the gesture is representational, but when he raises a clenched or flattened hand in a communist or fascist salute, he has moved into the realm of the purely symbolic.

Animal gestures and cries are largely non-symbolic. Usually they are either of the weeping and blushing kind, that is expressive cries or gestures, or they are representational, as when a chimpanzee pulls a companion in the direction it wants it to go. When a bird cries out on the approach of a predator, and so warns its companions, it is reacting automatically to the stimulus of seeing the enemy. Its cry triggers off reactions in its companions, which take to flight, but the bird utters the warning cry even if there are no companions present. The evolutionary process will obviously favour animals where such expressive cries trigger off suitable reactions, but the element of symbolism is small.

Its symbolical quality is one of the things that make human language such a powerful tool. The expressive cry or trigger stimulus can refer only to the immediate situation, to what is present to the senses, but the symbolical utterance can refer to things out of sight, to the past and the future, to the hypothetical and the possible.

The functions of language

Language is used for more than one purpose. The man who hits his thumb-nail with a hammer and utters a string of curses is using language for an expressive purpose: he is relieving his feelings, and needs no audience but himself. People can often be heard *playing* with language: children especially like using language as if it were a toy, repeating, distorting, inventing, punning, jingling, and there is a play element in the use of language in some literature. But when philosophers use language to clarify their ideas on a subject, they are using it as an instrument of thought. When two neighbours gossip over the fence, or exchange conventional greetings as they pass one another in the street, language is being used to strengthen the bonds of cohesion between the members of a society. Language, it seems, is a multi-purpose instrument. One function, however, is basic: language enables us to influence one another's behaviour, and to influence it in great detail, and thereby makes human co-operation possible. Other animals co-operate, for example many primates, and social insects like bees and ants, and use communication systems in the process. But human co-operation is more detailed and more diversified than that found elsewhere in the animal kingdom, and no non-human animal society has a division of labour or a system of production at all comparable to those of human societies. This human co-operation would be unthinkable without language, and it is obviously this function which has made language so successful and so important; other functions can be looked on as by-products. A language, of course, always belongs to a group of people, not to an individual. The group that uses any given language is called the *speech community*.

Language types

A human language, then, is a signalling system which operates with symbolic vocal sounds, and which is used by some group of people for the purposes of communication and social co-operation. There are about six thousand human languages spoken in the world today, which all fall under this definition of language, but nevertheless differ widely from one another. Various attempts have been made, therefore, to classify languages into different types.

One scheme distinguishes two main types of language, the analytic and the synthetic. An analytic language is one that uses very few bound morphemes, such as are seen in English prefixes and suffixes (re*fill*, slow*ly*) and in the inflections (grammatical endings) of English nouns and verbs (box*es*, talk*ing*, talk*ed*). Chinese, for example, is a highly analytic language: it has few bound forms, its words being mostly one-syllable morphemes or compounds of free morphemes. A synthetic language, by contrast, uses large numbers of bound morphemes, and often combines long strings of them to form a single word. Examples of highly synthetic languages are the Eskimo languages and Turkish. Most languages lie between these extremes, for the synthetic-analytic division is not a sharp one: rather it is a continuous scale, a continuum, with languages occupying various points between the two extremes. Its weakness as a system of classification is that languages are mixed: some are more synthetic or more analytic in some respects, some in others. It nevertheless has its uses: it makes sense, for example, to say that the English language in the course of its history has become less synthetic and more analytic.

Another well-known classification divides languages into four types: *isolating, agglutinative, flectional* (or *inflectional*), and *polysynthetic* (or *incorporating*). An isolating language uses no bound forms: words are invariable, and in the extreme case every word would consist of a single morpheme. Vietnamese and Chinese are examples of highly isolating languages. In agglutinative languages, such as Turkish and Finnish, there are many bound forms, and these are, as it were, stuck together to form words, without their shape being altered during the process: within a word, the boundaries between morphemes are clear-cut. In a flectional language, by contrast, the bound morphemes are not invariable, and a morpheme may signal several different features. For example, in Latin the noun *dominus* 'a master' has a genitive plural form *dominōrum*. The ending *-ōrum* signals three things: that the noun is plural, that it is genitive (so that the word means 'of masters'), and that its gender is either masculine or neuter. But the ending *-ōrum* cannot be broken up into three pieces, each of which signals one of these things, whereas in an agglutinating language there would indeed be three different suffixes joined together to signal the three features. In a polysynthetic language, large numbers of morphemes, both grammatical and lexical, can be combined into a single word, as in the Eskimo languages.

This fourfold system arose in the middle of the nineteenth century, and is still often used today. It is not wholly satisfactory, however. The various definitions given are not always completely clear, and the four classes are not quite mutually exclusive: the Eskimo languages, for example, are both agglutinative and polysynthetic. For this reason, attempts have been made in recent years to establish different systems of language-types. The two systems we have so far considered are both based on morphology, that is, the structure of words. Many recent linguists have instead concentrated on word-order, and tried to base a typology on it.

We have already noted that in English the normal order of the elements in a clause is Subject-Verb-Object, as in 'The dog bit John', whereas some languages prefer a different order: classical Latin, for example, normally has S-O-V order, as in 'Canis Marcum momordit', literally 'Dog Marcus bit', that is, 'The/A dog bit Marcus'. There are six possible combinations of Subject, Verb, and Object, and five of them are certainly attested in living languages, while the sixth (O-S-V) probably also exists, in a few languages in South America. Again, in English an adjective normally precedes its noun, as in 'White clothes', but in some languages it usually follows it, as in French 'Vêtements blancs', literally 'Clothes white'. In French the possessive also follows the noun, as in 'La mort de mon oncle', but in this case English has a choice: the possessive can come before the noun ('My uncle's death') or after it ('The death of my uncle'). In both English and French a relative clause comes after its governing noun, as in an example we have already seen: 'The women, who were wearing white clothes . . .'; but in some languages, such as Turkish, the order is the other way round. Again, both English and French use prepositions, which are placed before the noun phrase which they govern, as in the Preposition Phrase 'in white clothes', but some languages, again including Turkish, instead use postpositions, which are placed *after* the noun phrase which they govern.

One attempt to categorize languages by means of word-order divides them into those in which the head normally precedes the modifier ('operand-operator languages'), and those in which it normally follows it ('operator-operand languages'). So in operand-operator languages the Verb precedes the Object, the Noun precedes its adjectives and possessives and relative clauses, and the Preposition precedes the noun phrase which it governs; Welsh is an example of an operand-operator language. In operator-operand languages, the Object precedes the Verb, adjectives and possessives and relative clauses precede their Noun, and Postpositions are used instead of Prepositions; Turkish is an example of an operator-operand language. Unfortunately, a very large number of languages fail to conform exactly to either pattern: English, for example, is largely an operand-operator language, but places adjectives before the noun. Some advocates of the system therefore argue that the two types are ideals towards which languages strive: a mixed language is in process of transition from one type to the other. It is doubtful, however, whether this theory is supported by the actual data of language-change.

There are some methodological difficulties with such word-order studies, especially in finding cross-language definitions for the categories used: it is not certain, for example, that all languages have parts of the sentence that can be categorized as Subject, Verb, and Object. Some systems of language-typology avoid this particular difficulty by using non-syntactic features for the classification: for example, it is possible to use semantic categories such as Agent, Instrument, Experiencer, and Patient, instead of (or in addition to) syntactic categories like Subject and Object. None of the various approaches used, however, seems to have succeeded in establishing an all-embracing scheme of Language Types, and perhaps such an aim is in fact impracticable. They have, however, thrown much light on the structure of various languages and on the differences (and resemblances) between them.

Language universals

In recent years the study of language types has been closely linked to the search for language universals, that is, features which all languages possess, and must possess. Typology examines language variation, while the study of universals tries to establish the permissible limits of this variation, and both use the same kind of material. The search for linguistic universals was given considerable impetus by the work of Noam Chomsky. Because of the ease with which children learn language, Chomsky maintains that human language is innate: in the brain is a genetically transmitted 'language organ', which determines the syntactic and semantic properties of all languages. On Chomsky's view, therefore, all languages have the same underlying structure, and it should be possible to demonstrate the existence of universals. Not all specialists in the field, however, believe that *all* language universals are innate: some take the view that some universals may have psychological or functional explanations.

Some proposed universals are absolute, for example that all languages have vowels. It can be added that all languages have oral vowels (but not all languages have nasal vowels). There are also strong tendencies which are not quite universals: for example, nearly all languages have nasal consonants, but there are just a few that lack them. Some proposed universals are of the 'If A, then B' type: for example, 'If a language has V-S-O as its basic word-order, then it invariably has prepositions'. On the other hand, if a language has S-O-V as its basic word-order, then it will probably have postpositions; but this is not a universal, but a strong tendency, because there are counter-examples: classical Latin, for example, has S-O-V as its basic word-order, but has prepositions. Universals of the 'If A, then B' type are called *implicational* universals; and tendencies of this type are similarly called implicational tendencies.

2 The flux of language

Languages sometimes die out, usually because of competition from another language. For example, it is only during the past few centuries that English has become the universal language in Cornwall. Formerly there was a Cornish language, a Celtic language related to Welsh and Breton, but this was gradually displaced by English, and finally died out. The last known native speakers of Cornish were a few old people in the village of Mousehole, near Penzance, in the 1770s. A language can also become dead in another way. Nobody today speaks classical Latin as spoken by Julius Caesar, or classical Greek as spoken by Pericles, or the Old Icelandic spoken by the heroes of the Norse sagas. So classical Latin and classical Greek and Old Icelandic are dead languages. But, although dead, they have not *died*: they have changed into something else. People still speak Greek as a living language, and this language is simply a changed form of the language spoken in the Athens of Pericles. The people who live in Rome today speak a language that has developed by a process of continuous change out of the language spoken there in the time of Julius Caesar, though modern Italian developed out of the everyday language of the ancient Roman market-place and of the common soldiery, rather than out of the upper-class literary Latin that Caesar wrote. And the people who live in Iceland today speak a language that has developed directly out of the language of the great Icelandic sagas of the Middle Ages.

In fact all living languages change, though the rate of change varies from time to time and from language to language. The modern Icelander, for example, does not find it very difficult to read the medieval Icelandic sagas, because the rate of change in Icelandic has always been slow, ever since the country was colonized by Norwegians a thousand years ago and Icelandic history began. But the English, on the contrary, find an English document of the year 1300 very difficult to understand, unless they have special training; and an English document of the year 900 seems to them to be written in a foreign language, which they may conclude (mistakenly) to have no connection with Modern English.

Linguistic change in English

The extent to which the English language has changed in the past thousand years can be seen by looking at a few passages of English from different periods. Since it is convenient to see the same material handled by different writers, I have chosen a short passage from the Bible, which has been translated into English at many different times. The passage is from Chapter XV of the Gospel according to Luke, and is the end of the story of the Prodigal Son. Here it is first in a twentieth-century translation, the New English Bible, published in 1961:

> Now the elder son was out on the farm; and on his way back, as he approached the house, he heard music and dancing. He called one of the servants and asked what it meant. The servant told him, 'Your brother has come home, and your father has killed the fatted calf because he has him back safe and sound.' But he was angry and refused to go in. His father came out and pleaded with him; but he retorted, 'You know how I have slaved for you all these years; I never once disobeyed your orders; and you never gave me so much as a kid, for a feast with my friends. But now that this son of yours turns up, after running through your money with his women, you kill the fatted calf for him.' 'My boy,' said the father, 'you were always with me, and everything I have is yours. How could we help celebrating this happy day? Your brother here was dead and has come back to life, was lost and is found.'

You may feel that there is a certain unevenness of manner about that, but at any rate it is twentieth-century English, with nothing archaic or affected about it. Now let us look at the same passage as it appeared in the famous King James Bible of the year 1611:

> Now his elder sonne was in the field, and as he came and drew nigh to the house, he heard musicke & dauncing, and he called one of the seruants, and asked what these things meant. And he said vnto him, Thy brother is come, and thy father hath killed the fatted calfe, because he hath receiued him safe and sound. And he was angry, and would not goe in: therefore came his father out, and intreated him. And he answering said to his father, Loe, these many yeeres doe I serue thee, neither transgressed I at any time thy commandement, and yet thou neuer gauest mee a kid, that I might make merry with my friends: but as soone as this thy sonne was come, which hath deuoured thy liuing with harlots, thou hast killed for him the fatted calfe. And he said vnto him, Sonne, thou art euer with me, and all that I haue is thine. It was meete that we should make merry, and be glad: for this thy brother was dead, and is aliue againe: and was lost, and is found.

We have no great difficulty in understanding that passage, but nevertheless there are numerous ways in which it differs from present-day English. In its vocabulary, there are words which seem to us archaic, or at least old-fashioned: *nigh* 'near', *meete* 'fitting', *transgressed* 'broke, violated', *commandement* 'commands, orders'. One word looks familiar, but has an unfamiliar meaning: *liuing* does not mean 'living' in our sense of the word, but rather 'income, property, possessions'. In grammar, we notice the use of the personal pronoun *thou* and its accusative *thee*, together with the associated pronoun-determiner *thy*: and after *thou* the verbs have the inflection *-est* or *-st* (*gauest, hast*). The use of *thou* in the passage in fact shows the disadvantage of using translations for our illustrative material, for it does not reflect normal English usage in 1611. In Shakespeare's time, a father could address his son as *thou*, but the son could not, like the son in the passage, say *thou* in return, but would have to say *you* or *ye*; the usage in the passage is due to the influence of the original Greek. The passage uses the relative pronoun *which* ('thy sonne . . . which hath deuoured') where we should use *who*. In word-order, notice the sequence Verb-Subject-Object in 'neither transgressed I . . . thy commandement', and similarly Verb-Subject order in 'therefore came his father out'. The perfect tense of the verb *to come* is formed with the auxiliary *be*, not *have*: 'Thy brother *is* come', 'this thy sonne *was* come', where we should say 'has come', 'had come'. In the noun phrases *this thy sonne* and *this thy brother*, the determiner *this* and the pronoun-determiner *thy* occur together before the noun; today we should say 'this son of yours', 'this brother of yours'.

The spellings of the passage are quite close to modern ones, except for the use of *u* and *v*, which are not used to distinguish vowel from consonant: *v* is always used at the beginning of a word (*vnto*), and *u* is always used elsewhere (*serue, out, thou*). Notice, however, the spelling of *dauncing*, which does rather suggest a different pronunciation from *dancing*. There is in fact plenty of evidence to show that pronunciation in 1611 differed in many ways from pronunciation today, even when the spellings are the same. The vowels in particular were different, as we shall see later.

As our third example we can take the same passage as rendered by John Wycliffe, the first person to translate the entire Bible into English. Wycliffe died in 1384, and his translation probably dates from the last few years of his life. Like many Middle English texts, the passage uses two different kinds of letter g, namely ʒ and g. The ʒ (called 'yogh') is descended from Old English script, whereas g was introduced from the continent after the Norman Conquest. In the passage, ʒ usually corresponds to a modern *y*, as in ʒeeris 'years'; but in neiʒede 'drew nigh, approached', it corresponds to a modern *gh*, and was probably pronounced [ç] (like the consonant of Modern German *ich*). The punctuation of the passage has been modernized.

Forsoth his eldere sone was in the feeld, and whanne he cam and neiʒede to the hous, he herde a symfonye and a crowde. And he clepide oon of the seruauntis, and axide what thingis thes weren. And he seide to him, Thi brodir is comen, and thi fadir hath slayn a fat calf, for he receyued him saf. Forsoth he was wroth, and wolde not entre. Therfore his fadir gon out, bigan to preie him. And he answeringe to his fadir seide, Lo, so manye ʒeeris I serue to thee, and I brak neuere thi commaundement, thou hast neuer ʒouun a kyde to me, that I schulde ete largely with my frendis. But aftir that this thi sone, which deuouride his substaunce with hooris, cam, thou hast slayn to him a

fat calf. And he seide to him, Sone, thou ert euere with me, and alle
myne thingis ben thyne. Forsothe it bihofte to ete plenteously, and for
to ioye: for this thi brother was deed, and lyuede aȝeyn: he peryschide,
and he is founden.

This is much more remote from Modern English, especially in
vocabulary. There are many words and phrases which, while
perfectly comprehensible, sound archaic or old-fashioned, like
forsoth 'indeed' and *wroth* 'angry'. There are also words which are
quite strange to the modern reader, like *neiȝede* 'approached' and
clepide 'called'. There are familiar-looking words with unfamiliar
meanings, like *symfonye* 'musical instrument', *crowde* 'fiddle',
largely 'liberally, plenteously', *thyngis* 'goods', and *for* 'because' (in
'for he receyued him saf'). In grammar, there are noun-plural
endings in *-is* (*thyngis, hooris*, etc.), verb-plural endings in *-en* or *-n*
(*weren, ben*), verb past-tense endings in *-ide* (*clepide, axide*, etc.),
and past participles ending in *-n* (*comen, founden*). In spelling, only
u occurs in the passage, not *v*, but in Wycliffe's time they tended to
be used interchangeably, and not distributed as they are in the
1611 passage: the use of *v* initially and *u* elsewhere was a printer's
convention, which in England lasted until about 1630, but
manuscripts often use the two letters indiscriminately. The
passage also uses *i* instead of *j* (*ioye*); the letter *j* was in fact
merely a decorative variant of *i*, and the modern vowel-consonant
distinction in their use was not established until about 1630.
There are also numerous words where the spelling suggests a
pronunciation different from our own – *whanne* 'when', *oon* 'one',
etc. – though of course this piece of evidence alone is not sufficient
for us to determine their pronunciation. The word-order of the
passage, however, is very close to that of present-day English.

For our final example, we go back behind the Norman
Conquest, to a manuscript of the early eleventh century. As is
customary in modern editions of texts from this period. I mark
long vowels by putting a macron (short horizontal line) over them,
while short vowels are left unmarked. The symbol þ (called
'thorn') is equivalent to the modern *th*: the symbol æ (called 'ash')
is pronounced like the vowel of the word *hat* in RP. The
punctuation is modernized. As the English of this period is difficult
for the modern reader, I give only the opening of the passage.

Sōþlice his yldra sunu wæs on æcere; and hē cōm, and þā hē þām hūse genēalǣhte, hē gehȳrde þæne swēg and þæt wered. þā clypode hē ānne þēow, and ācsode hine hwæt þæt wǣre. þā cwæþ hē, þīn brōþor cōm, and þīn fæder ofslōh ān fætt cealf, forþām þe hē hine hālne onfēng.

Part of the difficulty of this lies in the number of unfamiliar words: *þā* 'when, then', *genēalǣhte* 'approached', *swēg* 'noise', *wered* 'multitude, band', *þēow* 'servant', *ofslōh* 'killed', *forþām þe* 'because', *hine* 'him', *onfēng* 'received'; these are all words that have died out from the language. In the later passages, some of them are replaced by words borrowed from French after the Norman Conquest (*approached, servant, received*). Even words which have survived may be used in an unfamiliar sense: the word *æcere* has developed into our *acre*, but means 'field', and *hālne* has become our *whole*, but means 'well, safe'. Even words unchanged in meaning appear in unfamiliar spelling, like *yldra sunu* 'elder son', and were obviously pronounced differently from their modern counterparts.

The passage also differs from present-day English in the way words change their endings according to their grammatical function in the sentence. This could be demonstrated from many words in the passage but three brief examples will suffice. The word for 'field' is *æcer*, but after the preposition *on* it has to add the ending *-e* (pronounced as an extra syllable), and so in the text we have the expression *on æcere*. The expression for 'the house' is *þæt hūs*, but 'to the house' is *þām hūse*, and this is the form that appears in the text; *æcere* and *hūse* are the *dative case* of the nouns *æcer* and *hūs*. The normal word for 'was' is *wæs*, as in the first sentence of the passage, but there is also a form *wǣre* (the so-called subjunctive form) which has to be used in certain constructions, like 'ācsode hine hwæt þæt *wǣre*' ('asked him what it was').

The passage also differs from present-day English in word-order. Translated literally word for word it runs as follows:

> Indeed, his elder son was on field; and he came, and when he the house approached, he heard the noise and the crowd. Then called he a servant, and asked him what it was. Then said he, Your brother came, and your father killed a fat calf, because he him safe received.

There we see three different types of word-order, different arrangements of Subject-Verb-Object. Some clauses have the normal present-day order of S-V-O: 'he heard the noise', 'your father killed a fat calf'. But some have the order V-S-O: 'then called he a servant', 'Then said he . . .'. This construction often occurs when the clause begins with an adverbial expression, especially adverbs like *then* and *there*. Yet other clauses have the order S-O-V: 'when he the house approached', 'because he him safe received'. This word-order occurs in subordinate clauses, opened in this case by the conjunctions *because* and *when*. These three types of word-order are common in the earliest forms of English, and are still found in Modern German. One of the major syntactic changes in the English language since Anglo-Saxon times has been the disappearance of the S-O-V and V-S-O types of word-order, and the establishment of the S-V-O type as normal. The S-O-V type disappeared in the early Middle Ages, and the V-S-O type was rare after the middle of the seventeenth century. V-S word-order does indeed still exist in English as a less common variant, as in sentences like 'Down the road came a whole crowd of children', but the full V-S-O type hardly occurs today.

The English language, then, has changed enormously in the last thousand years. New words have appeared, and some old ones disappeared. Words have changed in meaning. The grammatical endings of words have changed, and many such endings have disappeared from the language. The membership of 'closed class' word-forms, the grammatical words, has changed: the system of personal pronouns, for example, has lost the forms *thou* and *thee*. There have been changes in word-order, the permissible ways in which words can be arranged to make meaningful utterances. Pronunciation has changed. Taken all together, these changes add up to a major transformation of the language.

It can also be seen, even from the four passages that I have quoted, that the pace of change has varied. Between the New English Bible and the King James Bible there is a period of just three and a half centuries, but the differences between them are less than those between the King James Bible and Wycliffe's version, which are separated by only about two and a quarter centuries. The differences between the Wycliffe and the Pre-Conquest passage, too, are very great. If we were to study a large number of passages to fill in the chronological gaps, we should find that the twelfth century and the fifteenth century were periods of particularly rapid change in English. This makes it convenient to divide the history of the English language into three broad periods, which are usually called Old English, Middle English, and Modern English (or New English). No exact boundaries can be drawn, but Old English covers from the first Anglo-Saxon settlements in England to about 1100, Middle English from about 1100 to about 1500, and Modern English from about 1500 to the present day. These periods are often subdivided, giving such sub-periods as Late Old English (c. 900–1100) and Early Modern English (c. 1500–1650).

Mechanisms of linguistic change

All living languages undergo changes analogous to those we have just seen exemplified in English. What causes such changes? There is no single answer to this question: changes in a language are of various kinds, and there seem to be various reasons for them.

The changes that have caused the most disagreement are those in pronunciation. We have various sources of evidence for the pronunciations of earlier times, such as the spellings, the treatment of words borrowed from other languages or borrowed by them, the descriptions of contemporary grammarians and spelling-reformers, and the modern pronunciations in all the languages and dialects concerned. From the middle of the sixteenth century, there are in England writers who attempt to describe the position of the speech-organs for the production of English phonemes, and who invent what are in effect systems of phonetic symbols. These various kinds of evidence, combined with a knowledge of the mechanisms of speech-production, can often give us a very good idea of the pronunciation of an earlier age, though absolute certainty is never possible.

When we study the pronunciation of a language over any period of a few generations or more, we find there are always large-scale regularities in the changes: for example, over a certain period of time, just about all the long [a:] vowels in a language may change into long [e:] vowels, or all the [b] consonants in a certain position (for example at the end of a word) may change into [p] consonants. Such regular changes are often called *sound laws*. There are no universal sound laws (even though sound laws often reflect universal tendencies), but simply particular sound laws for one given language (or dialect) at one given period. We must not think of a sound law, however, as a sudden change which immediately affects all the words concerned. If [b] changes to [p] in a given language, the change may first appear in words which are frequently used, and gradually spread through the rest of the vocabulary. Indeed, the sound law may cease to operate before all the relevant words have been affected, so that a few are left with the earlier pronunciation.

One cause which has been suggested for changes in pronunciation is geographic and climatic, for example that people living in mountain country are subject to certain changes in pronunciation compared to plainsmen, but the evidence for this is unconvincing. Other people have suggested biological and racial factors: it has been said, for example, that races with thick lips have difficulty in producing certain speech-sounds. Once again, no really convincing evidence has been produced; and if a child of any racial origins is brought up from birth in a normal English-speaking family, it will grow up speaking English just like a native. Moreover, the theory would obviously be most useful for explaining changes in a language when it is adopted by one people from another. But in these circumstances the theory is unnecessary: the influence of one language on another is quite enough to explain such changes, without racial characteristics being invoked.

During childhood, we learn our mother tongue very thoroughly, and acquire a whole set of speech habits which become second nature to us. If later we learn a foreign language, we inevitably carry over some of these speech habits into it, and so do not speak it exactly like a native. For example, we have seen that in most phonetic contexts the English /p/ phoneme is pronounced with a following aspiration, producing a kind of [pʰ] sound, and the same is in fact true of the English /t/ and /k/ phonemes. But it is not true of the similar phonemes in French or Italian, where the voiceless plosives are pronounced without any following aspiration. Many English speakers of French and Italian, even competent ones, carry over their aspirated voiceless plosives into those languages, and this is one of many features that make them sound foreign to native speakers. In bilingual situations, therefore, the second language tends to be modified. Such modifications may not persist: an isolated Polish or Pakistani immigrant to Britain will usually have grandchildren who speak English like natives, because the influence of the general speech environment (peer-group, school, work) is stronger than that of the home. But if a large and closely-knit group of people adopt a new language, then the modifications that they make in it may persist among their descendants, even if the latter no longer speak the original language that caused the changes. This can be seen in Wales, where the influence of Welsh has affected the pronunciation of English, and the very characteristic intonation-patterns of Welsh English have been carried over from Welsh, even among those who no longer speak it. Many historical changes may have been due to a linguistic substratum of this kind: a conquering minority that imposed its language on a conquered population must often have had its language modified by its victims.

It is also possible that fashion plays a part in the process of change. It certainly plays a part in the spread of change: one person imitates another, and people with the most prestige are most likely to be imitated, so that a change that takes place in one social group may be imitated (more or less accurately) by speakers in another group. When a social group goes up or down in the world, its pronunciation may gain or lose prestige. It is said that, after the Russian Revolution of 1917, the upper-class pronunciation of Russian, which had formerly been considered desirable, became on the contrary an undesirable kind of accent to have, so that people tried to disguise it. Some of the changes in accepted English pronunciation in the seventeenth and eighteenth centuries have been shown to consist in the replacement of one style of pronunciation by another style already existing, and it is likely that such substitutions were a result of the great social changes of the period: the increased power and wealth of the middle classes, and their steady infiltration upwards into the ranks of the landed gentry, probably carried elements of middle-class pronunciation into upper-class speech.

Besides spreading changes that have already taken place, fashion may actually cause changes in pronunciation. The important thing about a fashion is that it's exclusive: as soon as the fashion has penetrated to a less prestigious social group, it's time to move on. This can be seen in clothes: fashionable people may find it flattering to be imitated, but as soon as the new fashion has really caught on, they need to change to something else, to mark themselves off as different. It may be the same with language, for social groups use characteristic styles of language to mark themselves off from other groups. A group with high prestige may find that its style of speech is being imitated by other groups, and then its members may (perhaps unconsciously) begin to change it, perhaps by exaggerating its distinguishing characteristics.

Another suggested cause for changes in pronunciation is the fact that children grow. The vocal organs of children, it is argued, are a different size from those of adults; they learn to mimic the noises that their parents make, but on what is in effect a different instrument; as they grow up, they go on moving their vocal organs in the same way, but the sounds that they produce are now different, because the organs are changed. There are two serious objections to this theory, however. The first is that, if this were indeed a major cause of phonological change, we should then expect all changes of pronunciation to be in the same direction, irrespective of language or period, and this is certainly not the case. The second objection is that humans appear to have the capacity, probably innate, to allow for different sizes of vocal tract when they interpret speech: the voices of a young child, of a woman, and of a deep-voiced man all have different pitch-levels, but this does not cause problems of understanding. When the man utters the vowel [ɪ] he may in fact produce the same acoustic signal as the woman when she says [e], or the child when it says [æ], but we have an inbuilt mechanism that allows us to interpret their vowels correctly, provided we hear them as part of a longer utterance. This fact makes it unlikely that growth of the vocal tract leads to changes in pronunciation.

A less specific variant of the argument is that the imitation of children is imperfect: they copy their parents' speech, but never reproduce it exactly. This is true, but it is also true that such deviations from adult speech are usually corrected in later childhood. Perhaps it is more significant that even adults show a certain amount of random variation in their pronunciation of a given phoneme, even if the phonetic context is kept unchanged. This, however, cannot explain changes in pronunciation unless it can be shown that there is some systematic trend in the failures of imitation: if they are merely random deviations they will cancel one another out and there will be no nett change in the language. For some of these random variations to be selected at the expense of others, there must be further forces at work.

One such force which is often invoked is the principle of ease, or minimization of effort. We all try to economize energy in our actions, it is argued, so we tend to take short cuts in the movements of our speech-organs, to replace movements calling for great accuracy or energy by less demanding ones, to omit sounds if they are not essential for understanding, and so on. Such changes increase the efficiency of the language as a communication-system, and are undoubtedly a factor in linguistic change, though we have to add that what seems easy or difficult to a speaker will depend on the particular language that has been learnt. Suppose we have a sequence of three sounds in which the first and the third are voiced, while the middle one is voiceless: the speaker has to carry out the operation of switching off voice before the second sound and then switching it on again before the third. An economy of effort could be obtained by omitting these two operations and allowing the voice to continue through all three sounds. Such a change would be seen if the pronunciation of *fussy* were changed to *fuzzy*, the voiceless /s/ being replaced by the voiced /z/ between the two vowels. Changes of this kind are common in the history of language, but nevertheless we cannot lay it down as a universal rule that *fuzzy* is easier to pronounce than *fussy*. In Swedish, for example, there is no /z/ phoneme, and Swedes who learn English find it difficult to say *fuzzy*, which they often mispronounce as *fussy*. For them, plainly, *fussy* is the easier of the two pronunciations, because it accords better with the sound-system of their own language.

The change from *fussy* to *fuzzy* would be an example of **assimilation**, which is a very common kind of change. Assimilation is the changing of a sound under the influence of a neighbouring one. For example, the word *scant* was once *skamt*, but the /m/ has been changed to /n/ under the influence of the following /t/. Greater efficiency has hereby been achieved, because /n/ and /t/ are articulated in the same place (with the tip of the tongue against the teeth-ridge), whereas /m/ is articulated elsewhere (with the two lips). So the place of articulation of the nasal consonant has been changed to conform with that of the following plosive. A more recent example of the same kind of thing is the common pronunciation of *football* as *foopball*. Sometimes it is the second of the two sounds that is changed by the assimilation. This can be seen in some changes that have taken place in English under the influence of /w/: until about 1700, words like *swan* and *wash* rhymed with words like *man* and *rash*; the change in the vowel of *swan* and *wash* has given it the lip-rounding and the retracted tongue-position of the /w/, and so economized in effort.

Assimilation is not the only way in which we change our pronunciation in order to increase efficiency. It is very common for consonants to be lost at the end of a word: in Middle English, word-final /-n/ was often lost in unstressed syllables, so that *baken* 'to bake' changed from /'ba:kən/ to /'ba:kə/, and later to /ba:k/. Consonant-clusters are often simplified. At one time there was a /t/ in words like *castle* and *Christmas*, and an initial /k/ in words like *knight* and *know*. Sometimes a whole syllable is dropped out when two successive syllables begin with the same consonant (*haplology*): a recent example is *temporary*, which in Britain is often pronounced as if it were *tempory*.

On the other hand, ease of pronunciation can lead to an extra phoneme being inserted in a word: in Old English, our word *thunder* was *þunor*, with no *d*. By normal development, *þunor* would have become *thunner*, not *thunder*, but at some stage a /d/ has been inserted in the pronunciation. Spellings with *d* are first found in the thirteenth century, and are completely normal by the sixteenth. Why was a /d/ inserted in the word? Probably because the pronunciation *thunder* actually calls for less precise movements of the speech-organs. The /d/ arose from a slight mistiming in the transition from the nasal /n/ to the following phoneme (which was probably a syllabic /r/ rather than a vowel). This transition calls for two simultaneous movements of the speech-organs: (1) the nasal passages are closed by the raising of the soft palate, and (2) the tongue is moved away from the teeth to unblock the mouth-passage. If the two movements are not carried out simultaneously, but the nasal passages are closed before the tongue moves, a /d/ will be heard between the /n/ and the following phoneme, as the stop is released. Similar mistimings produced the /b/ in the middle of the words *thimble* and *bramble* (Old English *þymel*, *brēmel*). Sometimes, too, ease of pronunciation apparently leads us to reverse the order of two phonemes in a word (*metathesis*): this has happened in the words *wasp* and *burn*, which by regular development would have been *waps* and *brin* or *bren*.

The changes produced in pursuit of efficiency can often be tolerated, because a language always provides more signals than the absolute minimum necessary for the transmission of the message, to give a margin of safety: like all good communication-systems, human language has built in to it a considerable amount of redundancy. But there is a limit to this toleration: the necessities of communication, the urgent needs of humans as users of language, provide a counterforce to the principle of minimum effort. If, through excessive economy of effort, an utterance is not understood, or is misunderstood, the speaker is obliged to repeat it or recast it, making more effort. The necessities of communication, moreover, may be responsible for the selection of some of the random variations of a phoneme rather than others, so that a change in pronunciation occurs in a certain direction. This direction may be chosen because it makes the sound inherently more audible: for example, open nasal vowels seem to be more distinctive in quality than close ones, and in languages which have such vowels it is not uncommon for a nasal [e] to develop into a nasal [a].

In considering such changes, however, we cannot look at the isolated phoneme: we have to consider the sound-system of the language as a whole. The 'safeness' or otherwise of a phoneme for communicative purposes does not depend solely on its own inherent distinctiveness: it depends also on the other phonemes in the language with which it can be contrasted, and the likelihood that it may be confused with them. Let us imagine that in the vowel-system of a language there is a short [e], as in *bet* (see for example the vowel-diagram in Figure 4, p. 14 above); in one direction from it there is a short [æ] (as in *bat*), and in another direction a short [ə] (as in the first syllable of *about*); but in the upward (closer) direction there is no short vowel, no kind of short [ɪ] for example. Suppose now that random variations occur in speakers' pronunciations of these three vowels. When the variations of [e] go too far in the direction of [æ] or [ə], the speaker will be forced to correct them, to avoid misunderstanding. But when the variations are in the direction of [ɪ], there is no such necessity for checking or correction. The result will be a shift in the centre of gravity of the [e], which will drift up towards [ɪ]. Moreover, the movement of [e] towards [ɪ] will leave more scope for variations in [æ], which may tend to drift up towards [e]. In this way, a whole chain of vowel-changes may take place.

In this example I have assumed that the contrast between the three vowels is important enough in the functioning of the language for speakers to resist any changes which threaten this contrast. This will be the case if large numbers of words are distinguished from one another by these vowels, in other words if the contrast between them does a lot of work in the language. The functional load carried by a contrast is a major factor when speakers decide (unconsciously) whether to let a change take place or not. There may be forces in the system making for the amalgamation of two phonemes, and if there are very few words in the language which will be confused with one another as a result then there will not be much resistance to the change; but if serious confusion will be caused by the amalgamation it will be resisted more strongly, and perhaps be prevented.

This does not mean, on the other hand, that a phoneme with a small functional load will necessarily be thrown out of the system, either by being lost or by being amalgamated with another phoneme. It also depends on the degree of effort required to *retain* the phoneme, which may be quite small. For example, the contrast in English between the voiced /ð/ and the voiceless /θ/ phonemes carries a very small load; there are a few pairs of words that are distinguished from one another solely by this difference, like *wreathe* and *wreath*, and *mouth* (verb) and *mouth* (noun); but in practice the distinction between the two phonemes is of very small importance, and it would cause no great inconvenience if they were amalgamated, for example by both evolving into some third, different, phoneme. On the other hand, it takes very little effort to retain the distinction between them. They belong to a whole series of voiced and voiceless fricatives (/v/ and /f/, /z/ and /s/, /ʒ/ and /ʃ/), and so fall into a familiar pattern; and if we abolished the distinction between them we should not economize in the number of *types* of contrast that we made; we should still have to distinguish fricatives from other types of consonant, and between voiced and voiceless fricatives.

The stability of /ð/ and /θ/ thus results from the fact that they are, in André Martinet's terminology, 'well integrated' in the consonant system of English. An even better integrated group of consonants in present-day English is the following:

Voiceless plosives	/p/	/t/	/k/
Voiced plosives	/b/	/d/	/g/
Nasals	/m/	/n/	/ŋ/

Each of these three series uses the same places of articulation: the two lips pressed together for /p/, /b/, /m/; the tip of the tongue pressed against the teeth-ridge for /t/, /d/, /n/; the back of the tongue pressed up against the soft palate for /k/, /g/, /ŋ/. So, using only three articulatory positions, and three distinctive articulatory features (plosiveness, nasality, voice), we get no fewer than nine distinct phonemes. This group is very stable, because the loss of any one of the nine would produce negligible economy in the system: if, say, /ŋ/ were to disappear, we should still have to be able to produce nasality for /m/ and /n/, and we should still have to be able to articulate with the back of the tongue against the soft palate for /g/ and /k/. So even if /ŋ/ carried a very small load in the language we should still be unlikely to get rid of it. For the same reason, if there were a hole in the pattern, it would stand a good chance in time of getting filled. If there were no /ŋ/ in present-day English, but there was some other consonant which was not very well integrated in any sub-system, then any variations in this consonant that moved it in the direction of [ŋ] would tend to be accepted, because they would represent an 'easier' pronunciation – easier, that is, in terms of the economy (and therefore efficiency) of the system as a whole.

Changes in morphology, syntax, vocabulary, and word-meaning, while they can be complicated enough, are less puzzling than changes in pronunciation. Many of the same causes can be seen at work. The influence of other languages, for example, is very obvious: nations with high commercial, political, and cultural prestige tend to influence their neighbours: for centuries, French influenced all the languages of Europe, while today the influence of the English language is penetrating all over the world, largely because of the power and prestige of the United States. This influence is strongest in the field of vocabulary, but one language can also influence the morphology and syntax of another. Such influence may occur if languages in a given area are in intimate contact over an extended period, and also when a religion spreads and its sacred books are translated: in the Old English period there were many translations from the Latin, and there is some evidence that Latin syntax influenced the structure of Old English.

In the realm of vocabulary and meaning, the influence of general social and cultural change is obvious. As society changes, there are new things that need new names: physical objects, institutions, sets of attitudes, values, concepts; and new words are produced to handle them (or existing words are given new meanings). Sentimentality, classicism, wave mechanics, parliaments, post-Impressionism, privatization – these are human inventions just as much as steam engines or aircraft or nylon: and people inevitably invented names for them. Moreover, because the world is constantly changing, many words insensibly change their meanings. It is particularly easy to overlook shifts of meaning in words that refer to values or to complexes of attitudes: for example, in Shakespeare's day the adjective *gentle* meant a good deal more than 'kind, sweet-natured, mild, not violent', for it referred to high birth as well as to moral qualities, and had a whole social theory behind it.

As in pronunciation, so at the other levels of language, we see the constant conflict between the principle of minimum effort and the demands of communication. Minimization of effort is seen in the way words are often shortened, as when *public house* becomes *pub*, or *television* becomes *telly*, and also in the laconic and elliptical expressions that we often use in colloquial and intimate discourse. But if economy of this kind goes too far, some kind of compensating action may be taken, as when in Early Middle English the word *ea* was replaced by the French loan-word *river*, and in the seventeenth century the bird called the *pie* was expanded to the *magpie*. In such ways, the redundancy which has been removed from the language by shortenings may be reinserted by lengthenings.

There is also interplay between the needs of the users and the inherent tendencies of the language-system itself. One way in which the language-system promotes change, especially in grammar, is through the operation of **analogy**, which also tends to produce economy. Analogy is seen at work when children are learning their language. A child learns pairs like *dog/dogs*, *bed/beds*, *bag/bags*, and so on. Then it learns a new word, say *plug*, and quite correctly forms the plural *plugs* from it, on analogy with these other pairs. Analogy, then, is the process of inventing a new element in conformity with some part of the language system that you already know. The way in which analogy can lead to change is seen when the child learns words like *man* and *mouse*, and forms the analogical plurals *mans* and *mouses*. Ultimately such childish errors are usually corrected, but analogical formations also take place in adult speech, and quite often persist and become accepted. In Old English there were many different ways of putting a noun into the plural: for example, *stān* 'stone', *stānas* 'stones'; *word* 'word', *word* 'words'; *scip* 'ship', *scipu* 'ships'; *synn* 'sin', *synna* 'sins'; *tunge* 'tongue', *tungan* 'tongues'; *bēo* 'bee', *bēon* 'bees'; *bōc* 'book', *bēc* 'books'; *lamb* 'lamb', *lambru* 'lambs'. The form *stānas* has developed quite regularly into our plural *stones*, but, sometime during the past thousand years, all the others have changed their plural ending to the -(*e*)*s* type, by analogy with the many nouns like *stone*. The rarer a word is, the more likely it is to be affected by analogy. The unusual noun-plural forms in present-day English, which are the ones that have managed to resist the analogy of the plural in -(*e*)*s*, are mostly very common words, like *men*, *feet*, and *children*, or at any rate are words which *were* very common a few centuries ago, like *geese* and *oxen*.

Language families

The process of change in a language often leads to divergent development. Imagine a language which is spoken only by the population of two small adjacent villages. In each village, the language will slowly change, but the changes will not be identical in the two villages, because conditions are slightly different. Hence the speech used in one of the villages may gradually diverge from that used in the other. If there is rivalry between the villages, they may even pride themselves on such divergences, as a mark of local patriotism. Within the single village, speech will remain fairly uniform, because the speakers are in constant contact, and so influence one another. The rate at which the speech of one village diverges from that of the other will depend partly on the degree of difference between their ways of life, and partly on the intensity of communication between them. If the villages are close together and have a good deal of inter-village contact, so that many members of one village are constantly talking with members of the other, then divergence will be kept small, because the speech of one community will be constantly influencing the speech of the other. But if communications are bad, and members of one village seldom meet anybody from the other, then the rate of divergence may well be high. When a language has diverged into two forms like this, we say that it has two **dialects**.

Suppose now that the inhabitants of one of the villages pack up their belongings and migrate *en masse*. They go off to a distant country and live under conditions quite different from their old home, and completely lose contact with the other village. The rate at which the two dialects diverge will now increase, partly because of the difference of environment and way of life, partly because they no longer influence one another. After a few hundred years, the two dialects may have got so different that they are no longer mutually intelligible. We should now say that they were two different **languages**. Both have grown by a process of continuous change out of the single original language, but because of divergent development there are now two languages instead of one. When two languages have evolved in this way from some earlier single language, we say that they are *related*. The development of related languages from an earlier parent-language can be represented diagrammatically as a family tree, thus:

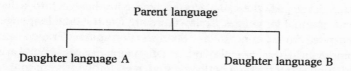

As we shall see later, this kind of diagram is in some ways inadequate, and we must certainly avoid thinking of languages as if they were people. But as long as we bear this in mind, we shall find that family trees are a convenient way of depicting the relationships between languages.

Languages descended from Latin

There are numerous examples in history of divergent development leading to the formation of related languages. For example, when the Romans conquered a large part of Europe, North Africa, and the Near East, their language, Latin, became spoken over wide areas as the standard language of administration and government, especially in the western part of the Empire. Then, in the fourth century of our era, the Empire began to disintegrate, and, in the centuries which followed, was overrun by barbarian invasions – Huns, Slavs, Germans – and gradually broke up. In the new countries that eventually emerged from the ruins of the western

Empire, various languages were spoken. In some places, both Latin and the local languages had been swept away and replaced by the language of an invader – in England, by Anglo-Saxon, in North Africa, by Arabic. But in other places Latin was firmly enough rooted to survive as the language of the new nation, as in France, Italy, and Spain. But, because there was no longer a single unifying centre to hold the language together, divergent development took place, and Latin evolved into a number of different new languages. In general, the further a place was from Rome, the more the new language diverged from the original Latin.

In the early Middle Ages there was a whole welter of local dialects developed from Latin: each region, with its own feudal court, would have its own local dialect. But, as the modern nation-states developed, these dialects became consolidated into a few great national languages. Today there are five national languages descended from Latin: Italian, Spanish, Portuguese, French, and Romanian. There are also other languages derived from Latin which have not become national languages, but which are spoken by some large group with a common culture: such are Romansh (spoken in parts of Switzerland and of Italy). Provençal (spoken in southern France), Catalan (spoken in Catalonia and the Balearic Isles), and Sardinian (spoken in southern Sardinia). Languages descended from Latin are called *Romance* languages. We can draw a family tree of the Romance languages, thus:

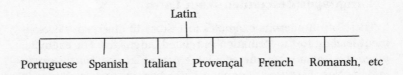

Each of the Romance languages has developed its own morphology and syntax, but they all bear signs of their common origin in Latin. The most obvious resemblances are in vocabulary: each language has undergone considerable changes in pronunciation, but the Latin origin of large numbers of words is quite evident. For example, the Latin word for 'good' is *bonus*: this has become Italian *buono*, Spanish *bueno*, French *bon*, Portuguese *bom*, and Romanian *bun*. The Latin *homo* 'man' has become Italian *uomo*, Spanish *hombre*, French *homme*, Portuguese *homem*, and Romanian *om*. The members ‘of such a related group of words are said to be **cognate**.

Some language families

This process of divergent development leading to the formation of new languages has occurred many times in human history, which is why there are now around six thousand different languages in the world. An examination of these languages shows that many of them belong to some group of related languages, and some of these groups are very large, constituting what we can call language families. A language which has arisen by the process of divergent development may itself give rise to further languages by a continuation of the same process, until there is a whole complex family of languages with various branches, some more nearly and some more distantly related to one another.

An example of such a family is the Semitic group of languages. At the time of the earliest written records this was already a family with many members: in Mesopotamia were the East Semitic languages, Babylonian and Assyrian, while round the eastern shores of the Mediterranean were the West Semitic languages, such as Moabite, Phoenician, Aramaic, and Hebrew. The East Semitic languages have died out, and the most successful surviving Semitic language is undoubtedly Arabic, a South Semitic language which, with some dialectal variations, is spoken along the whole northern coast of Africa and in a large part of the Near East. Also surviving are Syriac, Ethiopian, and Hebrew, the last of which is a remarkable example of a language being revived for everyday use after a long period in which it had only been used for religious purposes.

But the Semitic languages are themselves related to another family, the Hamitic languages, and at some time in the remote past (certainly long before 3000 BC) there must have been a single

Hamito-Semitic language which was the common ancestor of all Semitic and Hamitic languages. The language of ancient Egypt belonged to the Hamitic group; today, of course, the language of Egypt is a form of Arabic, but a descendant of the ancient Hamitic language of Egypt, Coptic, survived until about the fifteenth century, and is still used as the liturgical language of the Coptic Church. Surviving Hamitic languages are spoken across a large part of North Africa, and include Somali and the many dialects of Berber.

Another large language family is the Ural-Altaic. This has two main branches, the Finno-Ugrian and the Altaic (though some authorities deny that these branches are in fact related). The Finno-Ugrian group includes Hungarian, Finnish, Estonian, and Lapp, while the Altaic includes Turkish and Mongol. If you have ever visited Finland or Hungary, or seen newspapers from those countries, you may have been struck by the complete unfamiliarity of the language, whereas in most European countries there are many words that can be guessed, or which at any rate do not seem to be difficult to remember when once learnt. For example, the English numerals *one*, *two*, *three* are quite like German *eins*, *zwei*, *drei* and Swedish *en*, *två*, *tre*, and even French *un*, *deux*, *trois*; but the Finnish words are *yksi*, *kaksi*, *kolme*, and the Hungarian *egy*, *kettő*, *három*, which are quite strange to us. The reason is, of course, that English and most other European languages belong to a family quite unrelated to the Ural-Altaic.

A family with an enormous number of speakers is the Sino-Tibetan, which includes Thai, Burmese, Tibetan, and the various dialects of Chinese (not all of which are mutually intelligible). Japanese is not related to this group (though it has been deeply influenced by Chinese), but may possibly be related to Korean. In Southern India and Sri Lanka can be found Dravidian languages, which include Tamil and Telegu. In Malaya and the Pacific islands is the Malayo-Polynesian family, including Malayan, Melanesian, and Polynesian. In Africa, there are numerous language families, including the Nilo-Saharan, the Niger-Congo, and the Chadic. Of the better-known African languages, Yoruba and Igbo both belong to the Kwa branch of the Niger-Congo family, and Swahili and Zulu to its Bantu branch, while Hausa belongs to the Chadic family, which is perhaps related to Hamitic.

These are all families with large numbers of speakers, but there are many smaller ones, like the Eskimo languages, various families of languages among the American Indians, the Papuan languages of Australia and New Guinea, and the Caucasian languages by the Caspian Sea, including Georgian. In addition, there are isolated languages which have no known family connections, such as Basque, spoken by nearly a million people in the French and Spanish Pyrenees.

Attempts have been made to demonstrate relatedness between various recognized language-families, and thus to amalgamate them into superfamilies. It would not be surprising if many of the world's languages, or indeed all of them, went back ultimately to some common ancestor. To prove such relatedness, however, is quite another matter, after thousands of years of divergent development, and the proposed superfamilies must, at any rate for the present, be regarded as speculative.

Convergent development

The process of divergent development, then, has produced an enormous number of languages out of a smaller number of earlier ones (possibly out of one original one). There are, however, forces that work the other way, that may even reduce a language family or branch to a single language again. For example, Latin was only one of a number of related languages, dialects of Italic, which were spoken in the city-states of ancient Italy. At one time, some of these other Italic languages, such as Umbrian and Oscan, may have been at least as widespread and important as Latin. But as the Romans conquered Italy, their language conquered too, and eventually the other Italic languages died out. So we have the differentiation of a language into a number of variants, and then, for political reasons, one of these variants becomes dominant and the others disappear. Something similar has happened with the Semitic languages: many of these have died out, and one form, Arabic, has become the dominant one, because it was the language of the expansionist armies of Islam.

The same centralizing tendency can often be seen at work even when there is no question of conquest. Within a single political unit, like a modern national state, there is usually one form of the language which has higher prestige than the others, and which acts as a brake on the divergent tendencies in the language. This prestige-dialect may be the language of the ruling class, or it may simply be the educated speech of the capital, which is often the cultural as well as the administrative centre, and so exerts great influence on the rest of the country. Usually, such a prestige-dialect underlies the standard literary form of the language, which influences the whole country through books and education. The existence of a standard language discourages further divergence, because many people try to make their usage more like the standard, especially if they wish to make their way in administration and government, or if they are social climbers. It may also lead to the actual dying out of other dialects. In Old English there were many dialects, but Modern English is very largely descended from just one of them, a dialect of the East Midland region; some features from the other dialects have survived, but most of them have disappeared.

A standard literary language may continue to be influential even after the political decline of the group that made it important. An example of this is the Greek *koinē*, the standard literary language of the eastern Mediterranean from the time of Alexander the Great in the fourth century BC. This language was a modified form of the Attic dialect of Athens, which became the literary standard for the Greek-speaking world in the fifth century BC, when Athens was politically and culturally the dominant city of Greece. Athenian political dominance lasted less than a century, but the prestige of Athenian literature and of Athenian speech remained, and from it developed the koinē. This word means 'shared, common, popular', and it was indeed the common language of a large area for something like a thousand years. It is, for example, the language in which the New Testament was written. In the fourth century of our era, the sons of Constantine divided the Roman Empire, the younger son taking the eastern part and the elder son the western part, and this division became permanent. The administrative language of the Western Empire, ruled from Rome, was Latin; but the administrative language of the Eastern Empire, ruled from Constantinople, was the Greek koinē.

3 The Indo-European languages

We have talked about related languages and language families. What languages is English related to? If you know any European languages, you may well have been struck by resemblances between them and English. For example, German *Vater*, *singen*, *leben*, and *Stein* resemble their English translations *father*, *sing*, *live*, and *stone*. Resemblances alone do not prove relationship, however: the resemblances must be systematic. Consider then Table 3.1, which shows a number of words of similar meaning in modern English, German, and Swedish.

Table 3.1 *Similarities in English, German and Swedish*

English	German	Swedish
stone	Stein	sten
bone	Bein	ben
oak	Eiche	ek
home	Heim	hem
rope	Reif	rep
goat	Geiss	get
one	ein	en

The thing to notice here is not just that the words look alike, but that there are regular correspondences: words with English /əʊ/ have German *ei* and Swedish *e*. Such correspondences arise when related languages are produced by divergent development, because, as we have seen, the changes in pronunciation in any one language or dialect follow regular sound laws.

There are indeed certain anomalies in the table. German *Bein* does not mean 'bone' but 'leg'; the Swedish word *ben*, however, means both 'bone' and 'leg', and the same was once true of the German word. German *Reif* means 'ring, hoop', but formerly it also meant 'rope'. The English word *one* apparently does not fit the pattern, for it has the wrong pronunciation; if we go back a thousand years, however, we find that *one* is descended from an Old English word *ān* (pronounced with a long [ɑ:], as in *father*), and the other words in the table also have this long *ā* in Old English: *stān, bān, āc, hām, rāp, gāt*. Obviously we should expect Modern English *one* to rhyme with *stone*, but something irregular has happened. In fact our present-day pronunciation of *one* has been taken over from one of the regional dialects (perhaps to avoid confusion with *own*), but the expected pronunciation is found in *alone* and *atone*, which historically are derived from *all one* and *at one*.

The Germanic languages

This last example suggests that, when we look for family relationships between languages, it is desirable to go back to the earliest known forms of the languages. Table 3.2 shows the same seven words as they appear in Old English, Gothic, Old High German, and Old Norse. Gothic was the language of the Goths, who invaded the Roman Empire, Old High German was the ancestor of modern standard literary German, and Old Norse was the early form of the Scandinavian languages, as found for example in the medieval Icelandic sagas.

Table 3.2   *Similar words in four ancient languages*

Old English	Gothic	Old High German	Old Norse
stān	stains	stein	steinn
bān	–	bein	bein
āc	–	eih	eik
hām	haims	heim	heimr
rāp	raip	reif	reip
gāt	gaits	geiz	geit
ān	ains	ein	einn

Here again there are regular correspondences: words which have *ā* in Old English have *ai* in Gothic, *ei* in Old High German, and *ei* in Old Norse. The spelling *ei* perhaps represented a pronunciation [ei] (somewhat like *ay* in English *may*), while Gothic *ai* perhaps represented [ai] (somewhat like the *i* of English *mine*). It seems likely that the original phoneme from which they all developed was similar to the Gothic one, though we cannot know exactly.

This is only one correspondence, but a fuller examination of these languages shows regular correspondences between their sound-systems, and confirms that they are indeed related. The correspondences are not always obvious, and there are difficulties and complications. One source of confusion is seen if we examine the word *boat*, which comes from Old English *bāt*. In this case, however, the other languages fail to correspond. The German word is *Boot*, where we might have expected **Beiss* (the asterisk shows that the form is a hypothetical one, and has not been recorded). The Swedish form is not **bet*, but *båt*, which would correspond to an Old Swedish *bāt*; and the usual Old Norse word is *bátr*. There is, however, a rarer Old Norse word *beitr*, found in poetry, and this does correspond to the English word, whereas the other forms seem to make no kind of sense. What is the explanation? What happened, almost certainly, is that the Scandinavians borrowed their *bátr* from Old English *bāt*: it is an example of a *loan-word*, a word taken over bodily from one language to another. And the German word *Boot* was also borrowed from English, but at a later date, after Old English *ā* had developed into Middle English [ɔ:] (a vowel similar to that of present-day English *law*). You may find it surprising that the Scandinavians, a famous sea-faring people, should borrow such a word as *boat* from the English, but you must remember that the Anglo-Saxons and their cousins the Frisians were famous as deep-sea sailors and pirates before the Scandinavian Vikings had been heard of: the Saxons were the terror of the seas in the days of the late Roman Empire, at a time when the ancestors of the Danes and Norwegians were still probably longshoremen.

Another source of complication can be illustrated by the word for a waste place. This is German *Heide*, Old High German *heida*, Swedish *hed*, Old Norse *heiðr*, and Gothic *haiþi*. (The Old Norse letter ð was pronounced as [ð], and the Gothic letter þ as [θ].)

From this we might expect to find an English form *hoath, but of course the word is in fact *heath* (though *hoath* does exist in English place-names). Our word *heath* is quite regularly descended from Old English *hæþ*. In this case the clue to the difference from the other languages is given by the -*i* at the end of the Gothic word. It can be shown that, in prehistoric Old English, an [i] or [i:] or [j] caused a change in the vowel of the preceding syllable, provided it was in the same word. The prehistoric Old English form of *heath* was something like *hāþi; the final -*i* caused the *ā* to change to *æ*, and was later itself lost by a regular sound law. Dependent sound-changes of this kind (often called 'combinative changes') greatly complicate the task of establishing correspondences.

Although complicated, however, it can be done, and has been done for this group of languages. In addition to the languages already mentioned the group contains others, such as Dutch, Danish, and Norwegian. The languages of this group are called *Germanic* languages. Besides the regular correspondences in their sound-systems, they resemble one another closely in structure: they have the same or similar features of morphology and syntax. For example, in English there are two main ways of putting a verb into the past tense: in one group of verbs we change the vowel, as in *I sing, I sang*, while in the other we add an ending containing a /d/ or a /t/, as in *I live, I lived*. Exactly the same is true in the other Germanic languages: German *ich singe, ich sang*, but *ich lebe, ich lebte*; Swedish *jag sjunger, jag sjöng*, but *jag lever, jag levde*.

English and French

English, then, belongs to the group of Germanic languages. But does this group form part of any larger family of languages? One possibility which may have occurred to you, if you know French, is a close relationship between French and English. Enormous numbers of English words closely resemble French words of similar meaning: to English *people* corresponds French *peuple*; *battle* is *bataille*; *to change* is *changer*, and one could easily give whole strings of French words of this kind – *musique, art, palais, collaboration, collision, danger, danse, machine,* and so on. This, however, is a false trail. You will remember that we need to look at the earliest recorded forms of a language when determining its family relationships. If we go back to the earliest known forms of English, all these words resembling French words simply do not exist. As we go back in time such words become fewer and fewer, and when we get back to the period before the Norman Conquest they have disappeared entirely. They are in fact *loan-words*, taken from French, or in some cases direct from Latin. There are many such borrowed words in English, but they have not destroyed its essentially Germanic character and it retains typical Germanic structural features and a central core of Germanic words. Such are the common grammatical words (the, and, is), the numerals (one, two, three), and everyday lexical words for the closest members of the family (father, mother, brother, son) and for the parts of the body (head, foot, arm, hand). Such core-words are less often borrowed from other languages than more peripheral parts of the vocabulary, and so provide a better guide to family relationships.

The Indo-European languages

We see, then, that our attempt to compare Modern English with Modern French was misguided. We should instead have gone back to the ancestor of French, which is Latin, and compared it with the earliest known forms of the Germanic languages, and we should have looked especially at grammatical features and at words from the central core of the vocabulary. Let us try a comparison of this kind, throwing in a couple of other ancient languages for good measure. We can begin with the numerals from one to ten: these are given in Table 3.3 for classical Latin, classical Greek, and Sanskrit, an ancient language of northern India; to represent the Germanic languages I give Old English and Gothic. Both here and later, the transcription of Greek and Sanskrit words has been simplified: Greek has been put into the Latin alphabet, and accents omitted; in Sanskrit words, accents have been omitted, and some of the symbols simplified.

Table 3.3   *Numerals 1–10 in five ancient languages*

	Latin	Greek	Sanskrit	Gothic	Old English
1.	ūnus	heis	eka	ains	ān
2.	duo	duo	dvau	twai	twēgen, twā
3.	trēs	treis	trayas	–	þrīe
4.	quattuor	tettares	catvāras	fidwor	fēower
5.	quīnque	pente	panca	fimf	fīf
6.	sex	hex	sat	saihs	siex
7.	septem	hepta	sapta	sibun	seofon
8.	octō	oktō	astau	ahtau	eahta
9.	novem	ennea	nava	niun	nigon
10.	decem	deka	dasa	taihun	tīen

The resemblances between the Latin, Greek, and Sanskrit are quite striking. Moreover, there are things that suggest regular correspondences: where Latin and Sanskrit begin a word with *s*, Greek begins it with *h*; where Latin and Greek have *o*, Sanskrit has *a*. The resemblances to the Germanic languages are less close, but nevertheless clear enough, and they would be even clearer if we took into account certain related words and variant forms: for example, in Greek there is a word *oinē*, which means 'the one-spot on a dice', and this corresponds more closely than *heis* to the Latin and Germanic words for 'one'. There are also signs of regular correspondences between the Germanic forms and the others. For example, at the beginning of a word Germanic has *t* for their *d*, and it has *h* where they have *k* or *c*. Let us follow up just one possible correspondence. In the words for 'five', Greek and Sanskrit have *p* (*pente, panca*) where the Germanic languages have *f* (*fimf, fīf*). Can we find further evidence for this relationship? Consider Table 3.4.

Table 3.4   *Similarities in five ancient languages*

Old English	Gothic	Latin	Greek	Sanskrit
fæder ('father')	fadar	pater	pater	pitar-
nefa ('nephew')	–	nepos	–	napāt
feor ('far')	fairra	–	perā	paras
faran ('go, fare')	faran	(ex)-perior	peraō	pr-
full ('full')	fulls	plēnus	plērēs	pūrna-
fearh ('pig')	–	porcus	–	–
feþer ('feather')	–	penna	pteron	patra-
fell ('skin')	fill	pellis	pella	–

The words have the same or closely related meanings in the different languages. There are small variations: Sanskrit *napāt* means 'grandson', not 'nephew', but in fact Old English *nefa* could also mean 'grandson'. And in all these words we have Germanic *f* corresponding to *p* in the other three languages. Similar series of correspondences can be established for the other phonemes of these languages. And the correspondences are not confined to phonology (sound-systems): the Germanic languages also show detailed resemblances to Latin, Greek, and Sanskrit in morphology and syntax, for example in their inflectional systems (grammatical endings of words). It is certain that these languages are related.

But the family does not end here. Similar detailed resemblances, both in phonology and in grammar, can be demonstrated with a large number of other languages, including Russian, Lithuanian, Welsh, Albanian, and Persian. In fact English belongs to a very extensive family of languages, with many branches. This family includes most of the languages of Europe and India, and is usually called Indo-European.

The branches of Indo-European

One branch of Indo-European is Indo-Iranian, or Aryan, so called because the ancient peoples who spoke it called themselves Aryas, from a root *ārya-* or *airya-*, meaning 'noble, honourable'; the very name of Iran is ultimately derived from the genitive plural of this word. The branch has two groups, the Indian and the Iranian. To the Indian group belongs the language of the ancient Vedic hymns from North-West India, which go back by oral tradition to a very remote past, perhaps to about 1200 BC, though the first written texts are much later. A later form of this language is classical Sanskrit, which was standardized in the fourth century BC, and has since been the learned language of India (rather like Latin in western Europe). Modern representatives of the group are Bengali, Hindi, and other languages of Northern India, together with some from further South, like Sinhalese. The other Aryan group, Iranian, includes modern Persian, and neighbouring languages such as Ossetic, Kurdish, and Pashto (or Pushtu), the official language of Afghanistan. An ancient form of Iranian is found in the Avesta, the sacred writings of the Zoroastrians, perhaps dating back to 600 BC.

Another branch with ancient texts is Greek, which has a literature from the seventh century BC. The Homeric epics, which were long handed down by oral tradition, go back even earlier, to the ninth or tenth century BC (though not to the time of the Trojan War itself, which was about 1200 BC). Some years ago, tablets from Crete written in a script called Minoan Linear B were deciphered by Michael Ventris, and revealed a form of Greek which was in use there in about 1400 BC. The Greek branch includes all the various ancient Hellenic dialects, and it is from one of these, Attic, that Modern Greek is descended.

Two branches which have some things in common are the Italic and the Celtic. For example, both branches have a verb-inflection in *-r*, used to form the passive voice, as in Latin *amātur* '(he/she/it) is loved', and Welsh *cerir fi* 'I am loved'. The *-r* ending is similarly found in deponent verbs, that is ones which are passive in form but active in meaning: corresponding to the Latin deponent verb *sequitur* '(he/she/it) follows' is Old Irish *sechithir*.

Italic consisted of a number of dialects of ancient Italy, including Oscan, Umbrian, and Latin. The earliest Latin texts date from the third century BC. Of the other Italic languages we have only fragments.

Celtic, once widely diffused over Europe, can be divided into three groups: Gaulish, Britannic, and Gaelic. Gaulish was spoken in France and northern Italy in the time of the Roman Republic, and was spread abroad by Celtic military expeditions to central Europe and as far as Asia Minor. It died out during the early centuries of the Christian era, and is known only from a few inscriptions and from names of people and places preserved in Latin texts. Britannic was the branch of Celtic spoken in most of Britain before the Anglo-Saxon invasions. It survived into modern times in three languages: Cornish, which is known in texts from the fifteenth century and which died out in the eighteenth; Welsh, which has literary texts going back to the eleventh century; and Breton, which has literary texts from the fourteenth century. Breton is not a descendant of Gaulish: it was taken across to Brittany by refugees from Britain during the period of the Anglo-

Saxon conquests. Gaelic was the Celtic language of Ireland. It spread to the Isle of Man in the fourth century, and to Scotland in the fifth, thus giving rise to the three main branches of Gaelic – Irish Gaelic, Scottish Gaelic, and Manx. Its earliest records are inscriptions from the fourth or fifth century AD. A characteristic difference between Britannic Celtic and Gaelic Celtic is the treatment of Indo-European *kw*, which appears as *p* in Britannic but as *c* in Gaelic: Welsh *pen* 'head', *pair* 'cauldron', but Old Irish *cenn*, *coire*. For this reason the two groups of speakers are sometimes called 'P-Celts' and 'Q-Celts'.

Among the phonological characteristics of Celtic are the treatment of Indo-European *p*, and the treatment of Indo-European long *ē*. In most positions, Indo-European *p* was lost in Celtic: with Latin *plēnus* and Greek *plērēs* compare Old Irish *lan* and Welsh *llawn* 'full', and with Latin *pater* compare Old Irish *athir* 'father'. (The *p* in Welsh *pump* 'five' is not from Indo-European *p* but from Indo-European *kw*: compare Latin *quīnque*.) In Celtic, Indo-European long *ē* became long *ī*: with Latin *rēx* 'king' compare Old Irish *rī* (genitive *rīg*), Gaulish -*rīx*, and Welsh *rhi*.

Another two branches of Indo-European that have things in common are Baltic and Slavonic. The Baltic languages include Lithuanian, Lettish (or Latvian), and Old Prussian (which died out in the seventeenth century). The Slavonic branch has many members, which fall into three main groups: Eastern Slavonic includes Russian, Ukrainian, and Byelorussian; West Slavonic includes Polish, Czech, and Wendish; while South Slavonic includes Serbo-Croat, Slovenian, and Bulgarian. The earliest recorded Slavonic, called Old Church Slavonic, is the language of certain religious writings of the tenth and eleventh centuries AD, emanating from Bulgaria.

There are still three minor branches unmentioned: Albanian, Armenian, and Tocharian (an extinct language of Chinese Turkestan, which has some affinities with Italic and Celtic). Then there is the large Germanic branch. And finally we have to add Anatolian, of which the main representative is Hittite, one of the languages of the Hittite empire in Asia Minor round about 1500 BC, which is recorded in numerous texts in a cuneiform writing. Hittite is certainly related to Indo-European, though much of its vocabulary is non-Indo-European. Some scholars have argued that it represents a very early branching-off from the parent language, so that its relation to the other branches of Indo-European is that of cousin rather than sister.

Even from this brief survey, you will see what an enormous and complicated family the Indo-European languages are. It will also be seen how large a part they play in the modern world. Altogether, well over a thousand million people speak an Indo-European language as their mother-tongue today: of these, over three hundred million speak a Germanic language, about three hundred million a Romance language, about two hundred and seventy million an Indian language, and about the same number a Slavonic language; the other branches are all small. Only one other language family is comparable to this in size: the Sino-Tibetan family also has over a thousand million native speakers. The Hamito-Semitic, Ural-Altaic, Japanese-Korean, Dravidian, Niger-Congo, and Malayo-Polynesian families have roughly one hundred million native speakers each – about one tenth the size of the Sino-Tibetan or the Indo-European.

Who were the Indo-Europeans?

The Indo-European family of languages, with its numerous branches and its millions of speakers, has developed, if we are right, out of some single language, which must have been spoken thousands of years ago by some comparatively small body of people in a relatively restricted geographical area. This original language we can call Proto-Indo-European (PIE). The people who spoke it or who spoke languages evolved from it we can for convenience call Indo-Europeans, but we must remember that this does not imply anything about race or culture, only about language. People of very different races and cultures can come to be native speakers of Indo-European languages: such speakers today include Indians, Afghans, Iranians, Greeks, Irishmen, Russians, Mexicans, Brazilians, and Norwegians. It is probable, of course, that the speakers of Proto-Indo-European, living together in a limited area, had a common culture, whatever race or races they consisted of. But who were

they? Where did they live? And how did they come to spread
over the world?

The traditional view has been that the Indo-Europeans were a
nomadic or semi-nomadic people who invaded neighbouring
agricultural or urban areas and imposed their language on them.
The archaeologist Colin Renfrew has however recently argued
that we do not necessarily have to envisage conquering armies or
the mass-movement of populations. He believes that the initial
expansion of the Indo-Europeans was simply the pushing out of
the frontiers of an agricultural people, who over centuries
introduced agriculture into the more thinly populated country
round their periphery, inhabited by hunters or food-gatherers.
This process would require a longer time-scale than the traditional
view of mass migration: Renfrew thinks that the expansion began
in about 7000 BC, whereas the traditional view had dated it to
4000 BC or later. At present there is insufficient evidence for us to
decide between Renfrew and the traditionalists, and the matter
must be left open. But, even if Renfrew were right about the *initial*
expansion of the Indo-Europeans, his theory could hardly account
for the later spread of Indo-European speech. By the beginning of
our era, Indo-European languages were spoken over vast areas:
from Ireland in the West to India in the East, from Scandinavia in
the North to Crete in the South; it is difficult to believe that
expansion on this scale could be brought about by the gradual
pushing-out of the frontiers of agriculture. In historical times,
moreover, there is plenty of evidence for the spread of Indo-
European languages through conquest and colonization, or even
by mass-migration into unoccupied territory, as when Norwegians
emigrated to Iceland.

But, whatever the method by which the dispersal of the Indo-
Europeans began, where did it begin from? It is plain, for a start,
that, immediately before their dispersal, the Indo-Europeans were
not living in any of the advanced cultural centres of the ancient
world, such as the Nile valley, Mesopotamia, or the Indus valley.
When they appeared in such places it was as intruders from
outside. They appeared on the fringes of the Mesopotamian area
around 1500 BC, when a dynasty with Indo-European names are
found ruling a non-Indo-European people, the Mitanni, who lived

on the upper Euphrates. At about the same time, Hittite was being used in Anatolia, and some of the Aryas (the speakers of the Indo-Iranian branch of Indo-European) were in North-West India: their earliest records, the Vedas, suggest that at this time they were in the Punjab, and were in conflict with the earlier inhabitants of India. It would seem, therefore, that the Aryas had entered India from the North-West, from Iran or Afghanistan, and, since the Indian and Iranian branches of Indo-European are closely related, it seems likely that the Indians and the Iranians had lived together for some time, perhaps on the Iranian plateau, before the Indian group moved on to the Indian subcontinent. At this date, however, we know nothing about the Iranians, who do not impinge on the histories of other peoples until they come into conflict with Mesopotamian peoples many centuries later: references to the Medes and Persians are found in Assyria from the ninth century BC.

In Europe we have no very early records of the Indo-Europeans, except for the Greeks. From Ventris's decipherment of Minoan Linear B we know that a form of Greek, Mycenean, was in use in Crete and on the Greek mainland by 1400 BC. Greek traditions suggest that the Hellenes had moved into the Balkans from the North, perhaps around 1900 BC. If this were so, they may well have come from the valley of the Danube. The records of Italic are later, but we can perhaps equate the Italic-speaking peoples with a culture that appeared in northern Italy in about 1500 BC, and spread southwards; some elements in this culture suggest that it was an offshoot of a lake-dwelling people in the Alps. The Celtic-speaking peoples also first appear in the region of the Alps, and their great period of expansion began in the middle of the first millennium BC; they are often identified with the bearers of two Iron Age cultures, the Hallstatt and the La Tène; these cultures came to Britain from the Continent, the former in about 500 BC, the latter in the third and second centuries BC, supplanting the existing Bronze Age culture. The Germanic-speaking peoples are first heard about from the Romans not long before the beginning of our era; they were then living in northern Germany and Scandinavia. At the same time, the Slavs were living north of the Carpathians, mainly between the Vistula and the Dnieper; they

appear to have been living there for many years before they began
to expand in the early years of the Christian era.

The Indo-European languages of which we have early records
had already diverged markedly from one another. It seems likely,
therefore, that the dispersal of the Indo-Europeans must have
begun by 3000 BC at the latest, and that it may have begun very
much earlier. But where did it begin from? Here one of the sources
of evidence is the languages themselves.

At one time it was argued that the languages which preserve
most fully the features of Proto-Indo-European will belong to
peoples who have stayed near the original Indo-European
homeland, and not moved away to changed conditions and to
contacts with other peoples. But the assumption behind this
argument is unsafe: there is a good deal of evidence to suggest
that, when a language expands geographically, it is the dialects of
the original homeland which change most, at any rate in
phonology and grammar, and the dialects on the perimeter
which are most conservative. This, however, does not help us
much with our Indo-European problem, because the movements
of the early Indo-Europeans seem to have been very complicated,
with many successive overlapping waves of immigration.

Another line of approach is to examine the family relationships
of the Indo-European languages, to try to see which belong most
closely together. From this we might hope to work out which
branches migrated together, in what order different groups broke
away, and so on. One possible family tree would be the following.
First we divide into two main branches, Eastern and Western:

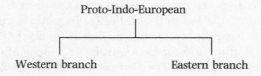

Then each of these branches is subdivided; first the Western
branch:

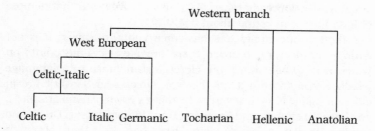

And then the Eastern branch:

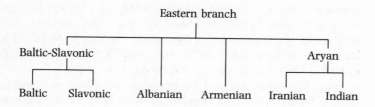

The first division into an Eastern Group and a Western Group is important. The groups are marked by a number of differences in phonology, grammar, and vocabulary, which suggests that there was an early division of the Indo-Europeans into two main areas, perhaps representing migrations in different directions. One of the distinctive differences in phonology between the two groups is the treatment of Proto-Indo-European palatal *k*, which appears as a velar [k] in the Western languages, but as some kind of palatal fricative, [s] or [ʃ], in the Eastern languages. Thus the word for 'hundred' is Greek *he-katon*, Latin *centum*, Tocharian *känt*, Old Irish *cet*, and Welsh *cant* (the *c* in each case representing [k]), but in Sanskrit it is *satam*, in Avestan *satəm*, in Lithuanian *szimtas*, and in Old Slavonic *seto* (modern Russian *sto*). For this reason, the two groups are often referred to as the *Kentum* languages and the *Satem* languages. On the whole, the Kentum languages are in the West and the Satem languages in the East, but an apparent anomaly is Tocharian, right across in western China, which is a Kentum language. The division into Kentum and Satem languages had already taken place when we get our first glimpse of Indo-European round about 1500 BC.

Although our family tree has some value, however, it is not entirely satisfactory, because there are always some points on which a language shows the closest resemblance to a language which is *remote* from it on the tree. Greek and Sanskrit are in different major branches, but nevertheless resemble one another a good deal in syntax, and to some extent in vocabulary. Greek and Iranian are in different major branches, but they agree in changing Indo-European *s-* at the beginning of a word into *h-*: the word for 'seven' is Latin *septem*, Sanskrit *saptan*, and Old English *seofon*, but in Greek it is *heptá* and in Old Iranian *haptan*. Moreover, no amount of juggling with the family tree can completely remove discrepancies of this kind. In fact, it is impossible to depict the relationships of the Indo-European languages in an entirely satisfactory way by means of a model in which branches divide and subdivide.

These facts make sense if we envisage Proto-Indo-European as having broken up into a number of dialects *before* the dispersal began (which is what could be expected anyway). For, under such conditions, changes will spread from various centres within the region, and the boundaries of one change will not necessarily coincide with those of another. The speakers in a given area may pick up one new pronunciation from their neighbours to the East, and another from their neighbours to the West, so that their speech combines features of different dialect regions. At the same time, another change may spread down from the North, and stop halfway across their area, so that some of them have it and some not. In this way, dialect features will appear in various permutations and combinations throughout the whole region.

This, in fact, is the kind of situation which is often found in studies of modern dialects. One small example of this is given in Figure 6, which shows the dividing lines, or **isoglosses**, for two pairs of features in the traditional rural dialects of Northern England. One line shows the boundary between two pronunciations of the vowel of the word *house*: North of the line, it is a pure vowel, [u:], while South of the line it is some kind of diphthong, [au] or [əu]. The second line shows the limit of occurrence of one

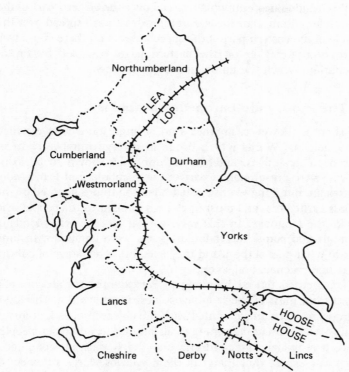

Figure 6   Two intersecting isoglosses in the traditional rural dialects of Northern England

particular word, namely, *lop*, meaning 'flea': this word is found only East of the line, not west of it; it is in fact a loan from Scandinavian, and it looks as though it has spread across the region from the East. The crucial point is that these two lines run in quite different directions, and cut one another, so that all possible combinations of the four features occur.

To return to Proto-Indo-European, it is clear that, if this kind of thing went on before the dispersal, the family resemblances between the various branches have only a limited value as a guide to their prehistoric migrations. It also enables us to see how a Kentum language, Tocharian, can occur in the Far East. We can imagine the fricative pronunciation of palatal *k* as an innovation in Proto-Indo-European which spread over the eastern part of the speech area from some focus. But it need not have spread over the whole of the eastern part of the speech area, and there could well have been a region on the eastern edge, occupied by Proto-Tocharian, which the innovation never reached.

The Proto-Indo-European vocabulary

There is, however, another kind of linguistic evidence which may help us. Words which occur in a large number of Indo-European languages, and which cannot be shown to be loan-words, were presumably a part of the vocabulary of Proto-Indo-European. But if the words existed, then the things denoted by the words existed too, and must have been familiar to the people who spoke the language. In this way, we can deduce what kinds of animals and plants the Indo-Europeans were familiar with (and hence what part of the world they lived in), what stage of culture they had reached, and so on.

The method, indeed, has dangers. For example, the absence of a word from most of the languages does not prove that the Indo-Europeans were unacquainted with the object in question: loss of words is a common happening in all languages, and when peoples have been widely dispersed and met widely different conditions, we must expect that many of them will lose large numbers of words. On the other hand, the absence of a whole group of words, covering an entire field of activity, may well be given some weight.

Another danger is that we may be deceived by loan-words. When a group of people learn a new technique or become familiar with new objects, they often take over the appropriate names from the people from whom they learn the technique or acquire the objects. So several branches of the Indo-Europeans may well have borrowed the vocabulary of, for example, agriculture from the same people, or from peoples speaking similar languages. While, however, it is likely that the Celts and the Germans might borrow the same words from their neighbours, it is not very likely that they would also borrow the same words as the Indians and Iranians. We can guard against the danger of loan-words by giving the most weight to words that are found both in European and in Asiatic languages, and only such words are counted as original Indo-European in what follows.

The common vocabulary thus obtained gives some support to the traditional view that the Indo-Europeans, before their dispersal, were a nomadic or semi-nomadic pastoral people. They had cattle and sheep, for there are common words for both of these: for example, our *ox* is Welsh *ych*, Sanskrit *uksan-*, and Tocharian *okso*, and our *ewe* is related to Latin *ovis* and Sanskrit *avi-*. Cattle were obviously highly prized: the Old English word *feoh*, corresponding to Sanskrit *pacu-* and Latin *pecu*, meant both 'cattle' and 'wealth'; the Latin word for 'money, wealth' was *pecunia*; and cattle figure prominently in the early writings of Indo-European peoples. They also had other domestic animals, including the dog, and possibly the pig, the goat, and the goose, but there is no common word for the ass, nor for the camel – our name for this animal goes back, via Latin and Greek, to a loan from a Semitic language. The Indo-Europeans certainly had horses, for which a rich vocabulary has survived, and they also had vehicles of some kind, for there are words for wheel, axle, nave, and yoke. They had cheese and butter, but no common word for milk has survived, which shows how chancy the evidence is. No large common vocabulary has survived for agriculture: such a vocabulary is found in the European languages, but this may obviously date from after the dispersal. There are, however, common words for grain, and Greek and Sanskrit have cognate words for plough and for furrow, so there is some support for Renfrew's view that the Proto-Indo-Europeans were agriculturalists. There is however no common word for beer (which is an agriculturalist's product), while there is a word for mead. On the other hand, there is no common vocabulary for hunting or fishing.

There are a number of common words for tools and weapons, including arrows, and there is evidence to suggest that at one time the tools and weapons were made of stone: the Latin verb *secāre* 'to cut' is related to *saxum* 'a stone, rock', and the latter is identical with Old English *seax*, which meant 'knife'. At one time, it seems, a stone could be a cutting implement. The Proto-Indo-Europeans knew metal, however, for there are two common words for copper and bronze, one of which survives as our *ore* (Latin *aes*, Sanskrit *ayas*), and there are also words for gold and silver. There is, however, no common terminology for the techniques of metallurgy. The vocabulary shows a familiarity with pottery and also with weaving. There are also words for house and for door, which suggests a dwelling more substantial than a tent, but there is no common word for window.

They knew both rain and snow, but their summer seems to have been hot, which suggests a continental climate. The wild animals they knew included wolves, bears, otters, mice, hares, and beavers, but apparently not lions, tigers, elephants, or camels, so presumably they lived in a cool temperate zone. There has been some argument about the common Indo-European words for the beech tree, the eel, and the salmon. The beech does not grow in North-East Europe, or anywhere east of the Caspian, so it has been argued that the home of the Indo-Europeans must have been farther West. The eel and the salmon are not found in the rivers that flow into the Black Sea, so it has been argued that this region too must be ruled out. There are, however, two weaknesses in this argument. The first is that the climate has changed since the times of the Proto-Indo-Europeans: around 4000 BC, the climate of southern Russia was wetter and warmer than it is today, and there were many more trees, especially along the banks of streams and rivers; these trees almost certainly included beech. The second weakness is that we cannot be absolutely certain that these words originally referred to the species in question. For example, it is possible that the word for 'salmon' (German *Lachs*, Swedish *lax*, Russian *losósi* 'salmon', Tocharian *laks* 'fish') did not originally refer to the true salmon, but to a species of *Salmo* found North of the Black Sea.

It seems that rivers and streams were common, but there is no word for the sea or the ocean, so they were apparently an inland people. There is a word for a ship, seen in Latin *navis* and Sanskrit *naus*, but originally this may well have been the name of a vessel used for crossing rivers, or for fishing in them.

There is a large common Indo-European vocabulary for family relationships, and it seems that the family played an important role in their social organization. The linguistic evidence suggests that this family went by male descent, and that when a woman married she went to live with her husband's family. For example, there is a widespread Indo-European word for daughter-in-law (seen in Latin *nurus*, Greek *nuos*, Sanskrit *snusā*), but no such widespread word for son-in-law; and there are common words for husband's brother, husband's sister, and husband's brothers' wives, but no such common words for the wife's relatives.

This view of the Indo-European family is supported by the Indo-European names of Gods. There are a few common to the European and Asiatic languages, and they seem to be personifications of natural forces; they do not, however, include a Great Mother Goddess or an Earth Goddess. Prominent among them, however, is a Sky God: the Greek Zeus, the Sanskrit Dyaus, the Old English Tīw (whose name survives in our word *Tuesday*). He was a Father God, as we can see from his Latin name, Jupiter, which means 'Sky Father'. In historical times, we sometimes find societies with Indo-European languages which have a Great Mother goddess, for example Minoan Crete. The names of such deities, however, appear not to be of Indo-European origin, and it is to be presumed that the cult has been taken over from a non-Indo-European people, possibly one which has been invaded and conquered.

The home of the Indo-Europeans

A certain amount has emerged from all this about Proto-Indo-European culture, but not enough to pin it down to a particular locality. Arguments have been advanced for several different areas as the Indo-European homeland: Scandinavia and the adjacent parts of northern Germany, the Danube valley, especially the Hungarian plain, Anatolia (now in Turkey), and the steppes of the southern Ukraine, north of the Black Sea.

At one time the Scandinavian theory found a good deal of support, especially in Germany, and was often linked with a belief that the Germanic peoples were the 'original' Indo-Europeans. But the theory has serious weaknesses. Scandinavia does not tally very well with the evidence from comparative philology: it is a maritime region (whereas there is no common Indo-European word for sea or ocean), and it is not very suitable terrain for horse-drawn vehicles, which belong rather to the steppes. Nor is there an Indo-European word for amber, which was one of the most sought-after products of the Baltic region. Moreover, the great changes in pronunciation that the Germanic languages underwent in prehistoric times, and the simplification of the tense-system of their verbs, make one suspect that they had been learned by some conquered people, possibly speakers of a Finno-Ugrian language.

In the 1920s, a persuasive case was put forward by the archaeologist V. Gordon Childe for locating the Indo-European homeland in the steppes of the Ukraine, north of the Black Sea. He argued that speakers of Proto-Indo-European should be identified with a certain 'corded-ware' or 'battle-axe' culture in that region. More recently, this line of argument has been developed by another archaeologist, Marija Gimbutas. She groups together a number of cultures (including Childe's 'corded-ware') under the title 'Kurgan', and argues that the bearers of these cultures were the Proto-Indo-Europeans. The material evidence from these cultures certainly corresponds very well with the comparative linguistic evidence, and also with what we know historically about the early Indo-European peoples. Gimbutas places the original Indo-Europeans rather farther to the east than Childe had done, north of the Caucasus range and around the lower Volga (north of the Caspian Sea). She dates the early Kurgan settlements in this region to the fifth millennium BC, claiming that, between 4000 BC and 3500 BC, the Kurgan culture spread westward as far as the Danube plain, and in the following five hundred years was to be found in the Balkans, Anatolia, much of eastern Europe, and northern Iran. Between 3000 BC and 2300 BC, continuous waves of Kurgan expansion or raids affected most of northern Europe, the Aegean area, the East Mediterranean area, and possibly Palestine and Egypt. The 'Peoples of the Sea' who raided and settled the coasts and islands of the East Mediterranean were possibly Kurgan.

Gimbutas is extremely persuasive, and her views are widely accepted. There are dissenting voices, however. As we have seen, Renfrew thinks that the Indo-European expansion began in Anatolia in about 7000 BC, and consisted in the slow spread of agriculture into the more sparsely populated land occupied by hunter-gatherers. He points out, moreover, that the spread of a material culture does not necessarily mean the actual movement of a people. The Russian linguists Gamkrelidze and Ivanov put great emphasis on the evidence of Semitic loan-words in early Indo-European, and place the Indo-European homeland in eastern Anatolia, to the South of the Caucasus range and West of the Caspian Sea. They date it earlier than 6000 BC, but are unable to identify any material culture which may have been Proto-Indo-European.

If Gimbutas is right, the peoples speaking the Proto-Indo-European language were a semi-nomadic pastoral people in the chalcolithic stage of culture, living on the South Russian steppes in the fifth millennium BC, where they formed a loosely linked group of communities with common gods and similar social organization. After 4000 BC, when the language had developed into a number of dialects, they began to expand in various directions, different groups ending up in Iran, India, the Mediterranean area, and most parts of Europe. In the course of their expansion, the Indo-Europeans overran countries which had reached a higher level of civilization than they had themselves: the Aryas, for example, conquered the civilizations of northern India, and the Persians those of Mesopotamia. This need not surprise us: primitive nomadic peoples have often overrun more advanced urban civilizations, and there is no need to postulate (as some people have done) some special intellectual or physical prowess in the Indo-Europeans. It merely shows that they had cultivated the art of war rather successfully (perhaps having profited from the technical advances of neighbouring urban cultures) and that they were under some kind of environmental pressure (like change of climate or exhaustion of pastures) that made them need to migrate or expand. Moreover, the urban civilization that is overrun may have internal weaknesses of a social or political kind, just as, much later, the Roman Empire had when it was overrun by the technically more backward Germanic peoples.

Perhaps, however, there is one technical factor which played a part in the expansion and conquests of the Indo-Europeans. This is the use of horse-drawn vehicles, which we have seen to be characteristic of Proto-Indo-European society. The evidence from comparative philology, indicating that the Proto-Indo-Europeans had wheeled vehicles, has indeed been challenged. It is supported, however, by later Indo-European history: when the Aryas invaded India they were fighting in horse-drawn chariots, and similar vehicles were used by other Indo-European peoples, like the Celts and Hellenes. And if Gimbutas is right in identifying the Indo-Europeans with Kurgan culture, there can be no doubt about the matter. The horse was a late introduction into the river valleys of the great early urban civilizations, in which the normal draught animal was the ass, and when the horse came to them, it came from the North. It is possible that in this respect the Indo-Europeans were ahead of their time, and that it was their use of wheeled vehicles, especially the fast horse-drawn chariot, that enabled them to overrun such a large part of the Eurasian continent.

4 The Germanic languages

The branch of Indo-European that English belongs to is called Germanic, and includes German, Dutch, Frisian, Danish, Swedish, and Norwegian. All these languages are descended from one parent language, a dialect of Indo-European, which we can call Proto-Germanic (PG). Round about the beginning of the Christian era, the speakers of Proto-Germanic still formed a relatively homogeneous cultural and linguistic group, living in the north of Europe. We have no records of the language in this period, but we know something about the people who spoke it, because they are described by Roman authors, who called them the *Germani*, which we for convenience can translate as 'Germans'. One of the best-known of these descriptions is that written by Tacitus in AD 98, called *Germania*.

Early Germanic society

Tacitus describes the Germans as a tribal society living in scattered settlements in the woody and marshy country of North-West Europe. He says that they hate cities and keep their houses far apart, living in wooden buildings, or sometimes, in winter, in pits dug in the ground and covered over with rubbish. They keep flocks, and grow grain crops, but their agriculture is not very advanced, and they do not practise horticulture. Because of the large amount of open ground, they change their ploughlands yearly, allotting areas to whole villages, and distributing land to cultivators in order of rank. The family plays a large part in their social organization, and the more relatives a man has the greater is his influence in his old age. They have kings, chosen for their birth, and chiefs, chosen for their valour, but in major affairs the whole community consults together; and the freedom of the Germans is a greater danger to Rome than the despotism of the Parthian kings. Chiefs are attended by companions, who fight for them in battle, and who in return are rewarded by the chiefs with gifts of weapons, horses, treasure, and land. In battle, it is disgraceful for a chief to be outshone by his companions, and disgraceful for the companions to be less brave than their chief; the greatest disgrace is to come back from a battle alive after your chief has been killed; this means lifelong infamy. The Germans dislike peace, for it is only in war that renown and booty can be won. In peacetime, the warriors idle about at home, eating, drinking, and gambling, and leaving the work of the house and of the fields to women, weaklings, and slaves. They are extremely hospitable, to strangers as well as to acquaintances, but their love of drinking often leads to quarrels. They are monogamous, and their women are held in high esteem. The physical type is everywhere the same: blue eyes, reddish hair, and huge bodies. The normal dress is the short cloak, though the skins of animals are also worn; the women often wear linen undergarments. Very few of the men have breastplates or helmets, and they have very little iron. They worship Mercury (Woden), and sacrifice animals to Hercules and Mars (Thor and Tiw). They set great store by auspices and the casting of lots. Their only form of recorded history is their ancient songs, in which they tell of the earth-born god Tuisto and his son Mannus, ancestor of the whole German race; the various sons of Mannus are the ancestors of the different German tribes. And Tacitus goes on to give an account of each of these tribes, its location and peculiarities.

To some extent, Tacitus is undoubtedly using the Germans as a means of attacking the corruptions of Rome in his own day: they are the noble savages whose customs are, in many ways, a criticism of Roman life. But at the same time he obviously has access to a great deal of genuine information about the Germans, and many of the details of his account are confirmed by what we know about the Germanic-speaking peoples in later times. When he wrote, they were already pressing on the borders of the Roman Empire, and Tacitus recognized them as a danger to Rome. Earlier they had probably been confined to a small area of southern Scandinavia and northern Germany between the Elbe and the Oder, but round about 300 BC they had begun to expand in all directions, perhaps because of overpopulation and the poverty of their natural resources. In the course of a few centuries they pushed northwards up the Scandinavian peninsula into territory occupied by Finns. They expanded westwards beyond the Elbe, into North-West Germany and the Netherlands, overrunning areas occupied by Celtic-speaking peoples. They expanded eastwards round the shores of the Baltic Sea, into Finnish or Baltic-speaking regions. And they pressed southwards into Bohemia, and later into South-West Germany. At the same time, the territory to their south ruled by Rome was also expanding, and by the time of Tacitus there was a considerable area of contact between Romans and Germans along the northern frontiers of the Empire. There was a good deal of trade, with a number of recognized routes up through German territory to the Baltic; there was considerable cultural influence by the Romans on the Germans (many of whom served their time as mercenaries in the Roman legions); and of course there were frequent clashes.

The branches of Germanic

As a result of this expansion of the Germanic-speaking peoples, differences of dialect within Proto-Germanic became more marked, and we can distinguish three main branches or groups of dialects, namely North Germanic, East Germanic, and West Germanic.

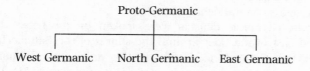

To North Germanic belong the modern Scandinavian languages – Norwegian, Swedish, Danish, Icelandic, Faroese, and Gutnish (the language of the island of Gotland). The earliest recorded form of North Germanic (Old Norse) is found in runic inscriptions from about AD 300; at this period it shows very little trace of dialectal variations, and it is not until the Viking Age, from about AD 800 onwards, that it begins to break up into the dialects which have developed into the modern Scandinavian languages. Here is a family tree for the North Germanic languages:

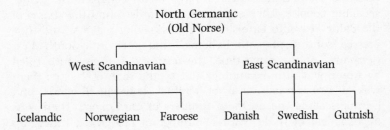

North Germanic differs from the other Germanic languages in a number of points of phonology and grammar. For example, Proto-Germanic /j/ is lost at the beginning of a word, so that corresponding to English *year*, German *Jahr*, and Gothic *jēr* we find Old Icelandic *ár* and Modern Swedish *år*. Proto-Germanic initial /w/ was lost before certain rounded vowels, so that corresponding to English *worm* and *wolf* we find Old Icelandic *ormr* 'snake' and *ulfr* 'wolf', both of which were also used as Scandinavian forenames. We have already noticed an example of one North Germanic grammatical peculiarity, the development of a postposed definite article: corresponding to the English forms 'a dog' and 'the dog' we find Swedish 'en hund' and 'hunden'. But if there is also an adjective before the noun, there has to be an element of the definite article both before and after: 'the big dog' is Swedish 'den stora hunden'.

The East Germanic dialects were spoken by the tribes that expanded East of the Oder around the shores of the Baltic. They included the Goths, and Gothic is the only East Germanic language of which we have any record. Round about AD 200

the Goths migrated south-eastwards, and settled in the plains
north of the Black Sea, where they divided into two branches, the
Ostrogoths east of the Dnieper and the Visigoths west of it. The
main record of Gothic is the fragmentary remains of a translation
of the Bible into Visigothic, made by the Bishop Wulfila or Ulfilas
in the middle of the fourth century. The Goths were later overrun
by the Huns, but a form of Gothic was being spoken in the Crimea
as late as the seventeenth century, and a few words of it were
recorded. It has since died out, however, and no East Germanic
language has survived into our own times. Here is a family tree for
the East Germanic languages:

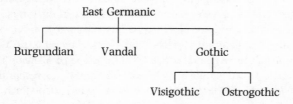

One of the phonological characteristics of Wulfila's text is that
the Proto-Germanic short vowels /e/ and /o/ appear as *i* and *u*: the
verb 'to steal' is Old English and Old High German *stelan*, and Old
Icelandic *stela*, but Gothic *stilan*; and corresponding to English *God*
and German *Gott* we find Gothic *guþ*.

To West Germanic belong the High German dialects of southern
Germany, the Low German dialects of northern Germany (which
in their earliest recorded form are called Old Saxon), Dutch,
Frisian, and English. The language most closely related to English
is Frisian, which was once spoken along the coast of the North Sea
from northern Holland to central Denmark, but which is now
heard only in a few coastal regions and on some of the Dutch
islands. Before the migration of the Anglo-Saxons to England, they
must have been near neighbours of the Frisians, and we can
postulate a prehistoric Anglo-Frisian dialect, out of which evolved
Old English and Old Frisian. Here is a family tree for the West
Germanic languages:

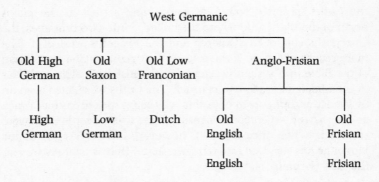

One of the phonological characteristics of the West Germanic languages is the development of numerous diphthongs, often found in positions where North and East Germanic have a pure vowel plus a consonant. So the Old Norse *höggva* and Modern Swedish *hugga* correspond to the Old English verb *hēawan* 'to cut, hew', and to Old English *brēowan* 'to brew' corresponds Old Swedish *bryggja*, Modern Swedish *brygga*. One lexical form found only in West Germanic is the word *sheep* (Dutch *schaap*, German *Schaf*, Old Frisian *skēp*), which has no known cognate elsewhere. Gothic used the forms *awi-* and *lamb*, while the Old Norse word was *fār* (Old Swedish) or *fær* (Old Icelandic): the Faroes are the 'Sheep Islands' (Old Icelandic *Færeyjar*).

The expansion of the Germanic-speaking peoples did not, of course, end in the time of Tacitus. During the break-up of the Roman Empire, Germanic military expeditions were made all over Europe and the Mediterranean: Goths swept through Spain and Italy, Vandals invaded North Africa, Franks and Burgundians settled in France, Anglo-Saxons occupied southern Britain. Later still, Scandinavian Vikings harried the whole of Europe, and established kingdoms in England, Ireland, Normandy and Russia. Often, however, such conquests were made by relatively small groups, whose language ultimately disappeared: Gothic and Vandal did not survive anywhere; Frankish disappeared in France, and French is a Romance language; the Vikings did not establish their language permanently anywhere except in Iceland and the Faroes. Of course, the Germanic languages often left traces on the languages that supplanted them: French has a few hundred loan-words from Germanic, including such a highly characteristic Germanic word as *guerre*, 'war'; the Langobards, or 'long beards', left their name in *Lombardy* when they invaded Italy in the sixth century AD; and the very name of *Russia* is a Scandinavian loan-word. And, even though so many dialects died out, there were in earlier times a great number of Germanic dialects spoken in Europe. Their consolidation into a small number of national languages was due to the rise of the modern nation-states: as we have seen, the existence of a coherent and centralized political unit favours the triumph of a single dialect (a prestige-dialect or standard literary language) within its area.

We have no records of the Proto-Germanic language from which all these languages are descended. We can, however, reconstruct it to quite a considerable extent by comparing the various daughter-languages. Especially valuable are languages with early literary records. We can also learn a good deal by comparing our reconstructions with the forms found in the other branches of Indo-European. Further minor sources of information are the Germanic names recorded by Latin and Greek authors, and the words borrowed from Proto-Germanic by other languages. For example, the Finnish word *kuningas*, meaning 'king', is plainly borrowed from Germanic, and it preserves a more archaic form of the word than any of the Germanic languages themselves (for example, Old Norse *konungr*, Old High German *kuning*, Old English *cyning*); the Proto-Germanic form was probably **kuningaz*.

The inflectional system of Proto-Germanic

The Proto-Germanic language, reconstructed in this way, has close affinities with the other Indo-European languages, together with certain peculiar developments of its own. Like the postulated Proto-Indo-European language, Proto-Germanic is a highly *inflected* language: that is, in its grammar it makes great use of variations in the *endings* of words. Not much of the Indo-European system of inflections is left in Modern English, which prefers other grammatical devices, and to get a better idea of what an inflected language is like, you need to look at something like classical Latin, or modern German.

The English sentence *The master beat the servant* could be rendered in Latin, word for word, as *Dominus verberāvit servum*, though classical Latin would normally prefer the order *Dominus servum verberāvit*. The important point is, however, that altering the order of the Latin words cannot alter the basic meaning of the sentence: if we write *Servum verberāvit dominus*, we are adopting a rather unusual word-order, and giving special emphasis to the word 'servant', but it still means 'The master beat the servant'. English uses word-order to indicate who is the beater and who the beaten, but in Latin this information is carried by the inflections -*us* and -*um*. If we wish to say that the servant beat the master, we must change these endings, and write *Servus dominum verberāvit*. In grammatical terminology, we are inflecting the nouns *servus* and *dominus* for **case**: the ending -*us* shows the nominative case, used for the subject of the sentence, and the ending -*um* the accusative case, used for the object of the sentence.

Latin nouns, moreover, have other inflections, which to some extent do the work which in Modern English is performed by prepositions (words like *of* and *with*). Thus the noun *dominus* has the following set of inflections:

	Singular	Plural
Nominative	dominus 'a master'	dominī 'masters'
Vocative	domine 'master!'	dominī 'masters!'
Accusative	dominum 'a master'	dominōs 'masters'
Genitive	dominī 'of a master'	dominōrum 'of masters'
Dative	dominō 'to, for a master'	dominīs 'to, for masters'
Ablative	dominō 'by, with, from a master'	dominīs 'by, with, from masters'

The Latin noun, it will be seen, has six different cases, and there are separate inflections for the singular and the plural.

Latin inherited its system of case inflections from Proto-Indo-European, and a somewhat similar system was inherited by Proto-Germanic, though both Latin and Proto-Germanic reduced the number of case-distinctions: for all practical purposes, they had only five or six cases, whereas Proto-Indo-European had at least eight. The cases preserved in Proto-Germanic were the nominative (showing the 'beater' relationship), the accusative (the 'beaten' relationship), the genitive ('of'), the dative ('to' or 'for'), and the instrumental ('by'). There are also traces of a vocative case (used in addressing somebody) and of a locative (corresponding to 'at'). As in Latin, there were separate inflections for the singular and the plural. In Proto-Indo-European, there had also been inflections for the *dual* number, that is, to indicate that there were *two* of a thing, but the dual survives only vestigially in the Germanic languages.

In Proto-Germanic, as in other Indo-European languages, there was no single set of case-inflections used for all nouns alike, but several different sets, some nouns following one pattern, and others another. That is, there were various **declensions** of nouns. All nouns, moreover, had grammatical gender: every noun had to be either masculine, feminine, or neuter. This grammatical gender had no necessary connection with sex or with animacy: the names of inanimate objects could be masculine or feminine, and the names of sexed creatures could be neuter. The words for *he*, *she*, and *it* had to be used in accordance with grammatical gender, not in accordance with sex or animacy. This is still, to some extent, the case in Modern German, where for example *das Mädchen* 'the girl', being neuter, has to be referred to as 'it', while *die Polizei* 'the police', being feminine, has to be referred to as 'she'.

So far we have been dealing with nouns, but similar considerations apply to adjectives (words like *good, happy, green, beautiful*). These were also inflected in Proto-Indo-European, and had to be put in the same case and number as the noun they were attached to. Moreover, adjectives had different inflections for different genders, and had to agree with the noun in gender. So in Latin the noun *dominus* 'master' is masculine, and 'a great master' is *magnus dominus*; but *domus* 'house' is feminine, and 'a great house' is *magna domus*; while *opus* 'work' is neuter, and 'a great work' is *magnum opus*. In Proto-Indo-European, the adjective inflections had been essentially the same as the noun inflections, but in many of the daughter-languages they became distinguished from them in various ways. This happened in Proto-Germanic, which developed two distinct sets of inflections for the adjectives, called the strong and the weak declensions of the adjective. The distinction between the strong and the weak forms of the adjective has not survived in Modern English, but it can still be found in many of the other Germanic languages. In Modern Swedish, for example, 'a good friend' is *en god vän*, but 'my good friend' is *min goda vän*. In the first phrase, the strong form of the adjective is used (*god*); in the second, the weak form (*goda*). In Swedish, the weak form is used after the definite article, after words like *this* and *that*, and after possessive words like *my* and *your*; otherwise the strong form is used. In Old English, similarly, the strong form of the adjective was used in *gōd mann* ('a good person'), and the weak form in *sē gōda mann* ('the good person').

Proto-Germanic, like Proto-Indo-European, also had a system of cases for the pronouns, articles, and similar words. Where Modern English has the one form *the*, Proto-Germanic had a whole series of forms according to the case, number, and gender of the noun that followed. This was still so in Old English, where 'the woman' is *sē wīfmann* (masculine), 'learning' is *sēo lār* (feminine), and 'the wife' is *þæt wīf* (neuter). The declension of the definite article is still found in Modern German, where the foreign learner is all too familiar with *der, die, das*. Similarly with the personal pronouns (*I, you, he*, etc.), which had different forms for different cases. Here, Proto-Germanic preserved dual forms as well as plurals, and these are found in some of the daughter-languages. In Old English, there is a form *ic* meaning 'I', and a form *wē* meaning 'we', but also a form *wit*, meaning 'we two'. Similarly, *þū* is singular 'thou', *gē* is plural 'you', and *git* is dual 'you two'.

Proto-Indo-European also had a great array of inflections for its verbs. Proto-Germanic retained many of these, but it simplified the system. For example, it had only two tenses of the verb, a present tense and a past tense: there were forms corresponding to *I sing* and *I sang*, but no forms with such meanings as 'I shall sing', 'I have sung', and so on. Within these two tenses, however, Proto-Germanic had different endings for different persons and numbers, like Latin, in which 'I sing' is *cantō*, 'he/she sings' is *cantat*, 'they sing' is *cantant*, and so on. Like Latin, Proto-Germanic had two sets of inflections for the verbs, one indicative and one subjunctive. The indicative was the normal form, while the subjunctive was used in various constructions implying doubt, uncertainty, or unreality. The subjunctive forms have been largely lost in Modern

English, which instead uses modal auxiliaries (*might*, *should*, etc.), but relics of them remain, for example in the use of *be* instead of *is* (as in the expression *if need be*), and in the difference between *he was* (indicative) and *he were* (subjunctive), as in the sentences 'If *he was* there he will tell us about it' and 'If *he were* here he would tell us about it'. Like Latin, Proto-Germanic had inflections to mark the passive; these did not survive in Old English, but are found in Gothic, where *haita* means 'I call', while *haitada* means 'I am called'.

It was in the verbs that Proto-Germanic made one of its own distinctive developments. From Proto-Indo-European it had inherited a whole series of verbs which showed change of tense by changing the vowel of their stem, like Modern English *I sing*, *I sang*, or *I bind*, *I bound*; these are called **strong** verbs. This alternation of vowels for grammatical purposes is highly characteristic of the Indo-European languages, and there were large numbers of strong verbs in Proto-Germanic. Alongside these strong verbs, however, Proto-Germanic invented a new type, called **weak verbs**. In these, the past tense is formed by adding an inflection to the verb-stem, as in *I walk*, *I walked*. This inflection had various forms: in Gothic, 'I seek' is *sōkja*, 'I sought' *sōkida*; 'I anoint' is *salbō*, 'I anointed' *salbōda*; 'I have' is *haba*, 'I had' *habaida*. There we have the endings *-ida*, *-ōda*, and *-aida*. All, however, have the consonant *d*, and either this or some other dental/alveolar consonant appears in the weak past-tense inflection in all the Germanic languages. In Proto-Germanic the inflections must have contained either a [d] or a [ð]. The origin of the weak conjugation of verbs is uncertain; one theory is that the ending was originally a part of the verb 'to do', rather as though 'he walked' had developed out of 'he walk did'; but no single theory seems able to explain all the facts. What is certain is that the weak verbs have become the dominant verb-forms in the Germanic languages. In Old English, for example, the weak verbs are already the majority. Since then, many strong verbs have changed over to weak, like the verb 'to help', which formerly had the past tense *healp*, but now has *helped*. And nearly all new verbs formed or borrowed by the language are made weak: for example, sixteenth-century loans such as *imitate* (from Latin) and *invite* (from French) have past tenses like *imitated, invited*; and when, in our own century, we invent a new verb such as *to garage* (formed from the noun), it seems inevitable that the past tense shall be *garaged*. So that today the strong verbs, which were the original type, are a small minority, and weak verbs are the norm.

The Phonology of Proto-Germanic

In pronunciation, Proto-Indo-European underwent considerable changes in developing into Proto-Germanic. The history of pronunciation in any language is full of detail and complication, and here we can consider only a few of the more prominent developments. One big change is in the matter of accent. The accent on a syllable depends partly on stress (acoustic loudness), partly on intonation (musical pitch), but some languages rely more on one than on the other. Proto-Indo-European probably made great use of musical accent, but in Proto-Germanic the stress accent became predominant. At the same time, there was a strong tendency in Proto-Germanic to adopt a uniform position for the stress on a word, by putting it on the first syllable. This was not the case in Proto-Indo-European, where the accent could fall on any syllable of a word, whether prefix, stem, suffix, or inflection. This so-called 'free accent' can still be seen in classical Greek: for example, the Greek word for 'mother' is *mētēr*, with the accent on the first syllable, but the genitive case ('of a mother') is *mētéros*, with the accent on the second syllable, or *mētrós* (a contracted form) with the accent on the final syllable. The tendency in Proto-Germanic to stabilize the accent on the first syllable of a word, together with the adoption of a predominantly stress type of accent (and also perhaps a tendency towards the even spacing of stressed syllables), had profound consequences. Above all, it led to a weakening and often to a loss of unstressed syllables, especially at the end of a word, and this is a trend which has continued in the Germanic languages throughout their history. For example, the Proto-Indo-European form of the infinitive of the verb 'to bear' was something like **bheronom*, which in Proto-Germanic became something like **beranan*. The final *-an* had been weakened and then lost before any of the

Germanic languages were recorded, and the Old English form is *beran*. Then the final *-an* became *-en*, giving early Middle English *beren*. In the course of the Middle English period the final *-n* was lost, and the word became *bere*, which was still a two-syllable word (with the final *-e* probably pronounced [ə]). At the end of the Middle English period, this final *-e* was lost in its turn, and the modern form has simply the single syllable *bear*. Similar processes of attrition, though not always as drastic as this, have taken place in the other Germanic languages.

The phoneme-system of Proto-Indo-European was reconstructed by a series of nineteenth-century scholars, culminating in the work of Karl Brugmann near the end of the century. Since then, additional evidence has come to light, notably the discovery of Hittite, and there have been great developments in linguistic theory. Some of Brugmann's views have therefore been challenged. For example, it has been suggested that Brugmann's PIE phoneme *b* did not in fact exist. On the evidence of Hittite, it has been argued that there was an additional series of consonants unknown to Brugmann, called laryngeals. Gamkrelidze and Ivanov have produced an alternative analysis of the PIE consonant-system: what Brugmann called voiced stops were in fact, they argue, glottalized voiceless stops. The debate continues, and in what follows I keep close to the traditional analysis.

In Proto-Indo-European as thus reconstructed, there was a rich array of stop consonants. This system underwent great changes in Proto-Germanic. The most important series of changes is called 'the first sound-shifting', or sometimes 'Grimm's Law', after the early nineteenth-century philologist Jakob Grimm, who analysed it. The main features of the first sound-shifting are shown in Table 4.1.

Table 4.1   *The first sound-shifting*

Aspirated voiced stops	Voiced stops	Voiceless stops	Voiceless fricatives
bh ⟶	b ⟶	p ⟶	f
dh ⟶	d ⟶	t ⟶	θ
gh ⟶	g ⟶	k ⟶	h

A few examples will show what is meant. PIE /p/ became Germanic /f/:

Latin	Greek	Sanskrit	Gothic	Old English
pedem	poda	padam	fōtus	fōt 'foot'
pecus	–	pacu	faihu	feoh 'cattle, money'
piscis	–	–	fisks	fisc 'fish'

PIE /t/ became Proto-Germanic voiceless /θ/; in some cases this has become voiced /ð/ in Modern English, as in the word *thou*:

Latin	Greek	Sanskrit	Old Norse	English
trēs	treis	trayas	þrír	three
tenuis	tanaos	tanu	þunnr	thin
tū	tu	tvam	þú	thou

Greek *tu* is the Doric form: the Attic dialect has *su*.

PIE /k/ became in Germanic the [x] sound heard in Modern German *ach* or Scots *loch*. In Old English and other early Germanic languages it usually appears with the spelling *h*. It was lost between vowels in prehistoric Old English, but can be seen in other Germanic languages. For example:

Latin	Greek	Welsh	Gothic	O.H. German	English
cordem	kardia	craidd	hairto	herza	heart
centum	-katon	cant	hund	hunt	hund(red)
decem	deka	deg	taihun	zehan	ten

The Indo-European voiced stops /b/, /d/, and /g/ became, in Germanic, the corresponding voiceless stops /p/, /t/, and /k/. The /b/ occurred only rarely in Proto-Indo-European, but examples of its development to Germanic /p/ can perhaps be seen in the English words *deep* (Lithuanian *dubs*), *thorp* (Lithuanian *troba* 'house', Latin *trabs* 'beam'), and *sleep* (related to Old Slavonic *slabu* 'weak'). The following are examples of the change from /d/ to /t/:

Latin	Greek	Sanskrit	Gothic	English
edō	edō	admi	itan	eat
decem	deka	daca	taihun	ten
vidēre	oida	veda	witan	to wit

In this last example, the Latin word *vidēre* means 'to see', and the remainder mean 'to know' or 'I know'. In Old English there was a verb *witan* 'to know', and from this we get the expression *to wit*, meaning 'namely'. The same root is seen in *witness* and *unwitting*.

The change of Indo-European /g/ to Germanic /k/ is seen in the following examples:

Latin	Greek	Gothic	English
ager	agros	akrs	acre
genus	genos	kuni	kin
gelidus	–	kalds	cold

Proto-Indo-European had a series of phonemes which appeared in Sanskrit as *bh*, *dh*, and *gh*, and in Greek as the letters phi, theta, and chi (transliterated in the Latin alphabet as *ph*, *th*, and *ch* respectively). The exact nature of the original sounds is disputed, but traditionally they have been called aspirated voiced stops, and represented by the symbols *bh*, *dh*, and *gh*. In Table 4.1 they are shown as changing into Proto-Germanic /b/, /d/, and /g/. However, this is not quite accurate, for in Proto-Germanic they almost certainly became the corresponding voiced fricatives. In many positions, however, they did develop into voiced stops in the various Germanic languages. The English verb *to bear* corresponds to Sanskrit *bharami* and Greek *phēro*; *brother* corresponds to Sanskrit *bhrātar* and Greek *phrātēr* 'clansman'; *door* is cognate with Greek *thura*; *red* is related to Sanskrit *rudhiras*; and Greek *chēn* is related to German *Gans* and English *goose*.

In addition to the three rows of phonemes shown in Table 4.1, it is believed that in Proto-Indo-European there was also a series of stops with labialization (lip-rounding), namely g^wh, g^w, and k^w. PIE k^w became PG /hw/: corresponding to Latin *quod*, we find Old Saxon *hwat* and Old English *hwæt* (Modern English *what*). PIE g^w became PG /kw/: Old English *cwene* 'woman', which became Modern English *quean*, corresponds to Greek *gunē* 'woman'. PIE g^wh appears in the Germanic languages either as *g* or as *w*, according to position, as in Old Norse *gunnr*, Old English *gūþ* 'battle, war', and Old English *snīwan* 'to snow'.

We do not know the exact dates of the first sound-shifting, but it may have begun around 500 BC, and possibly took several centuries to complete. It was followed by a smaller series of changes, usually called 'Verner's Law', in which voiceless fricatives became voiced if the preceding syllable was unstressed, but otherwise remained unchanged. This may have taken place in the first century of our era. Finally came the fixing of the accent on the first syllable of the word, which cannot have taken place until after the operation of Verner's Law.

The Proto-Germanic vowel system

Proto-Germanic also made changes in the PIE vowel system, though these were less extensive than the consonant changes. The three most important vowels in Proto-Indo-European were *a*, *e*, and *o*, each of which could be either short or long. There were also short *i* and *u*, which could operate either as unstressed vowels or as consonants (i.e. [j] and [w]) according to their position, and could also be combined with any of the three main vowels, long or short, to form diphthongs. There were also a disputed number of vowels used only in unstressed syllables, and a number of syllabic consonants.

In tracing vowel-changes in Proto-Germanic, or any of the later Germanic languages, we always have to distinguish between stressed and unstressed syllables, since these give different results. Henceforward, when I talk about vowel changes I shall be referring to stressed syllables unless I specify otherwise. For Proto-Germanic, let us look at just two vowel changes in stressed syllables: PIE short *o* became PG *a*, and PIE long *ā* became PG *ō*. Examples of the change from *o* to *a*:

Latin	Greek	Old Irish	Gothic	O.H. German	
octō	oktō	ocht	ahtau	ahto	'eight'
hortus	chortos	gort	gards	gart	'yard, garden, enclosure'
hostis	–	–	gasts	gast	'stranger, guest, enemy'

The stressed syllable in Germanic is the first in the word, and it is there that the change is seen. Examples of the change of *ā* to *ō*:

Latin	Greek	Old Irish	Gothic	O. Norse	Old English	
frāter	phrātēr	brāthir	brōþar	brōþer	brōþor	'brother'
māter	mātēr	māthir	–	mōþer	mōdor	'mother'

The Greek *phrātēr* meant 'clansman', not 'brother'. The Greek *mātēr* is from the Doric dialect, other dialects having *mētēr*.

The vowels played an important part in the grammar of Proto-Indo-European, because of the way they alternated in related forms (as in our *sing, sang, sung*), and this system descended to Proto-Germanic. There were several series of vowels which alternated in this way. Each member of such a series is called a **grade**, and the whole phenomenon is known as **gradation** (or **ablaut**). One such series in PIE, for example, was short *e*, short *o*, and zero: originally, the zero grade probably appeared in unaccented syllables. This series was used in some of the strong verbs: the e-grade appeared in the present tense, the o-grade in the past singular, and the zero grade in the past plural and the past participle (in which the accent was originally on the ending, not the stem). This is the series that was used in *sing, sang, sung*, though this fact has been obscured by the vowel changes which took place in Proto-Germanic. The original PIE stems of these words were something like **seng^wh-* (e-grade), **song^wh-* (o-grade), and **sng^wh-* (zero grade). In Proto-Germanic these became **sing-*, **sang-*, **sung-*, as seen for example in Old English *singan* ('to sing'), *sang* ('he/she sang'), *sungon* ('they sang'), *gesungen* ('sung'). The *e* changed to *i* because of the following *ng*, a normal combinative change in Proto-Germanic. PIE short *o* regularly changed to PG *a*, as we have already seen. The *u* appeared in the zero-grade form through the influence of the following syllabic *n*: in Proto-Germanic, the PIE syllabic consonants *m*, *n*, *l*, and *r* became *um*, *un*, *ul*, and *ur*, so that a syllable that originally had no vowel often appears in the Germanic languages with *u*.

Gradation is not confined to verbs, however. We see the alternation of *e* and *o* grades in the Greek verb *legō* 'I speak' and the related noun *logos* 'speech', and this same alternation, ultimately, lies behind the Modern English pairs *bind* and *band*, *ride* and *rode*, *learn* and *lore*. In some cases, related words appear with different grades in different languages; these must go back to variant forms in PIE. For example, the PIE word for 'knee' had the variant forms **gen-*, **gon-*, **gn-*. The *e* grade appears in Latin *genu* and the *o* grade in Greek *gonu*. In the Germanic languages it is the zero grade *gn-* that appears: by Grimm's Law this becomes *kn-*, as in Gothic *kniu* and Old English *cnēo* 'knee'.

These, then, are some of the main developments in Proto-Germanic: simplification of the inflectional system of PIE; the introduction of the weak declension of the adjective; the introduction of the weak verbs; the great consonant change known as the First Sound-Shifting (or Grimm's Law), and the smaller change known as Verner's Law; the change from predominantly pitch accent to predominantly stress accent; the fixing of the accent on the first syllable of the word; and of course a host of lesser changes, both in grammar and in pronunciation.

The Vocabulary of Proto-Germanic

Some of the vocabulary of Proto-Germanic also seems to be peculiar to it, since it is not paralleled in other Indo-European languages. In some cases this may be pure chance, a word having been preserved by Germanic and lost by the other branches, but no doubt some of the words were invented or acquired by the Germanic peoples after the dispersal of the Indo-Europeans. Among the words peculiar to Germanic are a number that have to do with ships and seafaring: words to which there are no certain correspondences in other Indo-European languages include *ship*, *sail*, *boat*, *keel*, *sheet*, *stay* ('rope supporting a mast'), possibly *float*, and *sea* itself. This tallies with the view that the Indo-Europeans originally lived inland: nautical vocabularies would then be developed independently by those peoples that reached the coast and took to the sea.

The Proto-Germans borrowed a number of words from neighbouring peoples, especially the Celts and the Romans, who were on a higher cultural level and so had things to teach them. The Celts were skilled in metallurgy, and the Germanic words for iron and lead (seen for example in Old English *īren*, *lēad*) were probably borrowed from them. From the Romans were borrowed many words to do with war, trade, building, horticulture, and food – all fields where the Germans learnt a good deal from their southern neighbours. The word *pile* (OE *pīl*) 'pointed stake' is from Latin *pīlum* 'javelin', and goes back to these early days, as does the word *street* (OE *strǣt*), taken from the Latin (*via*) *strāta* 'paved (road)', a tribute to the impression made on the Germans by Roman military roads. Tacitus described the Germans as living in ugly wooden houses, or even in pits covered with rubbish, but they learnt a good deal about building from the Romans, and borrowed the words which in Modern English have become *wall*, *tile*, *chalk*, *mill*, and *pit* (from Latin *puteus* 'a well'). They also learnt Latin trading terms, for there was a good deal of traffic between the two areas: the loans include the words which have become *pound*, *mile*, *cheap*, *monger*, and *mint* (originally meaning 'coin, money', from Latin *monēta*). Tacitus said that the Germans did not grow fruit trees or cultivate gardens, but again they seem to have been willing to learn, for they borrowed the words *apple*, *plum*, and *pear*, not to mention *wine*. As has happened so often since, culinary refinements also came to the north of Europe from the Mediterranean: the very word *kitchen* was borrowed from Latin, and so were *pepper*, *peas*, *mint* (the herb), *cheese*, *butter*, *kettle*, and *dish*. To judge from the linguistic evidence, the Germans were not so much impressed by Roman law, ideals of order, and so on, as by more concrete manifestations of Roman civilization – roads, buildings, food.

5 Old English

During the three or four centuries after Tacitus wrote his *Germania*, the Germanic peoples were in a state of flux and movement. We know little of their history in this turbulent period of migration and expansion, but we do know that, towards the end of these centuries of flux, our Germanic ancestors settled in England. There is some archaeological evidence that Saxons settled in East Anglia and the Vale of York while Britain was still a Roman province, but the main settlements were made after the Roman legions had withdrawn from Britain in AD 410, and the traditional accounts of the landing of Hengest and Horsa in Kent place it in the year 449.

The Anglo-Saxon settlement of Britain must not be thought of as the arrival of a unified invading army, but rather as the arrival and penetration of various unco-ordinated bands of adventurers in different parts of the country, beginning in the middle of the fifth century and going on all through the sixth. The struggle with the Romano-Celtic population was a long one, and Anglo-Saxon domination in England was not assured until late in the sixth century. We know little about this struggle: it was the age of King Arthur, and there are more legends than hard facts. But by about 700, the Anglo-Saxons had occupied most of England (the exceptions being Cornwall and an area in the North-West) and also a considerable part of southern Scotland. Wales remained a British stronghold.

Anglo-Saxons and Celts

The Anglo-Saxon conquest was not just the arrival of a ruling minority, but the settlement of a whole people. Their language remained the dominant one, and there are few traces of Celtic influence on Old English; indeed, the number of Celtic words taken into English in the whole of its history has been very small. The names of some English towns were taken over from the Celts, for example London and Leeds. Rivers often have Celtic names: Avon and Ouse are Celtic words for 'water' or 'stream'; Derwent, Darent, and Dart are all forms of the British name for 'oak river'; the Thames is the 'dark river'; while Trent apparently means 'trespasser', that is, a river liable to flooding. Among county names, Kent and Devon are Celtic, and so are the first elements in Cornwall and Cumberland; the latter means 'the land of the Cymry (that is, the Welsh)', and testifies to the long continuance of Celtic power in the North-West. A few words for topographical features are also borrowed from Celtic, like OE *cumb* meaning 'narrow valley, coomb'.

These few Celtic words in Old English were merely a drop in the ocean, however. Even in English place-names, where Celtic left its biggest mark, Celtic forms are far outnumbered by English ones, and only in areas where the Anglo-Saxons penetrated late are Celtic names at all common for villages. There are an enormous number of place-name elements of English derivation. Among the common ones are *ton* (OE *tūn* 'enclosure, farmstead, hamlet'), *ham* (OE *hām* 'homestead' and *hamm* 'meadow, water-meadow'), *ley* (OE *lēah* 'glade, wood'), *worth* (OE *worþ* 'enclosure'), *field* (OE *feld* 'open country'), and *ing* (OE *-ingas* 'the people of'). Thus Nottingham (OE Snotingeham) was 'the homestead of Snot's people', Buckingham was 'the meadow of Bucca's people', Langley was 'a long wood', and Aston and Easton were 'eastern farmstead (or village)'.

The failure of Celtic to influence Old English to any great extent does not mean that the Britons were all killed or driven out. There is in fact evidence that a considerable number of Britons lived among the Anglo-Saxons, but they were a defeated people whose language had no prestige compared with that of the conquerors, and the Anglo-Saxons had settled in such large numbers that there could be no question of their absorption by the Celts. The Old English word *wealh*, which originally meant 'foreigner', came to mean both 'Celt, Welshman' and 'servant, slave', which illustrates both the survival of the Britons among the Anglo-Saxons, and their low status. The OE *wealh* has survived as the second syllable of *Cornwall*, and also in the word *walnut* (OE *wealh-hnutu* 'foreign nut, walnut'). Our word *Welsh* is from the related adjective, OE *welisc*.

Angles, Saxons, and Jutes

The piecemeal way in which the Anglo-Saxons conquered England led to a profusion of small kingdoms, and no doubt to dialect differentiation. In any case there were probably dialect differences from the start, for the invaders came from more than one Germanic tribe. Bede, writing in about 730, tells us about this:

> They came from three very powerful Germanic tribes, the Saxons, Angles, and Jutes. The people of Kent and the inhabitants of the Isle of Wight are of Jutish origin and also those opposite the Isle of Wight, that part of the kingdom of Wessex which is still today called the nation of the Jutes. From the Saxon country, that is, the district now known as Old Saxony, came the East Saxons, the South Saxons, and the West Saxons. Besides this, from the country of the Angles, that is, the land between the kingdoms of the Jutes and the Saxons, which is called *Angulus*, came the East Angles, the Middle Ángles, the Mercians, and all the Northumbrian race (that is those people who dwell north of the river Humber) as well as the other Anglian tribes.

The land of the Old Saxons was in North-West Germany (in Schleswig-Holstein, and perhaps farther west too along the North Sea coast), and we can assume that the Saxons who invaded England came from this region. The Angles probably came from slightly farther north, from the Danish mainland and islands. The Jutes are more obscure: they may have come from Jutland, which is what Bede's account might suggest, but their culture seems to have had affinities with that of the Franks farther south, and some people believe that they came from the Rhineland. There is also evidence that, in addition to Angles, Saxons, and Jutes, the Germanic invaders of Britain included Frisians.

Whatever their exact origins, these groups were in any case closely related in language and culture, and regarded themselves as one people. For example, the word *Engle* 'the Angles' came to be applied to all the Germanic settlers in Britain, and the related adjective *Englisc* was similarly applied to all these peoples and their language, not just to the Angles. Political union came slowly, however. In the early days there was a medley of petty kingdoms, and some of their names are preserved in our modern counties:

Figure 7   Britain before the Vikings, showing Anglo-Saxon and British kingdoms. Farther north were Scots and Picts

Essex, Middlesex, and Sussex were the realms of the East, Middle, and South Saxons, while Norfolk and Suffolk were the north and south folk of the East Angles; the names of others survive only in the history-books, like the kingdoms of the Dere in Yorkshire and the Bernice in Northumberland. By a process of conquest and amalgamation, this medley of kingdoms was eventually reduced to seven, sometimes called the Heptarchy: Northumbria (Southern Scotland and England north of the Humber), Mercia (in the West Midlands), East Anglia, Essex, Sussex, Kent, and Wessex (based on central southern England). The approximate positions of these seven kingdoms are shown in Figure 7. Different kings managed to establish their suzerainty over other kingdoms at various times, but these dominations were often personal and temporary. In very broad terms, we can see a gradual shift southwards of the centres of power and civilization. In the seventh century, Northumbria was very powerful, and was a great centre of learning. In the eighth century this leadership passed to Mercia, and in the ninth century to Wessex; and it was the kings of Wessex who finally unified the country. In the late ninth century, the kings of Wessex, notably King Alfred, saved the South and West of England from the Danes, and in the tenth century Alfred's successors reconquered the North and the East. In the second half of the tenth century, Edgar not only ruled all England, but was recognized as overlord of Wales and Scotland as well. From this time, the unity of England was durable: the king might be Danish, like Cnut, or half-English, like Edward the Confessor, or Norman French, like William the Conqueror, but in any case he ruled a single country.

The West Saxon literary language

The unification of England under the West Saxon kings led to the recognition of the West Saxon dialect as a literary standard. The surviving texts from the Old English period are in four main dialects: West Saxon, Kentish, Mercian, and Northumbrian (the last two often being grouped together as Anglian); and there were certainly other dialects of which we have no records. The approximate boundaries of the four main dialect-areas are shown

Figure 8   The main dialect-areas of Old English

in Figure 8. The bulk of our records, however, are in the West
Saxon dialect. Many of the earlier manuscripts were destroyed in
the Viking conquests of the North and Midlands, and in the later
part of the period there was a tendency for the manuscripts to be
copied by West Saxon scribes and so put into West Saxon form.
For example, the Old English epic poem *Beowulf* was possibly
written in an Anglian dialect, but the only surviving manuscript is
in West Saxon.

One interesting thing is that, although West Saxon became
the literary standard of a united England in the late Anglo-

Saxon period, it is not the direct ancestor of modern standard English, which is mainly derived from an Anglian dialect. One difference between West Saxon and Anglian is preserved in the modern words *weald* (from West Saxon) and *wold* (from Anglian): before certain consonant-groups a vowel became diphthongized in West Saxon but not in Anglian, the Old English forms being Anglian *wald* and West Saxon *weald*, both meaning 'forest'. The same difference is seen in the word for 'cold': Anglian *cald*, West Saxon *ceald*. The modern word is quite regularly descended from the Anglian form; the West Saxon form would have produced a modern word **cheald*. Another West Saxon characteristic was the use of the diphthongs *ie* and *īe*, which did not exist in the other dialects. The West Saxon verb 'to hear' was *hīeran*; in Late West Saxon this became *hȳran*, which could be expected to develop into a modern form **hire* or **hure*; our word *hear* is in fact quite regularly descended from the Anglian form, *hēran*. In addition to such phonological differences, the Old English dialects differed in small ways in grammar and vocabulary.

Christianity and writing

We know little about the Anglo-Saxons until after their conversion to Christianity, which introduced them to writing. As elsewhere in medieval Europe, writing was in the hands of clerics, who often had strong views about what it was proper to record, so that we learn little about the ways of the heathen English from their writings. Some pagan lore has, however, remained fossilized in the language. The heathen gods Tīw, Wōden, and Thunor ('thunder', corresponding to the Scandinavian Thor) have given their names to Tuesday, Wednesday, and Thursday, while Wōden's consort Frīg ('Love') has given her name to Friday. More remarkably, the goddess of the rising sun or of spring, Ēastre, has probably given her name to the Christian festival of Easter. These pagan deities are also commemorated in place-names such as Tuesley, Wednesbury, and Thunderfield, and pagan practices are attested by place-names like Harrow (OE *hearh* 'temple') and Wye in Kent (OE *wīg* 'idol, shrine').

The conversion of the English to Christianity began in about the year 600, and took a century to complete. It was carried out from two directions, the Celtic church penetrating from the North-West and the Roman church from the South-East. With Christianity came writing. The English already had one form of writing, runes, but these were used only for short inscriptions, not for texts of any length. Runes had been used by the Germanic peoples from at least the third century AD, for carving or scratching inscriptions on stone, metal-work, or wood: the word *book* (OE *bōc*) originally meant 'beech'. The word *rune* also meant 'mystery, secret', and the inscriptions were evidently thought to have magical power (as often among early peoples). Runes go back ultimately to some form of the Greek alphabet, but, because of their use in inscriptions, have acquired a decidedly angular form. The best-known inscriptions are the Scandinavian ones, but the English also used a form of the runic alphabet which, from its first six letters, is known as the 'futhorc'. When the clerics introduced writing to England, they used a Celtic version of the Latin alphabet, but eked it out with runic symbols from the futhorc: for example, they used the symbol ρ ('wynn') to represent the OE /w/ phoneme.

In modern editions of OE texts (at any rate ones designed for students), it is customary to give the Latin letters their modern form, to use *w* instead of 'wynn', and to use special symbols only for some of the letters that represent a departure from the Latin alphabet. It is also common in modern editions to mark long vowels by putting a macron (short horizontal line) over them, while leaving the short vowels unmarked; the original OE manuscripts do not mark vowel-length. I shall follow modern conventions in these matters.

The Pronunciation of Old English

Old English script used the six vowel-symbols *a, e, i, o, u,* and *y,* and a seventh one, æ, called 'ash'. All of these could represent both long and short vowels. The probable pronunciations represented by the symbols are shown in Table 5.1. The pronunciations are those of Early West Saxon.

Table 5.1   *The vowel-sounds of Old English, Early West Saxon*

Symbol	Pronunciation	Resembling the vowel of
a	[a]	French *la*, German *mann*, Northern English *hat*
æ	[æ]	RP *hat*
e	[ɛ]	French *elle*, German *Bett*
i	[ɪ]	English *pin*
o	[ɔ]	English *law* (shortened)
u	[ʊ]	RP *put*
y	[y]	French *cru*, German *Hütte*
ā	[ɑː]	English *far*
ǣ	[æː]	London English *bad*
ē	[eː]	French *été* (lengthened), German *zehn*
ī	[iː]	German *sie*, English *tree*
ō	[oː]	German *wo*, French *chose*
ū	[uː]	English *food*
ȳ	[yː]	French *sûr*, German *führen*

All the symbols represent pure vowels, not diphthongs. To represent diphthongs, the Anglo-Saxons used digraphs (sequences of two symbols): *ea*, *eo*, *io*, and *ie*. These probably represented the pronunciations [ɛə], [eʊ], [ɪʊ], and [ɪə]; they too could be either short or long. Anglian texts also use the digraph *oe*; this however does not represent a diphthong, but the half-close front rounded vowel [ø(ː)], that is, some kind of [e(ː)] with lip-rounding.

Turning now to consonants, the use of double consonants was different from the one we are used to. In Modern English spelling, we use double-consonant symbols in two-syllable words to show that the preceding vowel is short: the spellings *written* and *copper* are used for words pronounced /ˈrɪtn/ and /ˈkɒpə/, which have short vowels; a single consonant-symbol is used if the preceding vowel is long or is a diphthong, as in *writer* and *coping*. But in Old English this is not so: the fact that a single consonant-symbol is used tells us nothing about the length of the preceding vowel. The Old English words for 'written' and 'copper' are *writen* and *copor*; these had short vowels, and were probably pronounced [ˈwrɪtɛn] and [ˈkɔpɔr]. However, we do find OE spellings with doubled consonants, like *assa* 'ass', *bucca* 'he-goat', and *cuppe* 'cup'. In such words the double-consonant symbol indicates that the consonant was in fact pronounced double or long, rather as in Modern Italian or Modern Swedish. The kind of pronunciation to aim at is heard in Modern English words like 'mis-spell', 'book-case', and 'lamp-post' (as contrasted with 'dispel', 'bookish', and 'lampoon', which have single [s], [k], and [p]).

Old English script normally uses sixteen consonant-symbols, which in modern editions are usually reproduced as *b, c, d, f, g, h, l, m, n, p, r, s, t,* þ, ð, and *w.* For *w* the scribes in fact used the runic symbol 'wynn', and for *g* they used ȝ, and some modern editions retain these. A few other symbols are sometimes found, for example *x,* which stands for *ks* or *hs.* Many of the symbols present no difficulty: the letters *b, d, l, m, p, t,* and *w* each represent a single phoneme which can be pronounced as in Modern English. The other symbols call for comment.

Old English had no symbol *v*: the symbol *f* was used to represent both [f] and [v]. The reason is that, in Old English, [f] and [v] were members of the same phoneme. When this phoneme occurred within a word (that is, not initially or finally) before a voiced sound, and was not doubled, it was pronounced [v]; in all other positions it was pronounced [f]. So [f] was used in *fæder* 'father', *fīf* 'five', *'hæft* 'handle', and *pyffan* 'to puff', while [v] was used in *giefan* 'to give', *seofon* 'seven', *hræfn* 'raven', and *lifde* 'he lived'. The pronunciation often corresponds to modern usage, but not always, since OE *fīf* was [fi:f], whereas our *five* is [faɪv]; and, unlike our word *puff,* OE *pyffan* was pronounced with a double [-ff-].

There were two other such pairs in Old English. There was a symbol *s,* but not normally a symbol *z,* and for a similar reason: [s] and [z] were members of a single phoneme, and the rules for their distribution were exactly the same as for [f] and [v]. So [s] occurred in *sǣ* 'sea', *hūs* 'house', *stānas* 'stones', *west* 'west', and *cyssan* 'to kiss', while [z] occurred in *nosu* 'nose' and *bōsm* 'bosom'.

The third pair that behaved in this way were the voiceless [θ] (as in *thin*) and the voiced [ð] (as in *this*). To represent this phoneme, the scribes used two symbols: the runic symbol þ, called 'thorn', and the symbol ð, called 'eth'. They did not, however, use one of these symbols for the voiceless sound and the other for the voiced, but used them both indiscriminately; this is only to be expected, since native speakers of a language do not usually notice differences between allophones of a single phoneme. For simplicity, I shall use only thorn in my transcriptions from Old

English. The distribution of the allophones was exactly the same as in the other two pairs: thus the voiceless [θ] was used in *þegn* 'thane, attendant', *treowþ* 'good faith', *þes* 'this', and *moþþe* 'moth', while the voiced [ð] was used in *baþian* 'to bathe' and *fæþm* 'embrace, fathom'.

In all three cases, Old English has a single phoneme consisting of a pair of voiced and voiceless allophones, where Modern English has two separate phonemes. The Old English arrangement was not inherited from Proto-Germanic, but arose in prehistoric Old English by processes of assimilation.

The letter *k* was not normally used, [k] being represented by *c*. However, when in prehistoric Old English this [k] preceded a front vowel, it developed into a palatal stop instead of a velar one, that is, it was articulated farther forward in the mouth, somewhere between [k] and [t]. In the course of the Old English period, the difference between the velar and the palatal variants became greater, and the palatal stop has developed into Modern English [tʃ] (as in *church*). Indeed, it had probably reached this stage by the end of the Old English period, so it is convenient to use the [tʃ] pronunciation when reading Old English. The Old English symbol *c*, then, can represent either [k] or [tʃ]. It is not always possible by looking at an Old English word to know which pronunciation to use, because the vowel following the *c* may well have changed since prehistoric times: thus *cēlan* 'to cool' and *cynn* 'kin' both have the velar stop [k], even though they have front vowels, because they derive from prehistoric OE forms *kōljan* and *kunni*. Often, the modern pronunciation can be a guide: thus the velar [k] was used in *cyssan* 'to kiss', *cǣg* 'key', *þancian* 'to thank', and *cæppe* 'cap, hood', while the palatal [tʃ] was used in *cinn* 'chin', *cēosan* 'to choose', and *cīdan* 'to quarrel, chide'. Originally, it is clear, the two sounds were merely variants of a single phoneme: [k] was the allophone used before back vowels and [tʃ] the allophone used before front vowels; but in the course of the Old English period they developed into two separate phonemes. The kind of process by which this happened can be illustrated by two words already given as examples: *cinn* (pronounced [tʃɪnn]) and *cynn* (pronounced [kynn]) (notice that even in word-final position the double-consonant is pronounced [-nn]). Originally, the contrast between the two words was carried by the vowels [ɪ] and [y], and the difference between the two initial consonants had no significance. But in late Old English, in many parts of the country, the [y] of *cynn* lost its lip-rounding and became [ɪ], so that the word was then *cinn*, pronounced [kɪnn]. At that stage, therefore, there was a pair of words, pronounced [kɪnn] and [tʃɪnn], which were distinguished from one another solely by the difference between [k] and [tʃ]; and this means that /k/ and /tʃ/ were now separate phonemes.

In most positions, OE [k] also became palatalized when it followed [s], and the combination represented by the OE spelling *sc* normally develops into Modern English [ʃ]. The [ʃ] pronunciation had been reached by the end of the OE period, so it is convenient to use it when reading OE texts. Examples are *scip* 'ship', *scrūd* 'dress, shroud', *fisc* 'fish', and *blyscan* 'to blush'. In some positions, however, [sk] remained unchanged, as in *ascian* 'to ask' and *tusc* 'tooth'.

OE *c* never represents a pronunciation [s], as it does in Modern English *centre*, *city*, and *lace*. This spelling-convention was introduced from French after the Norman Conquest, and is unknown in Old English.

The letter *g* was used in Old English to represent two different phonemes. On the one hand there was a /j/ phoneme, similar to the semi-vowel in Modern English *yes*, as in the words *gēar* 'year', *fæger* 'fair', *cǣg* 'key', and *geoc* 'yoke'. On the other hand there was a /g/ phoneme, similar to the consonant of Modern English *go*, as in the words *gōd* 'good' *gēs* 'geese', and *dogga* 'dog'. When, however, this phoneme occurred undoubled between vowels, a different allophone was used: instead of being a voiced velar stop, it was the voiced velar fricative [ɣ], made by narrowing the passage between the back of the tongue and the soft palate; this pronunciation would have been used, for example, in the words *fugol* 'bird' and *lagu* 'law'. In Middle English this velar fricative developed into the semi-vowel [w], and the words were written *fowel* and *lawe*; in Modern English they have become *fowl* and *law*. Often, the OE scribes did not distinguish in spelling between /g/ and /j/, but when /j/ occurred before a back vowel they tended to spell it *ge*, as in the word *geoc* already quoted; here the *e* probably does not indicate a diphthong, but is simply inserted to show the quality of the preceding consonant. Alternatively, the spelling *i* could be used for /j/ in such positions, and in fact the word is also found with the spelling *ioc*.

When the /g/ phoneme was doubled, it was usually spelt *gg*, as in *frogga* 'frog' and *dogga* 'dog', but sometimes the spelling *cg* was used instead, and we find *frocga*, *docga*. The spelling *cg*, however, was also used to represent a /dʒ/ phoneme (resembling that of Modern English *judge*), as in *ecg* 'edge', *brycg* 'bridge', and *secgan* 'to say'.

The spelling *n* represented an /n/ phoneme, as today, but when it occurred before [k] or [g] it was pronounced [ŋ] (like the *ng* of our *sing*). Examples are *þancian* 'to thank' and *finger* 'finger', pronounced ['θaŋkɪan] and 'fɪŋgər]. In Old English the spelling *ng* represents the pronunciation [ŋg], never just [ŋ]: so OE *hring* 'a ring' was pronounced [hrɪŋg], whereas the Modern English equivalent is [rɪŋ]. This means that, in Old English, [ŋ] was not an independent phoneme, as today, but was simply an allophone of the /n/ phoneme, the variant of /n/ which occurred before [k] and [g]. Indeed, in the standard language it did not become an independent phoneme until about the year 1600.

The letter *h* often represented a more strongly articulated consonant than it does today. At the beginning of a syllable it was probably the glottal fricative [h], much as today; but in other positions it was either [x] (like the *ch* of German *ach*) or [ç] (like the *ch* of German *ich*), according to the preceding vowel. So OE *hætt* 'hat' was [hætt], but *niht* 'night' was [nɪçt], and *dohtor* 'daughter' was ['dɔxtɔr]. The three sounds were allophones of a single phoneme, which we can call /h/.

The letter *r* also represented a more powerfully articulated consonant than it does today: OE /r/ was probably trilled, that is, produced by a rapid succession of taps by the tip of the tongue on the teeth-ridge, whereas the corresponding consonant in Modern English is usually an approximant. Moreover, OE /r/ was pronounced in positions where it does not occur today (at least in most British speech), namely before consonants and before a pause. So you have to pronounce the /r/ in OE words like *bearn* 'child' and *wæter* 'water'.

Indeed, in general, when you read Old English texts, you have to remember that every symbol must be pronounced: the *h* in *niht* 'night', the *c* in *cnēo* 'knee', the *e* at the end of *cwene* 'woman', both the *n* and the *g* in *singan* 'to sing', both *s*-sounds in *cyssan* 'to kiss', and so on. Also, you have to try to avoid being misled by relatively recent sound-changes in English, which are liable to affect our interpretation of spellings. For example, in Old English the quality of a vowel is not affected by a preceding /w/, or by a following /l/ or /r/, as it often is in Modern English (as in *watch, ball, burn*). Again, the first vowel in OE words like *cwene* 'woman' and *hopa* 'hope' must be pronounced short. And unstressed vowels must be given their full quality, and not all reduced to [ə], so that for example *bera* 'a bear' must be distinguished in pronunciation from *bere* 'barley'. In the matter of stress, be guided in general by Modern English.

It will be seen that some OE spelling-symbols are ambiguous, since they can stand for more than one phoneme: this is true of *c*, of *g*, and of *cg*. Most of the symbols, however, are unambiguous, and in the past it has been common practice for historical philologists to use letter-symbols rather than phonetic symbols when discussing the phonology of Old and Middle English. I shall follow this practice.

Sound changes in Old English

Old English shows certain phonological developments of its own compared with the other Germanic languages. The Proto-Germanic diphthongs were changed in Old English. For example, PG *ai* became OE *ā*, so that Old English has *stān* and *hām* where Gothic has *stains* 'stone' and *haims* 'village'. And PG *au* became OE *ēa*, so that Old English has *drēam* where Old Norse has *draumr* 'dream', and *bēam* where German has *Baum* 'tree, pole', and *ēare* where Gothic has *ausō* 'ear'.

In prehistoric Old English a number of combinative sound-changes took place. One with far-reaching effects was **front mutation** or **i-umlaut**. This was a series of changes to vowels which took place when there was an *i*, *ī*, or *j* in the following syllable. Subsequently, the *i*, *ī*, or *j* disappeared, or changed to *e*, but its original presence can be established by examining the cognate words in other languages. Front mutation, for example, accounts for the difference in vowel between the related words *dole* and *deal*. In Old English they are *dāl* ' portion' and *dǣlan* 'to divide, distribute', in which the *ǣ* is due to front mutation; this is clear if we look at the Gothic words, which are *dails* and *dailjan*.

OE *dǣlan* is a weak verb, and it is normal for the stem-vowels of OE weak verbs to show front mutation. The weak verbs were formed in two main ways: there are denominative verbs (formed from nouns or adjectives), and causative verbs (formed from strong verbs). OE *dǣlan* is an example of a denominative verb, formed from the noun *dāl*. Causative verbs were formed on the past-singular stem of strong verbs. The strong verb *rīsan* meant 'to rise', and the corresponding causative verb is *rǣran* 'to cause to rise, rear'. The Proto-Germanic past-tense singular was **rais-* (OE *rās* 'rose'), and from this was formed the causative verb **raisján*. The accent was on the ending, so by Verner's Law it became **raizján*. In West Germanic, PG /z/ became /r/, so the prehistoric OE form was **rārjan*, which by front mutation became **rǣran*. Front mutation is normal in all the forms of weak verbs. Their infinitive was formed with the suffix **-jan*, and their various other inflections also contained *i* or *j*. For example, in prehistoric Old English, the third-person singular ending of the present tense was **-iþ*, so that 'he divides' was **dāliþ*. The *i* caused front mutation of the *ā*, and then itself changed to *e*. This *e* was lost in some varieties of Old English, so that the recorded forms of the word are *dǣleþ* or *dǣlþ*.

The change from *ā* to *ǣ* was a movement to a closer and more frontal vowel, and this is the general direction of the changes caused by front mutation: it was obviously a kind of assimilation, the affected vowels being moved to a place of articulation nearer to that of the following vowel or *j*. Thus *ū* became fronted to *ȳ*, a change which accounts for the different vowels of *mouse* and *mice*, which have developed regularly from OE *mūs*, *mȳs*; the original plural form was **mūsiz*, but the *i* caused the *ū* to change to *ȳ*; then the ending **-iz* was lost, giving the OE plural *mȳs*.

Similarly, front mutation changed short *u* to *y*; this change is reflected in the different vowels of *full* and *fill*, which in Old English are *full* and *fyllan* (from earlier **fulljan*). In some positions, an unmutated *u* developed in prehistoric Old English into *o*; sometimes, therefore, we get a contrast between unmutated *o* and mutated *y*, as in the words *gold* 'gold' and *gyldan* 'to gild'. Other pairs of words illustrating the front mutation of *u* to *y* are OE *fox* 'fox' and *fyxen* 'vixen', *cnotta* 'a knot' and *cnyttan* 'to tie, knit', *lust* 'pleasure, desire' and *lystan* 'to please'.

Front mutation changed *ō* to *ē*, and this accounts for the different vowel of *food* (OE *fōd*) and *to feed* (OE *fēdan*). Other such pairs in Modern English are *doom* and *deem*, *goose* and *geese*, *tooth* and *teeth*, *blood* and *bleed*, *book* and *beech*. Even where the *ō* has been shortened since OE times, we still often have the spelling with *oo*, which shows that the vowel was once long. Finally, front mutation changed short *a*, *æ*, and *o*, which all became *e*; modern pairs illustrating these changes include *man* and *men*, *wander* and *wend*, *Canterbury* and *Kent*, *long* and *length*, *tale* and *tell*, *straight* and *stretch*.

Even from these few examples, you will see that front mutation made considerable changes in the pronunciation of English. But do not confuse pairs like *foot* and *feet*, where the vowel difference is caused by front mutation in prehistoric Old English, with pairs like *sing* and *sang*, where the difference goes right back to the system of vowel-gradation in Proto-Indo-European.

Other combinative changes in prehistoric Old English caused the diphthongization of pure vowels, often with different results in different dialects. One change, called 'breaking' or 'fracture', affected vowels before /l/ plus consonant, /r/ plus consonant, and /h/. So West Saxon and Kentish have the forms *ceald* 'cold', *earm* 'arm', and *eahta* 'eight', compared with Gothic *kalds*, *arms*, and *ahtau*. The Anglian dialects, however, have unbroken vowels in many positions, as in *cald* 'cold' and *æhta* 'eight'. Another prehistoric change was the diphthongization of some front vowels after initial [j] and palatalized [k], as in West Saxon *geaf* 'he gave', *giefan* 'to give', *gēar* 'year', and *gīe* 'ye, you'. The change also took place in Northumbrian in some positions, but not in Kentish or Mercian: the Mercian forms of those four words are *gæf*, *gefan*, *gēr*, and *gē*. These two types of diphthongization probably took place earlier than front mutation. At a later date than front mutation there was a third type of diphthongization, called 'velar umlaut', which was caused by an unstressed back vowel in the following syllable, when only a single consonant intervened; this process accounts for the diphthongs in such forms as *heofon* 'heaven'. It occurred extensively in Kentish and Anglian, but in West Saxon is found only before a limited number of consonants. The exact dates of these various sound-changes are unknown, but they must have taken place sometime between the middle of the fifth century and the middle of the eighth century.

Old English morphology

In grammar, Old English carried out some simplifications of the Proto-Germanic system. OE nouns have only four cases: nominative, accusative, genitive, and dative. Moreover, the number of commonly used declensions is reduced, the vast majority of nouns tending to be attracted into three or four large declensions. At the same time, there are fewer distinctive case-endings than in Proto-Germanic, because of the weakening and loss of sounds in unstressed syllables in prehistoric Old English, and the operation of analogy. A few distinctive endings remained: all nouns have the ending *-um* for the dative plural, and most have *-a* for the genitive plural, and many masculine nouns have a genitive singular in *-es* and a nominative and accusative plural in *-as*. But in no nouns is a distinction made between nominative plural and accusative plural, and in many nouns other distinctions are obliterated too. For example, the feminine noun *giefu* 'a gift' has the one form *giefe* for its accusative, genitive, and dative singular, and the masculine noun *guma* 'a man' has the one form *guman* for its accusative, genitive, and dative singular and its nominative and accusative plural. Old English in fact relied a good deal for its case-distinctions on the adjectives, which had preserved more distinctive endings than the nouns, and on the definite article *sē*, which still had a large number of forms for different cases and genders. Old English did still, however, make great use of its inflectional system, and to a great extent it still preserved grammatical gender.

In its verbal system, Old English inherited from Proto-Germanic a two-tense system (traditionally called 'present' and 'past'), with different forms for indicative and subjunctive. Proto-Germanic also had inflections for the passive, but these did not survive in Old English. As examples of verb-forms, let us look at the strong verb *helpan* 'to help'. In the present tense, Old English retained the person-distinctions in the indicative singular, as in *ic helpe* 'I help', *þū hilpst* 'you (sg) help', and *hē/hēo/hit hilpþ* 'he/she/it helps'. But in the plural it made no person-distinctions: *wē/gē/hīe helpaþ* 'we/ you/they help'. In the present subjunctive there was one form for the singular, *helpe*, and one for the plural, *helpen*. There were also imperative forms, that is, ones for giving commands: singular *help*, plural *helpaþ*. In the past tense there was a distinctive form for the second-person singular, *þū hulpe* 'you (sg) helped', as against first- and third-person *ic/hēo healp* 'I/she helped'; in the plural there was no distinction of persons, but the one form *hulpon* 'we/you/they helped'. In the past-tense subjunctive there was one form for the singular (*hulpe*) and one for the plural (*hulpen*). There was also a past participle, *holpen*, and a present participle, *helpende*. It will be seen that the verbal system, although simplified compared with Proto-Germanic, still had many more variant forms than Modern English.

In Old English, as in other Germanic languages, we also see the beginnings of a new tense-system using auxiliaries, and especially the development of forms for the perfect and for the passive, like Modern English 'I have helped' and 'I am helped'. The perfect tenses existed in Old English, but were not used as frequently or as consistently as they were later. The perfect tenses of transitive verbs (that is, those that take a Direct Object) were formed by the use of the verb *habban* 'to have' and the past participle of the verb. Originally, sentences like 'He had broken a leg' meant something like 'He possessed a broken leg'; and in fact in the Old English equivalent of this sentence the word *broken* was sometimes given an inflection to make it agree with *leg*. Thus in the Anglo-Saxon Chronicle (Parker MS) in the entry for the year 755 we read *oþ þæt hīe hine ofslægenne hæfdon*, literally 'until they him slain had', where the *-ne* of *ofslægenne* is the inflection for the accusative singular masculine, making it agree with *hine* 'him'. But even in the Old English period this habit of inflecting the past participle was dying out, and in a later manuscript of the Chronicle (Laud

MS) the same entry reads *oþ þet hig hine ofslægen hæfdon*. The perfect tenses of intransitive verbs (those with no Direct Object) were formed with the verbs 'to be' (*bēon, wesan*) or 'to become' (*weorþan*). So a translator of King Alfred's time writes *þā wæs þæs folces fela on ān fæsten opflogen* 'then had (literally 'was') much of that multitude fled into a fortress', in which *wæs opflogen* translates the Latin pluperfect *confūgerant*.

The passive too was formed with the verbs 'to be' or 'to become' and the past participle. We can take an example of the passive from the same text of King Alfred's time: *þær wearþ Alexander þurhscoten mid ānre flān* 'there was (literally 'became') Alexander pierced by an arrow'. Only transitive verbs can produce passives of this type, since it is the Direct Object of the active sentence that becomes the Subject of the passive one: 'An arrow there pierced Alexander' becomes 'There was Alexander pierced by an arrow'. In Old English, the passive could only be formed with verbs which took an Object in the accusative case. Many OE verbs took an Object in the dative case, and some an Object in the genitive. The verb *helpan*, for example, usually had a dative Object, occasionally a genitive one: *þū monegum helpst* 'you help many (people)' (where *monegum* is dative plural); *þonne þū hulpe mīn* 'when you helped me' (where *mīn* is the genitive of the pronoun). Such sentences could not be made passive in Old English; it was only after the dative case of nouns and pronouns had disappeared in Middle English that it became possible to say such things as 'Many people are helped by you'.

Old English syntax

Because of its inflectional system, Old English had greater freedom of word-order than Modern English. In Old English we can say *sē cyning hæfde micel geþeaht* 'the king held a great council'; and as a stylistic variant of this we can say *micel geþeaht hæfde sē cyning*: this is quite unambiguous, because the nominative article *sē* marks the subject of the sentence, but the word-order throws the emphasis on 'a great council'. But in Modern English we cannot use this second word-order, because 'A great council held the king' means something quite different. It is not that Old English lacked rules and preferences about word-order – we have already seen that it favoured three particular types of word-order for the clause: S-V-O, V-S-O, and S-O-V. These can be illustrated from a sentence of King Alfred's which begins as follows:

> þā ic þā þis eall gemunde, þā gemunde ic ēac hū ic geseah, ǣr þǣm þe hit eall forhergod wǣre and forbærned, hū þā circicean giond eall Angelcynn stōdon māþma and bōca gefylda . . .

This contains five clauses: (1) 'When I then this all remembered', (2) 'then remembered I also' (3) 'how I saw,' (4) 'before it all ravaged was and burnt up,' (5) 'how the churches throughout all England stood with treasures and books filled . . .'. Clause (1) is a subordinate clause, and has the S-O-V order often (but not invariably) found in such clauses. Clause (2) has V-S-O order (the Direct Object being the remainder of the whole sentence); this order is common when the clause begins with an adverbial expression, especially *þā* 'then' and *þǣr* 'there'. Clause (3) has the common S-V-O order (the Direct Object being Clause 5). Clause (4) is a subordinate clause in the passive; the verb is in the subjunctive, and is placed *after* the past participle 'ravaged'. Clause (5) has the order S-V, but the verb is intransitive, so there is no Direct Object; the nouns dependent on the past participle 'filled' (which are in the genitive plural) are placed before it.

The order V-S-O is normal in questions: *Hwȳ didest þū þæt?* 'Why did you that?', *Hæfst þū ǣnigne gefēran?* 'Have you any companion?'. Negation is achieved by use of the particle *ne*: *Fram ic ne wille* 'Away I do not intend (to go)'. If the *ne* was the first word in the sentence, the word-order V-S-O was likely: *ne mihte hē gehealdan heardne mēce* 'he could not hold the hard sword'. The *ne* occurred so frequently before certain words that it often coalesced with them, producing forms like *nis* 'is not' and *nolde* 'would not'. Multiple negation was common, that is, *ne* might occur several times in the same sentence: such repetitions, far from cancelling one another out, in fact made the negation more emphatic. Neither in questions nor in negative sentences does Old English make use of auxiliary *do*: where we say 'Why do you go?' and 'I do not go', Old English has *Hwȳ gāþ gē?* and *ic ne gā*.

The structure of the Noun Phrase is quite similar to that of Modern English, the normal pattern being Determiner-Adjective-Noun. Exceptions to this pattern are provided by the forms *eall* 'all', *bēgen* 'both', and adjectives ending in *-weard*. These precede the determiner, as in *eal þes middangeard* 'this entire earth', *bēgen þā gebroþru* 'both the brothers', and *on sūþeweardum þǣm lande* 'in the southern part of the land' (literally 'on southward the land'). It is however perfectly possible for adjectives to follow the noun, or for one to precede it and another to follow it: *Denum eallum* 'to all the Danes', *micle meras fersce* 'big fresh-water meres'. It is even possible for a determiner to follow the noun, especially if it is emphatic: *Ic eom micle yldra þonne ymbhwyrft þes* 'I am much older than this world'. Titles of rank usually follow the name they qualify: *Ælfred cyning* 'King Alfred'.

One big difference from Modern English is in the system of demonstratives. Today we have a threefold system: *the, this, that*. But in Old English there are only two demonstratives, *sē* 'the, that' and *þes* 'this'. On the other hand, the ternary modern system comprises only five different forms (*the, this, these, that, those*), whereas each of the OE demonstratives is declined through three genders, five cases (the fifth being the instrumental), and two numbers. In the plural, indeed, there is no distinction of genders, and in the singular there is some overlapping of forms, but even so there are about ten different forms of *sē*, and the same number of *þes*. One particular point to note is that the word *þæt* is simply the nominative and accusative singular neuter form of *sē*, not a contrasting demonstrative.

The vocabulary of Old English

To enlarge its vocabulary, Old English depended mainly on its own resources, not on borrowings from other languages. From Proto-Indo-European, the Germanic languages had inherited many ways of forming new words, especially by the use of prefixes and suffixes. Thus, in Old English, adjectives could be formed from nouns by means of such suffixes as *-ig*, *-lēas*, and *-ful*, giving words like *blōdig* 'bloody', *frēondlēas* 'friendless', and *þancful* 'thankful'. Conversely, nouns could be formed from adjectives: for example, there was a Proto-Germanic suffix *-iþō* (prehistoric OE *-iþa*) which could be added to adjectives to form abstract nouns: on the stem of the adjective *fūl* 'foul, dirty' was formed the prehistoric OE noun *fūliþa*; the *i* caused front-mutation and was later lost, leading to the recorded OE form *fȳlþ* 'impurity, filth'. Similar formations have led to such Modern English pairs as *merry* and *mirth*, *slow* and *sloth*, *strong* and *strength*, *true* and *truth*. Adverbs were commonly formed from adjectives by means of suffixes such as *-e* and *-līce*: so from the adjective *fæst* 'firm' was formed *fæste* 'firmly', and from *blind* was formed *blindlīce* 'blindly'.

There were large numbers of prefixes, many of which could be added to verbs. See King Alfred's sentence on p. 119 above: *forhergod* and *forbærned* are the past participles of the verbs *forhergian* and *forbærnan*, formed by the addition of the prefix *for-* to the verbs *hergian* 'to harry, ravage' and *bærnan* 'to burn'; the prefix *for-* has an intensive force, and in particular often signifies destruction, so that *forhergian* means 'destroy by harrying' and *forbærnan* 'destroy by burning'. Another common verbal prefix is *ge-*, which often has a perfective force, signifying the achievement or the completion of the action. So *sceran* means 'to cut', and *gesceran* 'to cut right through'; *rīdan* means 'to ride', and *gerīdan* 'to ride up to, conquer, occupy'. There is a well-known example of this perfective use of *ge-* in King Alfred's account of a voyage by the Norwegian Ōhthere:

þā siglde he þonan sūþryhte be lande swā swā he mehte on fīf dagum gesiglan.

The interesting thing here is the difference between *siglde* 'sailed' and *gesiglan* 'to get somewhere by sailing'. The sentence means 'Then sailed he from there southwards along the land as (far) as he was able to sail in five days'.

As well as using affixation, Old English formed new words by compounding. The difference is that an affix is a bound morpheme, whereas a compound word is formed by the joining of two or more free morphemes, So, for example, literature, arithmetic, grammar, and astronomy were called *bōccræft*, *rīmcræft*, *stæfcræft*, and *tungolcræft*, that is, book-skill, number-skill, letter-skill, and star-skill. Homelier compounds have survived to our own times, like *ēarwicga* 'earwig', *hāmstede* 'homestead', *sunnebēam* 'sunbeam', and *wīfmann* 'woman'.

Old English did however borrow a small number of words from other languages, especially for the concepts and institutions of Christianity. OE *cirice* or *cyrce* 'church' is derived from the Greek *kuriakón*, meaning '(house) of the Lord', and goes back to heathen days; similar forms are found in all the Germanic languages, whereas the Romance languages have words derived from the Latin *ecclesia*, like French *église*. Most of the words connected with Christianity, however, date from after the Conversion, and are from Latin (though Latin itself had borrowed many of them from Greek). They include OE *apostol* 'apostle', *biscop* 'bishop' (Latin *episcopus*), *munuc* 'monk' (Latin *monachus*), *mynster* 'monastery, church' (Latin *monastērium*), as well as words for abbot, disciple, nun, pilgrim, pope, and school.

But even in this field Old English made considerable use of its native language material. Sometimes existing words were simply transferred to Christian use, as with *Easter*, *hell*, and *holy*. Sometimes new words were coined from native elements: thus Latin *evangelium* was rendered as *gōdspell* 'good message', which has become our *gospel*, and *trinitas* 'trinity' was rendered as *þrīnes* 'threeness'.

Specimens of Old English

Let us end this chapter with brief examples of OE prose and verse. In these, punctuation has been modernized. First a few lines from the *Colloquy* of Ælfric, abbot of Eynsham, who was writing from about 990 onwards. Ælfric was the classic of OE prose-writers, and produced many homilies and lives of the saints. The Colloquy is a slighter work, a dialogue in Latin for use in the teaching of Latin. To this Latin work was added a gloss in Old English, probably not by Ælfric himself. Since it is an interlinear gloss, it follows the word-order of the Latin original, and so cannot be used as evidence for OE word-order. It begins with the pupils addressing the teacher:

Pupils: We cildra biddaþ þē, ēalā lārēow, þæt þū tǣce ūs sprecan, forþām ungelǣrede wē syndon, and gewæmmodlīce wē sprecaþ. (We children beg thee, oh teacher, that thou teach us to speak [Latin], because ignorant we are and corruptly we speak.)

Teacher: Hwæt wille gē sprecan? (What wish ye to say?)

Pupils: Hwæt rēce wē hwæt wē sprecan, būton hit riht sprǣc sȳ and behēfe, næs īdel oþþe fracod? (What care we what we say, provided that it correct speech be and seemly, not foolish or impious?)

The forms *tǣce* and *sȳ* are subjunctive: the indicative forms would be *tǣc(e)st* and *is* or *biþ*. The word *wille* is from the verb *willan* 'to wish, be willing, intend'; this verb is not used, like present-day *will*, merely to signal futurity or prediction. In referring to the future, Old English simply uses the so-called present tense: later in the Colloquy a character says *gē etaþ wyrta ēowre grēne* 'you will eat your vegetables uncooked', where *etaþ* translates the Latin future-tense form *manducābitis*. The pupils address their teacher as *þū* (singular), but he addresses them as *gē* (plural), whereas today we use *you* in both cases. In Old English, *thou* and *thee* were always singular, and *ye* and *you* always plural, but in Middle English times the custom arose of using *ye/you* as a polite or deferential way of addressing a single person, and this usage spread; *thou* and *thee* gradually dropped out of use in everyday speech, and finally disappeared (except in some regional dialects) round about 1700. The difference between *ye* and *you* was the same as that between *he* and *him*: one was nominative and the other accusative. This distinction was maintained until the sixteenth century: it is regularly observed in the King James Bible of 1611, though in everyday speech at that date *you* was the normal form for both nominative and accusative, and *ye* was dying out.

Originally, *you* was not the accusative form but the dative: OE *ēow* 'to you'. The original accusative form was *ēowic*, but during the OE period this was supplanted by *ēow*. The same thing has in fact happened with all the personal pronouns (except *it*): our words *him, me, us, her*, and *thee* originally meant 'to him', 'to me', and so on. The OE accusative forms were *hine, mec, ūsic, hīe*, and *þec*, but these fell out of use during the Old and Middle English periods, and were replaced by the dative forms.

A little later in the Colloquy, the teacher is talking to a ploughman, who has been describing the harshness of his life and the amount of work he has to do:

Teacher: Hæfst þū ǣnigne gefēran? (Hast thou any companion?)

Pupil: Ic hæbbe sumne cnapan þȳwende oxan mid gādisene, þe ēac swilce nū hās ys for cylde and hrēame. (I have a certain boy driving oxen with goad-iron, who likewise now hoarse is on account of cold and shouting.)

Teacher: Hwæt māre dēst þū on dæg? (What more dost thou during the day?)

Pupil: Gewyslice þænne māre ic dō. Ic sceal fyllan binnan oxan mid hig, and wæterian hig, and scearn heora beran ūt. (Certainly then more I do. I have to fill mangers of oxen with hay, and water them, and dung of them carry out [that is, carry out their dung].)

Teacher: Hig! hig! micel gedeorf ys hyt. (Oh! oh! Great labour is it.)

Pupil: Geleof, micel gedeorf hit ys, forþām ic neom frēoh. (Sir, great labour it is, because I not-am free.)

The phrase *ǣnigne gefēran* at the beginning of that extract illustrates the importance of the adjective in the OE inflectional system. The word *gefēran* could equally well mean 'companion' or 'companions', but the ending *-ne* added to *ǣnig* can only be accusative singular masculine, and shows that the correct translation is 'companion'; and similarly with *sumne cnapan* 'a certain boy'. Just as, in the first extract, *wille* did not correspond exactly to modern *will*, so in this one the word *sceal* does not correspond in meaning to modern *shall*, for *ic sceal* means 'I must, I am obliged to', and earlier meant 'I owe, I am in debt'. In the pupil's first speech occurs the word *þe*, which I have glossed as 'who'. The words *who* and *which* did exist in Old English (*hwā*, *hwilc*), but were indefinite or interrogative pronouns, not relatives. For the relative function, Old English used the indeclinable particle *þe*, or the declinable pronoun *sē* (identical in form with the definite article), or the two together. In Middle English, *which* and *that* were used as relatives, but *who* was not used in this way until Early Modern English, and even then not as frequently as today: in the 1611 Bible, the Lord's Prayer begins 'Our Father, *which* art in heaven'.

Finally, a few lines of OE poetry. Like much early Germanic poetry, this did not use rhyme, but alliteration. Each line of verse

was divided into two halves, and in each half there had to be two
fully stressed syllables, some of which alliterated with one another;
in other words, they began with the same letter, which usually
(but not always) represented the same phoneme; all vowels,
however, were allowed to alliterate together. The first stress of the
second half-line had to alliterate with one of the stresses of the first
half-line, normally the first one; sometimes the second stress of the
first half-line also alliterated with these two. Less frequently, the
second stress of the second half-line also alliterated. In the passage
below, line 1 alliterates on *b*, line 2 has vowel-alliteration (*eald,
æsc*), line 3 alliterates on *b*, line 4 on *h*, and so on. There were also
quite complicated rules about the permissible patterns of syllable-
length and stress in a half-line, though these became laxer in the
course of the OE period, as did the rules about alliteration. I have
chosen a famous passage from a late OE poem which celebrates an
actual historical event. In 991 the men of Essex, led by Byrhtnoth
their 'ealdormann' (the king's deputy and chief executive for the
county), fought a battle at Maldon against an invading force of
Norwegian vikings, who had sailed up the Blackwater. After a
bitter struggle, the English were defeated and Byrhtnoth killed,
and the end of the poem, from which my extract comes, tells how
his 'companions', in traditional Germanic style, remained on the
battlefield to die with their lord.

>Byrhtwold maþelode,   bord hafenode,
>Sē wæs eald genēat   æsc ācwehte;
>hē ful baldlīce   beornas lærde:
>'Hige sceal þē heardra,   heorte þē cēnre,
>mōd sceal þē māre,   þē ūre mægen lytlaþ.
>Her līþ ūre ealdor   eall forhēawen,
>gōd on grēote.   Ā mæg gnornian
>sē þē nū fram þīs wīgplegan   wendan þenceþ.
>Ic eom frōd fēores: fram ic ne wille,
>ac ic mē be healfe   mīnum hlāforde
>be swā lēofan men,   licgan þence.'

This can be rendered as follows:

>Byrhtwold spoke, lifted his shield,
>he was an old retainer, shook his ash (spear),

he full boldly exhorted the warriors:
'Mind must be the firmer, heart the more valiant,
Courage must be the greater, as our strength diminishes.
Here lies our lord, quite hewn down,
The noble man in the dust. Ever will he have cause to mourn
Who now thinks to depart from this battle.
I am old of life; hence I will not,
But by the side of my lord,
By the man so dear, I intend to lie.'

There, nine hundred years after Tacitus, and nearly four hundred after the conversion of the English to Christianity, still speaks the authentic voice of the Germanic heroic age, when the greatest infamy was for the companion to return alive when his lord had been slain. Like much heroic poetry, the passage is highly formal, moving forward with parallel phrases and near-repetitions, and it has a marked diction of its own. It opens, for example, with a standard epic tag, 'so-and-so spoke'. The stock of conventional poetic diction was very large, because of the need for alliteration: there were numerous words for warrior (like *beorn* in the passage), for weapons (like *æsc*), and for horse, ship, prince, and so on. Some of these are descriptive compounds: in *Beowulf*, for example, the sea is called *swanrād* 'the swan-road'. Some are decorative periphrases: a king can be called 'giver of rings' or 'giver of treasure' (since he was expected to bestow liberal gifts on his followers in return for their military service). An example of a poetic compound is the word *wīgplega* in the passage; I have glossed this as 'battle', but literally it means 'war-play'.

6 Norsemen and Normans

During the later part of the Old English period, two different groups of non-English speakers invaded the country. Both groups were Scandinavian in origin, but whereas the first had retained its Scandinavian speech, the second had settled in northern France and become French-speaking. Both of their languages, Old Norse and Old French, had a considerable influence on English.

The Vikings in England

The harrying of Europe by the Scandinavian Vikings, which took place between about 750 and 1050, was the last phase of the expansion of the early Germanic peoples. Its basic cause was perhaps overpopulation in a region of poor natural resources, but there were other contributory causes. The custom of leaving the inheritance to the eldest son meant that there were always younger sons wanting to carve out inheritances for themselves. Political conflicts drove many noblemen into exile. And then, in the late eighth century, Charlemagne destroyed the power of the Frisians, who had hitherto been the greatest maritime power of North-West Europe, and thereby left open the sea-route southward for the Vikings. At about the same date, the ancient craft of boat-building in Scandinavia reached the stage at which it could produce the magnificent ocean-going sailing-ships which served the Vikings for trade, piracy, and colonization.

The Vikings were great traders, but it is for their more predatory activities that they are most remembered. Their attacks varied from piratical expeditions by single ships to the invasion of a country by enormous fleets and armies. The word *viking* (Old Norse *víkingr*) perhaps means 'creek-dweller', and hence 'pirate'; there are cognate forms in Old English and Old Frisian, and the OE word, *wīcing* 'a pirate', is recorded in the days before the Scandinavian raids. The word suggests one of the great assets of the Scandinavian raiders – their skill and daring as sailors and navigators, which had carried them to North America ('Vinland') long before Columbus, perhaps earlier than the year 1000.

The Vikings consisted of Swedes, Norwegians, and Danes. The Swedes mostly went eastwards, to the Baltic countries and Russia, while the Norwegians and Danes tended to go westwards and southwards. The Vikings who attacked England were referred to by the Anglo-Saxons as *Dene* 'Danes', but there were also Norwegians among them. The first attacks probably took place round about 800, and by 838 they had become serious. At first they were mere piratical raids in search of plunder; then large groups took to spending the winter in England, as happened in 850 and in 854; then large armies stayed for longer periods, like the one that landed in East Anglia in 865 and operated as a single unit for no less than nine years; and finally came conquest and settlement, which began in the last few decades of the ninth century. The Vikings came very near to conquering the whole of England, but King Alfred held the South and the West against them, the turning-point being his defeat of Guthrum at Chippenham in 878; the boundary between Alfred's territories and the Danelaw ran roughly along a line from London to Chester (see Figure 9). In the tenth century, the West Saxon kings reconquered the North and East, but in the meantime the Vikings established kingdoms in those areas, and there was massive Scandinavian settlement.

The Scandinavian influx has left its mark on English place-names. Common Scandinavian place-name elements are *by* 'village, homestead' as in *Grimsby* 'Grim's village'; *thorp* 'secondary settlement, outlying farmstead', as in *Grimsthorpe*; *toft* 'building-site, plot of land', as in *Langtoft* (where the first element means 'long'); and *thwaite* 'woodland clearing, meadow', as in *Micklethwaite* 'large clearing'. Some place-names are more distinctively Norwegian, some more Danish: the element *thorp*, for

Figure 9   The division of England between King Alfred and the Danes in the late ninth century. Alfred held England south and west of the hatched line

example, was rarely used by the Norwegians in England, and is a good sign of Danish settlement (though it also occurs occasionally in Anglo-Saxon place-names as a variant of *throp*). The main areas of Norwegian settlement were in the North-West – in Lancashire and Cumbria; elsewhere in the Danelaw there were Danes, the densest settlements being in Derbyshire, Yorkshire, Nottingham-shire, Lincolnshire, Leicestershire, and Norfolk.

Scandinavian influence on English went a good deal farther than place-names, however. The English were not exterminated by the Scandinavian settlers, but the latter were sufficiently numerous to influence English speech. Old English and Old Norse were still reasonably similar, and Englishmen and Danes could probably understand each other, and pick up each other's language, without too much difficulty. In the later OE period we must visualize various bilingual situations. There would be Englishmen speaking Old Norse, and Danes speaking Old English, and when they didn't know a word in the other language they would use a word from their own, perhaps giving it a pronunciation and inflections that they thought appropriate to the other language. Sometimes they would use a word in the other language but give it the meaning of the corresponding form in their own language. And no doubt there were children of mixed marriages who spoke an intermediate dialect. Thus great mixing took place between the two languages. In the end, Old Norse died out in England (it was already dying in the time of King Cnut, at whose court English was spoken), and English triumphed, but not before a good deal of Scandinavian had got mixed in with it. The final fusion of the English and Scandinavian peoples and cultures took place in the century following the Norman Conquest.

There are various ways of recognizing Scandinavian words in English, though in fact some words were practically identical in Old English and Old Norse, and would give the same result in Modern English. Some words, however, can be identified as of Scandinavian origin, because of their phonological form. Thus the word *awe* is certainly of Scandinavian origin: the Old English form is *ege*, pronounced ['ɛjɛ], the first vowel having been changed by front-mutation and the *g* palatalized to [j] by the following vowel, and it would lead to a modern form **ey* (just as OE *legen* has produced our word *lain*). But neither the front-mutation nor the palatalization occurred in Old Norse, where the word was *agi*, and this, if borrowed in Late Old English, would develop quite regularly into modern *awe*. Another pair of words with Old English [j] and Old Norse [g] was *ǣg* and *egg*; the OE word became ME *ey*, a form found in Chaucer; our word *egg* comes from the Scandinavian. Similarly, Old English sometimes has [tʃ] where Old Norse retains [k], so that *church* is English and *kirk* Scandinavian, *ditch* English and *dike* Scandinavian. Again, Germanic [sk] did not become palatalized in Old Norse as it did in Old English, so that a word of Scandinavian origin will have [sk] where one of English origin has [ʃ]: thus *shirt* is English and *skirt* Scandinavian (both words meaning originally 'a *short* garment'); and similarly with *shrub* and *scrub*.

Among the vowels, one difference is that PG *ai* becomes *ei* in Scandinavian but *ā* in Old English: thus Old Norse *nei* corresponds to OE *nā*, the former giving Modern English *nay*, the second *no*. Other examples include the interjection *hail!* (cognate with OE *hāl*, Modern English *whole*) and *swain* (cognate with OE *swān* 'herdsman'). PG *au* became *ēa* in Old English, but remained *au* in Old Norse, so that *lēas* corresponds to *lauss*; our *loose* comes from the Scandinavian form, but the OE form survives as the suffix *-less*, in words like *homeless* (OE *hāmlēas*). Such phonological tests are not foolproof, for in some cases a dialectal variant in Old English can produce the same result as Scandinavian influence, but on the whole they are the most reliable guide.

But even when phonological evidence is lacking or doubtful, we can sometimes be confident that a word comes from the Scandinavian. Often, for example, a word is not recorded in Old English, but is recorded in Old Norse. An example is the verb 'to take', which is from Old Norse *taka*; this is not found in Old English, which uses the verb *niman*. In Middle English we find both verbs, but *take* is found in areas where there was Scandinavian influence, and *nim* in areas free from such influence. The verb *to nim* survived into Early Modern English, in the sense 'to steal', and is responsible for the name of Shakespeare's Corporal Nym, who was adept at *nimming* other people's property; the past participle has survived as the word *numb*, which originally meant 'taken, seized' (OE *numen*). Other examples include *anger, to cast, to die*, and *ill*, from Old Norse *angr, kasta, deyja*, and *illr*; Old English used instead the words *wræþþ, weorpan, steorfan*, and *yfel*, which have become *wrath, warp, starve*, and *evil*.

Sometimes the Old Norse and Old English words would produce the same modern English form, but with different meanings. Old Norse *dvelja* meant 'dwell', but OE *dwellan* meant 'lead astray'. Our word *gate* is descended regularly from the OE plural form *gatu*, but in northern dialects there is another word *gate*, meaning 'way, road, street', from Old Norse *gata*. In London, places such as Aldgate and Newgate really were at gates in the city wall; but in cities such as Leeds and York, *-gate* is the Scandinavian form: Briggate and Kirkgate are 'Bridge Street' and 'Church Street'.

In other cases the form of the modern word may come from one language and the meaning from the other: thus the OE word for 'bread' was *hlāf*, which has become our *loaf*, while OE *brēad* usually meant 'fragment'; but ON *brauð* did mean 'bread', so the modern word has its form from Old English but its meaning from Old Norse. The word *dream* is more peculiar. Old English *drēam* means 'noise, sound, joy, mirth, revelry', and is commonly used in descriptions of the pleasures of the warriors relaxing in the hall over their ale or mead, and of the music accompanying those pleasures; it is never used in Old English texts to mean 'dream', for which the word is *swefn*. This, however, was the meaning of the Old Norse *draumr*, and it might seem that here again the modern word has the English form and the Scandinavian meaning. This is by no means certain, however, because the early examples of *dream* in its modern sense (recorded from the thirteenth century) appear not to be confined to areas subject to strong Scandinavian influence. Perhaps the true explanation is that there was an OE word *drēam* meaning 'dream', but that it occurred only in everyday speech, not in the literary language; it is noteworthy that the corresponding Old Saxon form, *drōm*, means both 'joy' and 'dream'.

Most of the Scandinavian loan-words first appear in writing in the Middle English period, but their form shows that they had been taken into English in the late OE period, for they have undergone the sound-changes that mark the transition from Old to Middle English. They do not appear earlier in writing because at that time there was no literary tradition in the Danelaw, and most surviving texts are in the West Saxon dialect, which was the one least influenced by Old Norse. A few loans, however, do occur in OE texts. In the early days of the Viking raids there was probably not much opportunity for conversation between Englishmen and Vikings; the only loans from this period are a few words for Viking ships and weapons, which have not survived into the modern language. Later, when the Vikings had begun to settle in England, a number of words were borrowed relating to law and administration, for the Danes had a highly developed legal sense; they include *thrall*, and the word *law* itself.

But what is most striking about the Scandinavian loan-words as a whole is that they are such *ordinary* words. The English and the Scandinavians had very similar cultures, and the fusion of the two peoples was a close one; many of the words taken over, in consequence, were homely everyday ones, words belonging to the central core of the vocabulary. Thus the word *sister* is Scandinavian (the Old English is *sweostor*), and the names of such close family relationships are part of the central core of vocabulary. So are the names of parts of the body, yet the words *leg* and *neck* are Scandinavian. Other common nouns include *bag*, *cake*, *dirt*, *fellow*, *fog*, *knife*, *skill*, *skin*, *sky*, and *window*. Everyday adjectives include *flat*, *loose*, *low*, *odd*, *ugly*, and *wrong*, and among everyday verbs are *call*, *drag*, *get*, *give*, *raise*, *smile*, *take*, and *want*. Moreover, some grammatical words are from Scandinavian, namely the conjunctions *though*, *till*, and *until*, and the pronouns *they*, *them*, and *their*, which in Old English were *hīe*, *him*, and *hiera*. The Scandinavian pronouns no doubt had an advantage because they were less likely to be confused with the words for *him* and *her*. They were first used in the northern dialects, and spread southwards during the Middle English period; *they* spread faster than the other two, and Chaucer and his contemporaries in South-East England in the fourteenth century used *they* for the nominative but English forms like *hem* and *hire* for 'them' and 'their'. The form *hem* meaning 'them' still survives as *'em* (initial /h/ being regularly lost in unstressed words). The borrowing of such central grammatical words as personal pronouns shows the strength of the Scandinavian influence.

When the Scandinavian words appear in English texts they are given English inflections. Occasionally, however, a Scandinavian inflection was mistakenly apprehended as part of the stem, and incorporated in the English word. Thus there was an Old Norse ending *-t* which was added to adjectives to mark the neuter gender, and also to form adverbs. So the adjective þverr 'adverse, contrary' had the neuter form þvert, and this has been taken over into English as *thwart*; the same ending has survived in *want* and *scant*. The Old Norse reflexive ending *-sk*, meaning 'oneself', has been preserved in *bask* 'to bathe oneself' and the archaic *busk* 'to prepare oneself'.

The total number of Scandinavian loans is in fact rather small, compared with the number of words later borrowed from French and Latin; on the other hand, many of them are words in very frequent use, and there is a Scandinavian enclave in the very central regions of the English vocabulary. In the areas of densest Viking settlement, a larger vocabulary of Scandinavian loan-words is preserved in regional dialects, so that there are still parts of England and Scotland where you can hear good Scandinavian words like *big* 'to build', *hoast* 'cough', *laik* 'to play', *lait* 'to search', *lathe* 'barn', and *lie* 'scythe'.

The Norman Conquest

The Norman Conquest of 1066 was not such a violent break in English history as people sometimes imagine. There was already strong French influence in England before the Conquest, at any rate at the higher levels of society: Edward the Confessor was half Norman, and his court had close relations with France. It is certainly true, however, that the Conquest had a profound influence on the English language. For some centuries, English ceased to be the language of the governing classes, and there was no such thing as standard literary English; and when English did once again become the language of the whole country it had changed a good deal under the influence of the conquerors.

The rulers of Normandy had originally been Scandinavian Vikings, who occupied parts of northern France and were eventually recognized by the French crown: in 912, Rollo became the first Duke of Normandy, and accepted the king of France as his overlord. By the middle of the eleventh century, however, the Normans had long lost their Scandinavian speech: they spoke French, and were essentially French in culture. People sometimes talk, therefore, as though the Norman Conquest were the coming of a higher civilization to the backward and barbaric Anglo-Saxons. This, however, is a misapprehension. Six hundred years had passed since the Anglo-Saxon invasion of Britain, and in that time the English had developed a sophisticated civilization. The Normans demonstrated their superiority in military techniques, for they had the new heavy cavalry that had been developed on the continent by the Franks, while the Anglo-Saxons still fought on foot behind a wall of round shields. The Normans also showed themselves superior at the construction of castles, and after the Conquest they built some fine churches and cathedrals. But it is difficult to see in what other ways they were culturally superior to the people they conquered.

The Anglo-Saxons had a fine literature, both in verse and in prose. They had traditions of scholarship which went back to the seventh century, and when Charlemagne, at the end of the eighth century, wanted to reform his educational system, he imported an Englishman to do it for him. This tradition had been badly disrupted by the Viking invasions, but there was a revival under West-Saxon leadership in the second half of the tenth century. The Anglo-Saxons were also fine artists and craftsmen: they produced beautiful carved crosses, and jeweller's work, and illuminated manuscripts to compare with any in the world. They were also famous for their needlework, and the celebrated Bayeux Tapestry was probably made in England.

These people did not need William of Normandy and his adventurers to bring them civilization. French became the language of the upper classes in England simply because it was the language of the conquerors, not because of any cultural superiority on their part. What happened was that the native aristocracy were largely destroyed, and their lands were distributed to William's Norman followers, who became the new ruling class. Many key ecclesiastical positions, such as bishoprics and abbacies, were also given to Normans in the years following the Conquest, so that the church and education were dominated by them. French, therefore, was the language of the aristocracy and the court, and it remained so for over two hundred years. So anybody whose native tongue was English, and who wanted to get on in the world, had to learn French. The following comment on the situation was made in the late thirteenth century in a long history of England written in verse, usually known as the Chronicle of Robert of Gloucester:

> þus com, lo, Engelond in-to Normandies hond:
> And þe Normans ne couþe speke þo bote hor owe speche,
> And speke French as hii dude atom, and hor children dude also
>   teche,
> So þat heiemen of þis lond, þat of hor blod come,
> Holdeþ alle þulke speche þat hii of hom nom;
> Vor bote a man conne Frenss me telþ of him lute.
> Ac lowe men holdeþ to Engliss, and to hor owe speche ȝute.
> Ich wene þer ne beþ in al þe world contreyes none
> þat ne holdeþ to hor owe speche, bote Engelond one.
> Ac wel me wote uor to conne boþe wel it is,
> Vor þe more þat a mon can, þe more wurþe he is.

This can be translated as follows:

> Thus came, lo, England into Normandy's hand: and the
> Normans then knew how to speak only their own language,
> and spoke French as they did at home, and also had their
> children taught (it), so that noblemen of this land, that come of
> their stock, all keep to the same speech that they received from
> them; for unless a man knows French, people make little
> account of him. But low men keep to English, and to their own
> language still. I think that in the whole world there are no
> countries that do not keep to their own language, except
> England alone. But people know well that it is good to master
> both, because the more a man knows the more honoured he is.

This bears witness to the prestige of French, but also to the fact
that English was still spoken by the majority ('lowe men'). Now,
however, that English was no longer the language of upper-class
culture and administration, West Saxon lost its place as a standard
literary language. For three centuries there was no single form of
English recognized as a norm, and people wrote in the language of
their own region. Early Middle English texts give the impression of
a welter of dialects, without many common conventions in
pronunciation or spelling, and with considerable divergences in
grammar and phonology.

Figure 10   The main dialect areas of Middle English

Middle English dialects

Figure 10 shows the approximate boundaries of the main dialects of Middle English. You must remember, however, that a map of this kind, with sharply defined dialect boundaries, is a great simplification. A more accurate map would show numerous isoglosses marking the boundaries of various dialect features, and obviously these would not all run together along the dialect-boundaries shown on our map. A team at the University of

Edinburgh has indeed produced a dialect atlas of late Middle English, showing the regional distribution of the spelling-variants of nearly three hundred items, and this gives a much more refined picture of the Middle English dialects.

Nevertheless, our map is a useful one, since there are a number of major dialect features which are typical of the regions shown, and it does make sense to talk (for example) about an East Midland type of dialect, or a Northern type of dialect. The regions shown are Northern (divisible into Scots and Northern English), East Midland, West Midland, South-Eastern, and Southern. The separation of the Northumbrian dialect of Old English into the Scottish and Northern English dialects of Middle English is in part due to the political separation of the two regions, which led to the emergence of a Scots literary language in the course of the Middle English period. The marked difference between the East Midland and West Midland dialects of Middle English, which are both descended from the Mercian dialect of Old English, is due in part to the fact that the East Midlands were in the Danelaw, whereas the West Midlands were in the part of England held by King Alfred, so that the two areas were subjected to different influences. The South-Eastern dialect is descended from the Kentish dialect of Old English, and the Southern dialect (which can be subdivided into South-Western and Central-Southern) is descended from West Saxon.

There are many differences between these Middle English dialects, and we shall just look at a few examples of various kinds. First, a few differences in phonology. OE $\bar{a}$ remained north of the Humber, but south of the Humber it changed in the twelfth century into the half-open rounded vowel [ɔ:] (like that of present-day *law*); this phoneme is usually called Middle English $\bar{\varrho}$. In Modern English, ME $\bar{\varrho}$ has developed into /əʊ/, as in *home* and *boat*, whereas the Northern [a:] has developed into [ɛ:] or [e:], giving forms like Scots *haim*. The southern forms are normal in Modern English, both British and American, but there are a few words where a northern form has entered the standard language, the phoneme then being realized as /eɪ/. Thus the word *raid* is a northern dialectal variant of the word *road*: both come from OE *rād*, which originally meant 'a riding, a journey'; it is a telling comment on life in the turbulent North during the Middle Ages that a riding of Scots into England or of Englishmen into Scotland should come to mean a *raid*. Another such doublet is the pair *whole* and *hale*, both from OE *hāl*; the word *hail* (as a greeting) is from the Scandinavian version of the same word.

Another example of dialectal variation is the ME treatment of the OE front rounded vowel *y*, as in the word *cynn* 'kin'. In the North, in the East Midlands, and in Devon, Dorset and Wiltshire, this word appears as ME *kinn*. In Kent, and in parts of Essex, Middlesex, Sussex, and Suffolk, it appears as *kenn*. While elsewhere (mainly, that is, in the old West Saxon areas) it appears as *kunn*. These probably represented the pronunciations [kɪn], [kɛn], and [kyn] respectively. Similarly, OE long *ȳ* became ME *ī* or *ē*, or remained *ȳ*, in the same areas: OE *brȳd* 'bride' appears in ME in such forms as *brid*, *bred*, and *bruid*, probably representing the pronunciations [bri:d], [bre:d], and [bry:d]. Standard Modern English is descended from a dialect where OE *y* and *ȳ* normally developed into ME *i* and *ī*, the latter having developed into Modern English /aɪ/; so OE *cynn* and *mȳs* have become our *kin* /kɪn/ and *mice* /maɪs/. But we have inherited stray forms from other dialects: *merry* and *left* (opposite of *right*) come from the South Eastern dialect, for the OE forms are *myrige* and *lyft*; and *bury* (OE *byrgan*) has its pronunciation from Kentish but its spelling from the old West Saxon area; while *busy* (OE *bysig*) also has the Southern spelling, but has its pronunciation from the East Midlands or the North.

A characteristic of the dialects of the West Midlands and of the South East is the treatment of OE short æ. In the West Midlands and the South East this appears as *e*, but elsewhere as *a*: so OE *æppel* 'apple' is ME *eppel* in the West Midlands and the South East, but *appel* elsewhere; this development had in fact already taken place in Old English. Another characteristic of the West Midland dialect is its treatment of OE short *a* before nasal consonants: West Midland has *mon* 'man' and *thonc* '(kindly) thought, gratitude, thanks', where the other dialects have *man* and *thanc*. A characteristic of the southern dialects is the voicing of word-initial /f-/, /θ-/, and /s-/, which become /v-/, /ð-/, and /z-/; this is not always shown in the spellings (though you may be able to spot examples in the passage on p. 136 above), but it probably happened everywhere south of the Thames and the Severn, that is, in the South-Eastern and Southern dialects and in part of the South-West Midlands. The forms *vat* and *vixen* (OE *fæt* and *fyxen*) have come into the modern standard language from one of these southern dialects.

The grammatical differences between the ME dialects include differences in inflections, and in the forms of the personal pronouns. During the ME period, there was a tendency for northern forms to permeate southwards. The following examples show the kinds of difference that were typical in the late thirteenth century:

	'she comes'	'they come'
Northern	scho comis	thai come/comis
East Midland	sche comes/cometh	thei comen
West Midland	hue cometh/comes	hi comen
South Eastern	hi cometh	hi cometh
Southern	heo cometh	he cometh

The differences in vocabulary between the regions are most striking in the matter of loan-words. In the Northern and East Midland dialects there are numerous Scandinavian words; some of these permeated into the other dialects during the ME period, but many never became accepted outside the old Danelaw. French loan-words, on the contrary, first appeared most densely around London, the centre of fashion and administration, and spread northwards and westwards from there; by the fourteenth century, they were being used freely all over the country.

English versus French

While English was thus left without a standard literary dialect, the prestige languages in England were Latin and French. Latin was the language of the church, of scholarship, and of international communication; after the Conquest it was also important in administration, but here it gradually gave way to French. The invaders of 1066 spoke Norman French, a northern dialect of the language, and in England this developed characteristics of its own, and is then called Anglo-Norman. In the thirteenth century, however, when the Central French dialect of Paris had begun to exert a strong influence on the rest of France, the Anglo-Norman dialect lost some of its prestige in England: it was regarded as rather old-fashioned and rustic, and the courtly language was Central French.

In the thirteenth century, French was still being spoken at the English court, and literature was being written in French for the nobility of England; but it is this century that sees the tipping of the balance away from French and back to English. Although French was for a long time the prestige language in England, it was never the mother-tongue of the majority of the population. A considerable number of Normans settled in England after the conquest, but they never outnumbered the English in the way the Anglo-Saxon settlers must have outnumbered the Britons, and ultimately French died out in England. An event which contributed to the triumph of English was King John's loss of Normandy to the French crown in the opening years of the thirteenth century. Many of the English nobility had estates in Normandy as well as in England, and now had to decide which of the two they belonged to. A common solution was for one son to inherit the English estates, and another son the Norman estates, and this can be seen going on in the first half of the thirteenth century. Thus the ties with Normandy were severed, and the ex-Norman nobility gradually became English. The English crown, indeed, continued to hold lands in France, especially in southern Aquitaine, and went on importing Frenchmen to its court, but the English nobility were jealous of such royal favourites, and in the Barons' Wars against Henry III in the middle of the century there was a good deal of anti-foreigner propaganda. National feeling was beginning to arise in England, as in other countries of western Europe, and this must have raised the prestige of the English language.

The fourteenth century sees the definitive triumph of English. French was now rapidly ceasing to be the mother-tongue even of the nobility, and those who wanted to speak French had to learn it. Literature, even the most courtly literature, was written more and more in English, and in the second half of the century there was a great literary upsurge, with Chaucer as its major figure. English was also used more and more in administration. In 1362 the king's speech at the opening of Parliament was made in English, and in the same year an Act was passed making English the official language of the law-courts instead of French, though their records were to be kept in Latin.

The fourteenth century also saw the switch from French to English as the medium of grammar-school education. Here we have an interesting piece of contemporary evidence. During the first half of the century a monk of Chester called Ranulph Higden wrote in Latin a long work called *Polychronicon*; this was a universal history (a favourite medieval form), beginning at the Creation and coming down to Higden's own time. In 1385–87 this work was translated into English by John of Trevisa, writing in a South-Western dialect. In Book I of the work, Higden gives an account of the languages of Britain; the English, he says, have had Danes and Normans mixed in with them, and this has led to a corruption of the native language. He then continues (in Trevisa's translation):

> þis apeyring of þe burþtonge ys bycause of twey þinges. On ys for chyldern in scole, aʒenes þe vsage and manere of al oþer nacions, buþ compelled for to leue here oune longage, and for to construe here lessons and here þinges a Freynsh, and habbeþ suþthe þe Normans come furst into Engelond. Also gentil men children buþ ytauʒt for to speke Freynsh fram tyme þat a buþ yrokked in here cradel, and conneþ speke and playe wiþ a child hys brouch; and oplondysch men wol lykne hamsylf to gentil men, and fondeþ wiþ gret bysynes for to speke Freynsh, for to be more ytold of.

This can be translated as follows:

> This corruption of the mother-tongue is because of two things. One is because children in school, contrary to the usage and customs of all other nations, are compelled to abandon their own language, and to construe their lessons and their tasks in French, and have since the Normans first came to England. Moreover, gentlemen's children are taught to speak French from the time that they are rocked in their cradle and are able to speak and play with a child's trinket; and rustic men want to make themselves like gentlemen, and strive with great industry to speak French, in order to be more highly thought of.

This passage testifies to the high prestige that French still enjoyed when it was written (perhaps around 1330), and to the continued use of French in education (though it is no doubt significant that Higden protests against this). But when John of Trevisa translated this passage in 1385, he added a piece of his own, which was not in the original. It begins as follows:

> þys manere was moche y-used tofore þe furste moreyn, and ys seþthe somdel ychaunged. For Iohan Cornwal, a mayster of gramere, chayngede þe lore in gramerscole and construccion of Freynsh into Englysch; and Richard Pencrych lurnede þat manere techyng of hym, and oþer men of Pencrych, so þat now, þe ʒer of oure Lord a þousond þre hondred foure score and fyue, of the secunde kyng Richard after þe Conquest nyne, in al þe gramerscoles of Engelond childern leueþ Frensch, and construeþ and lurneþ an Englysch.

This can be rendered:

> This custom was much in use before the first plague [that is, the Black Death of 1349], and since then has somewhat changed. For John Cornwall, a licensed teacher of grammar, changed the teaching in grammar school and the construing from French into English; and Richard Pencrich learnt that method of teaching from him, and other men from Pencrich, so that now, in the year of Our Lord 1385, in the ninth year of King Richard II, in all the grammar schools of England children are abandoning French, and are construing and learning in English.

Trevisa goes on to say that this has the advantage that the children learn more quickly, but the disadvantage that they know no more French than their left heel, which is bad for them if they have to go abroad. He adds that to a great extent gentlemen have now given up teaching their children French.

The greatest stronghold of French in England was perhaps the king's court, but when Henry IV seized the throne in 1399, England, for the first time since the Norman Conquest, acquired a king whose mother tongue was English. In the fifteenth century the retreat of French became a rout. Not only was it no longer a native language in England, but now there were actually members of the nobility who could not speak French at all.

Henceforth, a fluent command of French was to be regarded as an accomplishment.

The New Standard English

With the re-establishment of English as the language of administration and culture came the re-establishment of an English literary language, a standard form of the language which could be regarded as a norm. In fact, there were *two* standard forms of English, that of England and that of Scotland, the latter now usually being called Middle Scots. Scotland was an independent kingdom, and the language of the lowlands and of the royal court, which they called 'Inglis', became its dominant language; the Highlands were still Gaelic-speaking, and there were also Norse speakers in the Western Isles and in the far North; but it was 'Inglis', descended from the Northumbrian dialect of Old English, that gradually spread and displaced the other languages. Of Middle Scots, more will be said later.

In England, as we have already seen, the new standard language which arose in the late Middle Ages was not descended from the West Saxon literary language. It was in fact based on the East Midland dialect of Middle English. This was probably due to the importance of the East Midlands in English cultural, economic, and administrative life. One of the two universities, Cambridge, was in this area. It was an extremely important commercial area, as well as being a rich agricultural region; we have to remember that, before the Industrial Revolution, the North of England lacked the economic importance that it has today: it was a primitive region, economically and socially backward compared with the South; and Norwich was one of the great cities of England at a time when Leeds, Liverpool, Manchester, and Sheffield were comparatively insignificant. Above all, an East Midland dialect was the basis of London speech, and London was the seat of government and the cultural centre of the nation, besides being by far the largest city in the country. The London dialect was in fact rather a mixed one, but in the fourteenth century it seems to have been basically East Midland in type, with influences from the neighbouring South Eastern and Southern dialects. These border influences on London speech explain some of the non-East-Midland forms in modern standard English, like the South-Eastern *merry* and *left* which we have already noticed. In the main, however, Modern English has forms descended from the East Midland dialect of Middle English, itself mainly descended from the Mercian dialect of Old English.

The establishment of a standard language did not take place overnight. In the fourteenth century, while Chaucer was writing in what was to become the standard language, Langland was writing his *Piers Plowman* in a South-West Midland dialect, while in the North-West Midlands there was a school of poets writing in that local dialect, the most famous of their products being *Sir Gawayne and the Green Knight*. But gradually the prestige of the London language grew, and in the fifteenth century its influence was increased by the introduction of printing. In the sixteenth century there was wide recognition of the language of the court at Westminster as the 'best' English, but even then it was no disgrace for a gentleman to speak with a regional accent. Nevertheless, the *literary* language had been largely standardized by the end of the fifteenth century, and in the Modern English period you cannot tell what part of the country people come from by examining their writings, as you could in the Middle English period.

French Loan-Words in Middle English

Although French died out in England, it left its mark on English. Its main effect was on the vocabulary, and an enormous number of French loan-words came into the language during the Middle English period. We have to treat the datings of these loans with some caution: there are fewer texts in Early Middle English than in Late Middle English, and some of the loans first recorded in the fourteenth century may have entered the language much earlier. Nevertheless, it seems clear that they came in fastest when French was dying out. In the eleventh and twelfth centuries, when French was the unchallenged language of the upper classes, the number of words borrowed by English was not great, but in the thirteenth, and still more the fourteenth century, there was a flood of loan-words. This is not surprising: when bilingual speakers were changing over to English for such purposes as government and literature, they felt the need for the specialized terms that they were accustomed to in those fields, and brought them over from French. It was not that English was deficient in such vocabulary: in almost every case there was already an English word for the concept, which was displaced by the French word; this is one of the reasons why so much of the vocabulary of Old English and Early Middle English now seems so unfamiliar to us.

The influx of French words differed in several ways from the influx of Scandinavian words. We have already seen that Scandinavian words spread down from the Danelaw, whereas French words tended to spread from London and the court, and locally from the lord's castle. Moreover, the French words were on the whole not such homely ones as the Scandinavian words: the Vikings had mixed in with the English on more or less equal terms, but the Normans formed a separate caste that imposed much of their culture on their subordinates. Many of the French loan-words reflect this cultural and political dominance: they are often words to do with war, ecclesiastical matters, the law, hunting, heraldry, the arts, and fashion. For the same reason, French words tended to penetrate downwards in society, whereas the Scandinavian words came in on the ground floor. Finally, the French words were entirely new ones, with no obvious resemblance to anything in English, whereas many of the Scandinavian loans were merely dialectal variants of their English counterparts.

As might be expected, titles of rank tended to be taken from French. These include (in their modern spellings) *baron, count, duke, marquess, peer, prince,* and *sovereign*; we did however retain the English words *earl, king, knight, lady, lord,* and *queen.* Words to do with administration include *chancellor, council, country, crown, government, nation, parliament, people,* and *state.* The law courts were long conducted in French, and we have borrowed the words *accuse, attorney, court, crime, judge, justice, prison, punish, sentence,* and *verdict.* French dominance of ecclesiastical life is reflected in such loans as *abbey, clergy, friar, parish, prayer, relic, religion, saint, saviour, sermon, service,* and *virgin.* Many of the military terms that were borrowed are now obsolete, but there are also *armour, battle, castle*, *tower*, and *war* (itself originally taken into French from Germanic). Words reflecting French dominance in the arts and fashion include *apparel*, *costume*, *dress*, *fashion*; and *art*, *beauty*, *chant*, *colour*, *column*, *music*, *paint*, *poem*, and *romance*. Also borrowed were many abstract nouns, especially the names of mental and moral qualities, such as *charity*, *courtesy*, *cruelty*, *mercy*, and *obedience*.

There are other indications of the aristocratic stamp of medieval French loan-words. Things connected with ordinary people tend to retain their English names, whereas upper-class objects often have French names. Thus we have English *home* and *house* but French *manor* and *palace*; English *child*, *daughter*, and *son*, but French *heir* and *nurse*; English *maid*, *man*, and *woman*, but French *butler* and *servant*; English *calf*, *ox*, *sheep*, and *swine*, but French *veal*, *beef*, *mutton*, and *pork*. In Modern English we often have French and Germanic words surviving side-by-side with similar meanings; in such cases the Germanic word tends to be more popular, and perhaps more emotionally charged, while the French word is often more formal, refined, or official. Thus we have such pairs as *doom* and *judgement*, *folk* and *nation*, *hearty* and *cordial*, *holy man* and *saint*, *stench* and *odour*.

If you know Modern French, you may sometimes be puzzled by the difference between an English word and the corresponding French word. Sometimes these differences are due to changes that have taken place in the pronunciation of both languages since medieval times. Thus our word *age* was borrowed from Old French *age*; our pronunciation retains the original [dʒ], while in Modern French it has become [ʒ]; on the other hand, Modern French retains the original vowel [a:], whereas in English it has developed into [eɪ]. Our word *chief*, similarly, is a Middle English borrowing from Old French *chef*; the initial consonant [tʃ] in our word is akin to the Old French one, whereas in Modern French this has developed into [ʃ]; on the other hand, Modern French has retained the original short vowel, whereas *chief* has developed a long vowel. Our word *chef* is a more recent borrowing of the same word, and so has a pronunciation resembling the Modern French one.

Some of the discrepancies between ME loan-words and Modern French words have other explanations, however. One cause is dialectal variation in Old French itself. Standard Modern French is descended from a Central French dialect of Old French, but the Normans spoke a Northern French dialect, which differed from it in a number of ways. For example, the Old French diphthong *ei* became *oi* in Central French, but remained *ei* in Anglo-Norman. Hence we have English *prey*, *strait*, and *veil* (from Anglo-Norman *preie*, *estreit*, *veile*), where Modern French has *proie*, *étroit*, and *voile*. (In Modern French, of course, the *oi* has remained in the spelling, but the pronunciation has become [wa].) In Central French, the groups [ga] and [ka] in word-initial position became [dʒa] and [tʃa], but this change did not take place in Norman French: this accounts for English *garden* and *catch* beside French *jardin* and *chasser*. This last word illustrates another difference: in Normandy, Old French *s* became *ch*, so that Norman had *cachier* 'to chase' and *lanchier* 'to throw' where Central French had *chacier* and *lancier* (Modern French *chasser*, *lancer*); the Norman words have given our *catch* and *launch*. As a final example, there was a difference in the treatment of [w] in Old French loan-words from Germanic: the [w] was retained in Norman, but changed to [g] in Central French, so that we have *wage*, *war*, and *wardrobe*, while Modern French has *gage*, *guerre*, and *garderobe*.

On the whole, however, only the early French loan-words were taken from Norman; in the thirteenth and fourteenth centuries, when the great bulk of the borrowings were made, it was Central French that was fashionable, and it was from this dialect that words were taken. But the borrowings from Norman are very thoroughly assimilated into English, and include more ordinary everyday words than the later borrowings from Central French, presumably because in many cases they were introduced by the Norman rank and file who came over at the Conquest. Thus the early loans include such words as *garden*, *hour*, *market*, *people*, and *wage*. In some cases, a word was borrowed in its Norman form, and then later borrowed again in its Central French form, so that we have both forms in Modern English, usually with different meanings. Such doublets include *catch* and *chase*, *cattle* and *chattel*, *warden* and *guardian*, and *wage* and *gage* 'pledge'.

When the words were first borrowed, they may have been given a French pronunciation, especially among bilingual speakers. But very soon they were adapted to the English phonological system, and given the English sounds which to the speakers seemed nearest to the French ones. This is normal when a word is borrowed from a foreign language. In recent times, for example, the word *garage* has been borrowed into English from French, but even speakers who know French pronounce the word in an English way: they do not, for example, use a French uvular [r], or a French [a]. Moreover, the word *garage* (at any rate in British speech) is now given an English kind of stress pattern, being stressed on the first syllable. The same kind of thing happened with many French loan-words in Middle English: at first, a word like *nature* was stressed on the second syllable, as this seemed most like the French way of saying it, but after a time the stress was moved to the first syllable, as this was more in conformity with English speech-habits. In Chaucer's poetry, such words can often be seen to fluctuate, being sometimes stressed one way, sometimes the other. In polysyllabic words, the stress was not always moved all the way to the first syllable, and the final stressing arrived at has been influenced by several different factors: compare *melody* with *melodious*, *advertise* with *advertisement*. Moreover, there are sometimes variant stressings in Modern English, as in *controversy*.

The early French loan-words were so well assimilated into English that they were soon felt as not in any way foreign. This made it easier for the language to accept later Romance and Latin loans; indeed, one of the results of the influx of French loans was to make English more hospitable to foreign words and less prone to use its own resources for word-creation. Where Old English invented words like *tungolcræft* 'star-skill' or *þrīnes* 'threeness', Middle and Modern English often borrow or adapt a word from abroad, like *astronomy* (from French which had borrowed it from Latin, which had itself borrowed it from Greek) and *trinity* (from French and Latin). But once they have been taken into English, such loan-words can be combined with native elements to form further words. French-English hybrids appear quite soon after the Conquest, the earliest types being French stems with English prefixes or suffixes, like *beautiful, faithless, gentleness, preaching,* and *ungracious.*

The dominance of French for so many centuries naturally had a great influence too on English literary traditions. Some of these were quite disrupted. The tradition of Old English historical writing in prose was lost, and when people like Robert of Gloucester begin writing history in English again, they write verse chronicles in the French manner. There must have been places, however, where some English literary traditions were preserved, and in the second half of the fourteenth century there was a flourishing school of poets using the alliterative line descended from Old English poetry. Chaucer, however, with his system of versification on continental models, makes such poetry look a little old-fashioned, for it was Chaucer's kind of poetry which was to triumph. Here, as in so many fields, the centuries of French linguistic domination made a deep impression on English culture.

7 Middle English

Old English did not disappear overnight at the Norman Conquest, nor did it immediately stop being written, for the West Saxon literary tradition was continued for a time in some of the great monasteries. But, in the years following the Conquest, changes which had already begun to show themselves in pre-Conquest Old English continued at an increased speed, and in less than a century we can say that the Old English period is over, and that Middle English has begun.

The Conquest, in fact, made the change from Old English to Middle English look more sudden than it really was, by introducing new spelling-conventions. An established literary language like late West Saxon tends to be conservative in its spelling: changes occur in pronunciation, but the scribes often go on writing the words in the traditional way. But the Norman scribes disregarded traditional English spelling, and simply spelt the language as they heard it, using many of the conventions of Norman French. Consequently, many changes that had not been reflected in OE spelling, or which had appeared only in occasional spellings, now emerged clearly.

New Spelling-Conventions

Quite apart from revealing hidden changes, the new orthography gave English writings quite a new look. A number of new consonant-symbols were introduced. A new symbol *g* was introduced for the stops represented by OE ʒ, and the OE symbol was retained only for the fricatives. Where Old English had used *f* to represent both [f] and [v], ME scribes used *u* or *v* for the voiced sound. Similarly, *z* was introduced besides *s*, though not consistently. The digraph *th* gradually replaced ð and þ, but ð is found up to about 1300, and þ remained quite common until about 1400; indeed, a debased form of þ survives even today in the initial *Y* of expressions like 'Ye Olde Tea Shoppe', in which *Ye* is simply a late medieval way of writing *þe*. It is to be noted that in Middle English there were separate phonemes /f/ and /v/, /s/ and /z/, and /θ/ and /ð/, where in Old English there had been pairs of allophones. In the spelling, however, this fact was only fully recognized for /f/ and /v/, and this still remains the case today.

Some of the remaining differences in orthography between Old and Middle English are shown in Table 7.1. Remember that we are not here discussing changes in *pronunciation*, but changes in *spelling*. The changes shown are *typical* ones: there is a great deal of variation from text to text, and, in Early Middle English, changes take place in what often seems a sporadic and haphazard way.

Table 7.1   *Old and Middle English spelling conventions*

Pronunciation	OE Spelling	ME Spelling	Examples in ME
[kw]	cw	qu	queen, quick
[ʃ]	sc	ss, sch, sh	fiss, fisch, fish
[dʒ]	cg	i, j, g	iuge, juge 'judge'; egge 'edge'
[k]	c	k, c	kinn, cool
[tʃ]	c	ch	chinn 'chin'
[s]	s	s, c	cyndre, sindir 'cinder', centre
[g]	ʒ	g	god, good 'good'
[j]	ʒ	ʒ, y	ʒer, yer, yeer 'year'
[x, ç]	h	h, ʒ, gh	liht, liʒt, light
[ɪ]	i	i, y	king, kyng
[i:]	ī	i, y	fir, fyr 'fire'
[e:]	ē	e, ee	quen, queen
[o:]	ō	o, oo	fod, food
[u:]	ū	ou, ow	hous, hows 'house'

The letter *y* was no longer used to represent a front rounded vowel, but was simply used as an alternative to *i*, so that ME *king* and *kyng* represent exactly the same pronunciation, as do ME *fir* and *fyr* 'fire'. The ME dialects that preserved the front rounded vowels [y] and [y:] from OE *y* and *ȳ* usually spelt them *u* or *ui*: OE *cynn* became *kunn*, and OE *fȳr* 'fire' became *fur* or *fuir*. OE [dʒ] never occurred in word-initial position, only medially and finally, but ME loan-words from French, like *judge*, have [dʒ] in initial position.

Not all these changes were improvements: both *q* and *y* were superfluous, and *ou* was not a very satisfactory spelling for [u:], because it was also used to represent two different ME diphthongs.

One oddity of ME spelling which is still with us was the result of a change of script. In place of the insular script of Old English, the Norman scribes introduced a continental style of handwriting. In this style, it was difficult to tell how many strokes had been made when letters like *m, n, v, w,* and *u* occurred together, and groups like *wu, un, uv,* and *um* were difficult to distinguish from one another. For this reason, scribes took to writing *o* instead of *u* when it occurred in groups of this kind. So for OE *sunu, cuman,* and *lufu,* we often find ME *sone, comen,* and *love.* But this was a change in spelling, not in pronunciation: the word *sun* (OE *sunne*) has always had the same vowel-sound as the word *son* (OE *sunu*), and the modern difference in spelling is a matter of chance.

Changes in pronunciation

We have already noticed some of the changes in pronunciation that took place in the transition from Old to Middle English: the development of OE *y* and *ȳ* in different areas, and the change of OE *ā* to *ǭ* south of the Humber. Alongside this ME *ǭ*, (pronounced [ɔ:]), there was a phoneme usually called ME *ǭ*, pronounced [o:] (as in Modern German *wo* 'where'), which was descended from OE *ō*. The two phonemes have been kept distinct to the present day: for example, OE *gāt* has became *goat*, while OE *gōs* has become *goose*. In Middle English texts, however, the two phonemes are not usually distinguished in the spelling, and it was not until Early Modern times that one came to be spelt *oa* and the other *oo*. Another similar awkward pair in Middle English are the phonemes usually called ME *ę̄* and ME *ẹ̄*. ME *ę̄* was descended from OE *æ* and *ēa*, and was pronounced [ɛ:], a half-open vowel similar to that of Modern French *faire*. ME *ẹ̄* was descended from OE *ē* and *ēo*, and was pronounced [e:], a half-close vowel similar to that of Modern German *zehn*. Once again, however, the two phonemes were not usually distinguished in ME spelling, and it was not until Early Modern times that it became common to spell the first as *ea* or *ei* and the second as *ee* or *ie*. The two phonemes were still kept distinct in the English of Shakespeare's day, but have fallen together in present-day English, so that we use the same vowel in *sea* (from OE *sǣ*) as in *see* (from OE *sēon*).

Other phonological changes which mark the transition from Old English to Middle English include the disappearance of OE æ, which in most dialects fell together with *a*; the monophthongization of all the Old English diphthongs, both long and short; the development of new ME diphthongs, especially by the fusion of a vowel with a following [j] or [w]; and the weakening of the vowels in unstressed syllables, all of them appearing as ME *e* (perhaps representing [ə]). For example, the OE words *fæder* 'father', *heorte* 'heart', *strēam* 'stream', *mægden* 'girl', *fugol* 'bird', and *lagu* 'law' appear in Middle English with such spellings as *fader* or *feder*, *herte*, *strem*, *meiden*, *fowel*, and *lawe*, though with much regional variation.

Late OE and Early ME Vowel-Lengthening

A sound-change which took place in late Old English, but which did not become apparent until the ME period, was the lengthening of short vowels before certain consonant-groups. In many cases the vowels were shortened again during the ME period, but long vowels remained in some dialects, especially before the groups *ld*, *mb*, and *nd*. Lengthening before these groups accounts for the modern forms of words like *old*, *bold*, *cold*, *told*. In Old English (Anglian) these had short *a* (*ald*, etc.); this was lengthened to *ā* during the ninth century, and in the twelfth century this *ā* regularly became *ǭ* south of the Humber, giving ME pronunciations like [ɔ:ld]. Other examples of lengthening before these three groups are provided by the words *field*, *child*, *comb*, *climb*, *blind*, and *ground* (OE *feld*, *cild*, *camb*, *climban*, *blind*, and *grund*). This lengthening did not take place, however, if the consonant-group in question was immediately followed by a third consonant. This accounts for the difference in vowel between *child* and *children*. In most such cases, however, either the long or the short vowel has been generalized in Modern English: thus our *lamb* is from the plural form (OE *lambru*, ME *lambre*), not from the singular (OE *lamb*), which had its vowel lengthened. The word *wind* 'moving air' probably has its short vowel by analogy with words like *windmill*, where the third consonant prevented the lengthening from taking place. In Middle English, *wind* normally had a long vowel, and as late as Shakespeare's time it rhymed with *kind* ('Blow, blow, thou winter wind . . .').

Another vowel-lengthening process, which has had far-reaching effects on both pronunciation and spelling, took place in Middle English itself, during the thirteenth century. This was the lengthening of short vowels in open syllables in two-syllable words. An open syllable is one which ends with a vowel. Where a single consonant occurs between vowels in an English word, the consonant normally belongs to the second syllable, and the first syllable is therefore open. Thus in the OE verb *bacan* 'to bake' the syllable-division is *ba-can*, and the first syllable is an open one. This word became early ME *baken* (still with short [a]), and then the vowel in the open syllable was lengthened to [a:] (like the vowel of French *tard*), which in Modern English has regularly developed into the [eɪ] of *bake*. When, however, there are two consonants between the vowels, the first consonant normally belongs to the first syllable, which is therefore a closed one. Thus in ME *thanken*, from OE *þancian*, the syllable-division was *than-ken*, and no lengthening took place.

The vowels which were regularly subject to this kind of lengthening were *a*, *o*, and *e*. When *o* was lengthened it became a long open vowel, and in the standard language it became identical with ME ǭ, so that today we have the same vowel in *boat* and *home* (from OE *bāt* and *hām*) as in *hope* and *throat* (from OE *hopa* and *þrote*). When *e* was lengthened it too became a long open vowel, and in the standard language it fell together with ME ę̄, so that today we have the same vowel in *sea* and *to lead* (from OE *sǣ* and *lǣdan*) as in *meat* and *steal* (from OE *mete* and *stelan*).

In some parts of Northern England and of East Anglia, the vowels *i* and *u* were also lengthened under the same conditions, and then became ME ẹ̄ and ǭ. A few of these lengthened forms have found their way into the modern standard language, for example *week* (OE *wicu*) and *evil* (Early ME *ivel* from OE *yfel*).

Because of the inflectional system of English, the conditions for lengthening were sometimes fulfilled in one form of a word, but not in another. For example, OE *cradol* 'a cradle' became ME *cradel*, and here lengthening of the *a* would occur. But the plural 'cradles' was OE *cradelas* (Early ME *cradeles*), and 'in a cradle' was *on cradole* (Early ME *on cradele*), and no lengthening would take place in these, because they were three-syllable forms. Similarly, OE *cran* 'a crane' would not have its vowel lengthened in Middle English, but the inflected forms, like *cranas* 'cranes' would do. In such cases Modern English has usually generalized one form or the other for each word: in the two examples given, it is the lengthened vowel that has been generalized, leading to our *cradle* and *crane*. In some cases, however, it is the short vowel that has been generalized: we use a short vowel in *vat*, *vats*, from the OE nominative singular *fæt*, not the long vowel which would have arisen from OE inflected forms like *fatu* 'vats'. Occasionally, both long and short forms have been retained, so that Modern English has two words where Old English had only one. OE *stæf* 'a staff' became ME *staf*, while the plural *stafas* became ME *staves*. From *staves* has been formed a new singular *stave*, and from *staff* a new plural *staffs*. In present-day English (RP), *staff* in fact has a long vowel, but this is a more recent development, dating from the seventeenth century.

This ME lengthening of vowels in open syllables of dissyllabic words has affected our spelling-conventions. In Early Middle English, words like *bake* had two syllables. After the first vowel had been lengthened, the final *-e* was lost, and such words became monosyllables. But the *-e* was often retained in the spelling, and so we tend in Modern English to regard a final *-e* as a mark of a preceding long vowel or a diphthong, provided there is only one consonant-symbol in between. Thus we use spellings like *home* and *stone*, where the final *-e* has no etymological justification, but is simply inserted to show that the *o* represents a long vowel or a diphthong. The Old English forms, of course, were *hām* and *stān*, and the modern words might well be spelt *hoam* and *stoan* (like *oak* and *road* and other such words that had *ā* in Old English).

Moreover, because of the lengthening in open syllables, we often insert two consonant-symbols in the spelling to show that the vowel is short: we write *backer* and *copper*, as distinct from *baker* and *coper*.

Middle English morphology

The Middle English period is marked by a great reduction in the inflectional system inherited from Old English, so that Middle English is often referred to as the period of weakened inflections. There were a number of causes for this. One was the mixing of Old English with Old Norse. Frequently, the English and Scandinavian words were sufficiently similar to be recognizable, but had decidedly different sets of inflections. In these circumstances, doubt and confusion would arise about the correct form of ending to use, and speakers in bilingual situations would tend to rely on other grammatical devices where these lay to hand. The existence and growth of such other devices must itself have contributed to the decay of the inflectional system, while itself being stimulated by this decay.

Another cause was phonological: the loss and weakening of unstressed syllables at the ends of words destroyed many of the distinctive inflections of Old English. As a result of these changes, OE word-final *-a*, *-u*, and *-e* all became ME *-e*. The endings *-an*, *-on*, *-un*, and *-um* all became *-en*, which was later reduced to *-e*. The endings *-as* and *-es* both became *-es*, while *-aþ* and *-eþ* both became *-eþ*. Moreover the final *-e*, which was all that was left of some of these endings, itself disappeared during the ME period: in the North, where the changes first took place, it was no longer pronounced by the mid-thirteenth century, and in the South it had disappeared by about 1400.

These changes had disastrous effects on the inflectional system, since many endings now became identical. For example, the OE noun *sunu* 'son' would become ME *sone* in all cases except the dative plural, which would become *sonen*, and even that would also later become *sone*. The same would be true of the differently declined nouns *giefu* 'gift' and *wine* 'friend'. As a result, the whole inflectional system became simplified. Among nouns, for example, the two declensions with the most distinctive of the remaining inflections tended to attract all the other nouns to themselves. At the same time, the number of different cases was reduced, especially in the declension of the adjective and of the definite article.

Among the nouns, two main declensions were generalized. One was the declension which in Old English had its nominative plural in -*as* (*stānas* 'stones') and its genitive singular in -*es* (*stānes* 'of a stone'). Both these endings became ME -*es*, so that both the nominative plural and the genitive singular were *stones*. The other declension was the one which in Old English formed both its nominative plural and its genitive singular in - *an*, which in Middle English became -*en*. Thus *ēage* was 'eye', and *ēagan* 'eyes' and 'of an eye'; in Middle English these became *eye* and *eyen*. Of these two declensions, the first became dominant in the northern dialects, in which all nouns tended to form the nominative plural and the genitive singular with -*es*, and forms like *eyes* are normal by about 1200. In the South, on the other hand, it was the -*en* declension that became dominant by the middle of the period, and many nouns that in Old English belonged to other declensions came to use the -*en* plural (though -*es* was common for the genitive singular). So we find forms like *devlen* 'devils' and *englen* 'angels', where Old English had *dēoflas* and *englas*. But in the course of the ME period the -*es* plural spread southwards and displaced -*en*, and by the fifteenth century it was almost universal, and of course our normal modern plural ending is directly descended from it. In Shakespeare's time we still find a few plurals in -*en* which have since disappeared, like *eyen*, *shoon*, *hosen*, *housen*, and *peasen* (the singular of which was *pease*, as still in *pease pudding*). And today we still have *oxen*, *children*, and *brethren*.

We still have a few relics of other declensions: there are the mutated plurals like *feet*, *geese*, *mice*, and *men*, where the vowel of the plural was changed by front mutation, and there is no plural ending; and there are uninflected plurals like *deer* and *sheep* which are descended from Old English neuter nouns in which the nominative and accusative plural had no ending (*dēor* 'wild animal', plural *dēor* 'wild animals'). We have also complicated things a little in Modern English by introducing a few learned plurals in words borrowed from Latin and Greek, like *formulae* and *nuclei* and *phenomena*, but on the whole we have pretty thoroughly generalized the Old English *-as* ending for the noun plural. We now spell it *-s* or *-es*, and (at any rate in South-Eastern England) pronounce it /-s/ or /-z/ or /-ɪz/ according to the preceding phoneme (compare *caps*, *cabs*, *matches*).

In Early Middle English we find all four of the OE noun-cases still preserved in both singular and plural, but in the course of the period there is a tendency to reduce the total number of forms to three: one for the nominative and accusative singular (like *eye*), one for the genitive singular (like *eyes* 'of an eye'), and one for all plural uses (like *eyen* 'eyes'). In the North, and later elsewhere, the plural and the genitive singular were identical, and there were only two forms, *eye* and *eyes*. A dative singular with the ending *-e* persisted for quite a time, especially in the South, but as the final unstressed *-e* was lost in all dialects by the fifteenth century this too disappeared. Occasionally, too, there are genitive plural forms in *-e* or *-ene* even in Late Middle English, as in *kingene king* 'king of kings'. But such forms disappear by the end of the ME period, and we reach the modern situation, where for most nouns we have only two different forms (*boy*, *boys*). We recognize a further two forms in our spellings, though not in pronunciation (*boy's*, *boys'*), and in fact a few nouns do have four distinct forms (*man*, *man's*, *men*, *men's*). We still have a few relics of the old case-system preserved as fossils in modern words and expressions. The word *alive* comes from OE *on līfe*, where *līfe* is the dative singular of *līf* 'life'. The final *-e* has been lost, of course, but we have retained the voiced [v], not the [f] of the nominative. In Lady Day and Lady Chapel, *Lady* represents an old genitive form (compare 'Lady Day' with 'the Lord's Day'). And the archaic word *whilom* comes from OE *hwīlum*, the dative plural of *hwīl* 'time, while', meaning 'at times'.

The same process of loss of case-distinctions took place in adjectives and demonstratives. In adjectives, the trend was towards the use of only two forms: the base-form (for example, *fair*), and a form with the ending *-e* (such as *faire*) which was used both for the plural and as the weak form. This stage has been reached in Chaucer, who writes 'the weder is fair' and 'she hadde a fair forheed', but 'faire wives' (where we have the plural form) and 'this faire Pertelote' (where the weak form is used after the demonstrative *this*). When the final *-e* was lost towards the end of the ME period, these two forms became the same, and the adjective became indeclinable, as it is today.

In Old English the definite article showed three genders (*sē* masculine, *sēo* feminine, *þæt* neuter), and was declined through all four cases, singular and plural, and in fact in the singular had a fifth case, the instrumental, *þȳ* or *þon*. The form *the* arose as Late Old English *þe*, which supplanted *sē* and *sēo*; it had its initial thorn from the influence of the other case-forms, which all began with *þ*. In the course of Middle English, the other forms disappeared, and *the* became used for all of them: Chaucer nearly always uses *the*, though he also has a plural form *tho* (from OE *þā*). By the end of the Middle English period we have reached the modern position, in which *the* is the only form of the definite article, and *that* (originally the nominative/accusative singular neuter form of the definite article) has become a contrasting demonstrative with its own distinct meaning.

We have seen that the definite article and the adjective played a large part in Old English in marking out distinctions of case and number. The loss of this function by the end of the Middle English period (when both the adjective and the definite article had become indeclinable) represented a major change in the structure of the language. It also meant that grammatical gender disappeared, and was replaced by 'natural gender'. That is, we now tend to refer to female creatures as *she*, male creatures as *he*, and inanimate objects as *it*. Things are indeed a bit more complicated than that: a ship for example can be *she*, and a dog (or even a human baby) can be *it*. But still we are a long way from the system of Early Old English, where *wīfmann* 'woman' was masculine, *lār* 'learning' was feminine, and *wīf* 'wife, woman' was neuter, and the forms of the pronoun, the adjective, and the definite article had to be chosen accordingly. Even in Late Old English, however, there is a strong tendency for women to be referred to as 'she' and men as 'he', whatever the gender of the noun that has been used.

Middle English syntax

As the inflectional system decayed, other devices were increasingly used to replace it. For one thing, word-order became more important: inflections were increasingly incapable of showing which noun was the subject of the sentence, and which the object, and this function was taken over by the use of the S-V-O word-order, which became the dominant one in the ME period. The S-O-V word-order found in some subordinate clauses disappeared in Early Middle English. The use of V-S-O order, especially after certain adverbs, persisted throughout the period, and is not uncommon as late as the seventeenth century. Indeed, the use of V-S order (but without an object) is still occasionally found today. But it was in the Middle English period that S-V-O was established as the normal type, as it still is. In the passage from Wycliffe (late fourteenth century) which we looked at in Chapter 2, every single clause has the S-V type of word-order.

Another device encouraged by the decay of the inflectional system was the use of separate words to perform the functions formerly carried out by word-endings. For example, prepositions like *in*, *with*, and *by* came to be used more frequently than in Old English. A few OE phrases with their modern equivalents will illustrate this: *hungre ācwelan* 'to die of hunger'; *meahtum spēdig* 'abundant in might'; *dæges and nihtes* 'by day and by night'; *mildheortnysse Drihtnes full is eorþe* 'the earth is filled with the mercy of God'. There are no prepositions at all in the original OE expressions, and the prepositions in the present-day glosses translate OE inflectional endings.

The Middle English verbal system

A similar tendency for inflections to be replaced by more analytic devices is also seen in the verb-system of Middle English. As we have seen, the OE verb had many inflections, but basically only two tenses, present and past. In Middle English and Modern English the system of inflections becomes much reduced, but a complicated system of tenses is built up by means of the primary auxiliaries (*be*, *have*, and later *do*) and the modal auxiliaries (*shall*, *should, will*, etc.). The future tense with *shall* and *will* is established in Middle English. In Old English, as we have seen *ic sceal* meant 'I am obliged to', and *ic wille* meant 'I wish to'. Indeed, *shall* and *will* have never entirely lost the connotation of obligation and desire respectively, but today their main function is to signal prediction or futurity, and this function (already hinted at in occasional OE usages) developed in the ME period. Thus a character in one of Chaucer's poems says:

> I shal myself to herbes techen yow
> That shul been for youre heele and for youre prow.

There *shal* is singular (from OE *sceal*) and *shul* is plural (from OE *sculon*), and the sentence means 'I shall myself direct you to herbs that will be for your health and for your benefit'. The tendency, when using the words as simple markers of the future, to confine *shall* to the first person (for example, 'I shall', 'we shall'), and *will* to the second and third (for example, 'it will', 'you will') is relatively recent, and even today is not universal: in Northern England you often hear 'Shall you go?', where a Londoner says 'Will you go?'.

As we have seen, the perfect tenses with *habban* or *bēon* and the passive forms with *bēon* or *weorþan* already existed in Old English, but they came to be used more frequently in Middle English. In the perfect, *have* spread at the expense of *be*, but *be* was common with verbs of motion and verbs of change of state, and this continued to be the case even in Early Modern English: 'Worcester *is stolne* away by Night: thy Fathers Beard *is turn'd* white with the Newes' (Shakespeare, *Henry IV.1*). In the passive, *be* supplanted *weorþan* (ME *werþe, worþe*), which had fallen out of use by the end of the ME period.

The continuous tenses, formed with *be* and the present participle ('He is coming', 'We were eating'), also arise in Middle English, but are not at all common until the Modern English period. There is indeed an OE construction using *be* and the present participle. Thus in the Anglo-Saxon Chronicle (755) we read *Ond hīe þā ymb þā gatu feohtende wǣron, oþ þæt . . .*, which is probably to be translated 'And then they went on fighting around the gates, until . . .'. The construction is here used for a continuous action with limited duration, and so is very similar to our continuous tenses. These continuous tenses, however, are probably not descended from the OE usage. It is more likely that they arose from ME sentences like *he was areading*, where *areading* has developed from *on reading*, and the sentence means 'he was engaged in the act of reading'. Later *areading* lost its first syllable, and we arrived at the modern sentence *he was reading*. Originally this *reading* was not part of the verb, but was a noun (OE *rǣding*), meaning 'the act of reading'. Many nouns of this kind originally ended in *-ung*, like OE *leornung* 'learning', but this changed to *-ing* in Middle English.

By the end of the Middle English period, therefore, the perfect, passive, and continuous markings of the verb were all well established, though much less frequently used than today. The ways in which they could be combined were also limited: as we shall see later, it was not until the eighteenth century that it became possible to use all possible combinations of them.

Specimens of Middle English

We can illustrate some of these points by looking at a couple more examples of ME writing, one early and one late. First an extract from the Peterborough Chronicle, which was a continuation of the Anglo-Saxon Chronicle, kept going at the monastery at Peterborough until 1154. Under the year 1137 there is a long annal describing the anarchy and miseries of King Stephen's reign, and I have taken an extract from this. The chronicler has been describing how all the great magnates disregarded Stephen, and used forced labour to build themselves castles. The word *me*, which occurs several times in the passage, is the unstressed form of *man*, used as in Old English as an impersonal 'one'. Punctuation is modernized, and abbreviations are silently expanded.

þa þe castles uuaren maked, þa fylden hi mid deoules and yuele men. þa namen hi þa men þe hi wenden ðat ani god hefden, bathe be nihtes and be dæies, carlmen and wimmen, and diden heom in prisun, and pined heom efter gold and syluer untellendlice pining, for ne uuæren næure nan martyrs swa pined alse hi wæron. Me henged up bi the fet and smoked heom mid ful smoke. Me henged bi the þumbes other bi the hefed, and hengen bryniges on her fet. Me dide cnotted strenges abuton here hæued and uurythen it ðat it gæde to the hærnes. Hi diden heom in quarterne þar nadres and snakes and pades wæron inne, and drapen heom swa. Sume hi diden in crucethur, ðat is in an ceste þat was scort and nareu and undep, and dide scærpe stanes þerinne, and þrengde þe man þærinne, ðat him bræcon alle þe limes. . . . . Warsæ me tilede, þe erthe ne bar nan corn, for þe land was al fordon mid suilce dædes, and hi sæden openlice ðat Christ slep, and his halechen. Suilc and mare þanne we cunnen sæin we þoleden xix wintre for ure sinnes.

This is very early Middle English, and not very easy for the modern reader. A fairly close translation is as follows:

When the castles were made, then filled they (them) with devils and evil men. Then seized they the people that they believed possessed any property, both by day and by night, both men and women, and put them in prison, and tortured them (with) indescribable torments in order to get gold and silver, for never were martyrs so tortured as they were. They ('One') hanged (them) up by the feet and smoked them with foul smoke. They hanged (them) by the thumbs or by the head, and hung corslets on their feet. They put knotted cords about their heads and tightened it so that it entered the brains. They put them in a cell in which were adders and snakes and toads, and killed them so. Some they put in a 'torturer', that is, in a chest which was short and narrow and shallow, and put sharp stones in it, and crushed the man in it so that all his limbs broke. . . . Wherever people tilled, the earth bore no corn, for the land was completely ruined with such deeds, and they said openly that Christ slept, and his saints. Such, and more than we are able to tell, we suffered nineteen years for our sins.

The orthography of the passage still shows the influence of the OE scribal tradition, for instance in the use of æ and of the spelling *sc* for [ʃ] (for example, *scort* 'short'). For [w], too, it sometimes uses wynn (*wæron* 'were'), but often instead uses *uu* (*uuaren* 'were'), and for [v] it most often uses *u*, not *f* (for example, *deoules* 'devils'). It uses both thorn and eth, but alongside these is now found *th* (*bathe* 'both'), and instead of *cw* we see the French spelling *qu* (*quarterne* 'cell, dungeon', from OE *cweartern*). OE *ā* is still represented by *a*, not *o* (for example, *þa* 'when', *mare* 'more, greater'), presumably because the change of *ā* to *ǭ* had not yet taken place in the part of the East Midland area where the text was written.

There are also points of grammar which remind us of Old English. The pronouns of the third-person plural are the English forms *hi, heom*, and *her(e)*, not the Scandinavian *they, them, their*. There is a verb which is strong (as in Old English) which is now weak (*slep* 'slept', from OE *slēp*). This is one of the verbs which changed from strong to weak during the ME period, and Chaucer uses both *he slepte* and *he sleep*. There is one example of S-O-V word-order in a subordinate clause ('the people that they believed any property possessed'), and a few examples of V-S-O order (such as, 'then seized they the people').

Despite these resemblances to Old English, however, there are also decided differences, and the text is clearly to be classified as Middle English. This is especially seen in the inflections, which are very much reduced compared to Old English. The adjectives have lost almost all their endings: there is a plural *-e* on some of them (such as *yuele*), but otherwise nothing. For example, *mid ful smoke* would in Old English have been *mid fūlum smocan*, with inflections for the dative singular. The definite article is almost invariably *þe* or *the*, as in *þe castles* and *bi the fet*, though there is one example of the plural *þa* (in *þa men*). In Old English, of course, the definite article was fully declined, and the equivalent of *bi the fet* would have been *bi þǣm fōtum*, the preposition *bi* governing the dative. For the nouns, the normal plural in the passage is *-(e)s* (*castles, bryniges*), and in several words this is used where in Old English there was a different one, for example *þumbes* and *snakes*, which had the OE plural forms *þuman* and *snacan*. There is however one plural ending *-en*, in the word *halechen* 'hallows, saints', from OE *hālgan*. Apart from these plural endings, the nouns have practically no inflections, except for one dative singular, the *-e* of *quarterne*. An interesting case is the phrase *be nihtes and be dæies*: this is a kind of halfway house between the Old English *nihtes and dæges*, in which the genitive inflection *-es* has an adverbial force, and the modern *by night and day*. The ME writer has introduced the preposition *by*, but has also retained the OE *-es* ending (perhaps apprehended as a plural).

In vocabulary, the passage shows very little French influence, having only *castles* and *prisun*. These are from Norman French, the former having initial [ka-] where Central French had [tʃa-] (Old French *chastel* from late Latin *castellum*, Modern French *château*). In several places where Modern English would use a French loan-word, the passage has an English word which is no longer used, like *halechen* 'saints' and *pining* 'torments'. Nor are there many Greek or Latin loans in the passage: the two words from Greek (*martyrs* and *devils*) are not new loans, but had been borrowed in Old English, and the only new classical loan in the passage is *crucethur* 'torture-box', probably from Latin *crūciātor*.

As we might expect from a text from the old Danelaw, however, there are more Scandinavian words, though fewer than in some later texts: *bathe* 'both', *bryniges* 'corslets', *carlmen* 'men', *drapen* 'killed', and *hærnes* 'brains'. Only one of these has survived in modern literary English, namely, *both*, from Old Norse *báðir*.

In reading the passage you may have been struck by the word *nadres* 'adders'. The OE word is *nǣdre*, and there are similar words in other Germanic languages (such as Gothic *nadrs*, German *Natter*). Why has the initial /n-/ been lost in Modern English? As we have already seen, word-final /-n/ in unstressed syllables was lost in Middle English, early in the North and later in the South; an example of this in the passage is the use of *me* as the unstressed form of *man*, meaning 'one, people' (like French *on* or German *man*). This final /-n/, however, was not lost under all circumstances: it was retained when it occurred immediately before a vowel, but lost when it occurred before a consonant or a pause. Because of this, double forms arose for many words, one form with final /-n/ and one without. For example, the unstressed form of OE *ān* 'one' led to the modern indefinite article: the vowel was shortened in Old English, because of the absence of stress, and then in Middle English the final /-n/ was lost before consonants but not before vowels, giving the two forms *a* and *an*, as in *a father* and *an uncle*. Similarly the unstressed form of OE *mīn* led to ME *my* and *mine* (*my father* but *mine uncle*). But when there are pairs in the language like *my nephew* and *mine uncle*, mistakes sometimes occur about the point of division between the two words, and there appear forms like *my nuncle*. The word *nuncle* did in fact exist, and is found in Shakespeare (for example, *King Lear* I.iv.117). The word *adder* is of this type, the expression *a nadder* having been apprehended as *an adder*. Other words that owe their modern forms to this kind of change are *apron* (Old French *naperon*), *newt* (OE *efete*), *nickname* (formerly *ekename* 'additional name'), and *umpire* (Old French *nompere*). Similarly, the pet-names Nan, Ned, and Nell are derived from 'mine Anne', 'mine Edward', and 'mine Ellen'.

It is also clear that in many words a final /-n/ would be retained in the inflected forms, while being lost (except before vowels) in the base-form. So OE *mægden* 'a girl' became ME *maide*, while *mægdenes* 'of a girl' became *maidenes*. In such cases analogy has generally operated to generalize one or other form: thus forms with final /-n/ have been generalized in *iron* and *seven*, and those without final /-n/ in *holly* (OE *holegn*) and *haughty* (Old French *hautein*). In a few cases, both forms have been preserved, so that in Modern English we have doublets like broke/broken, eve/even(ing), maid/maiden, morrow/morn, no/none, and ope/open. Moreover, because of the example of such pairs, we have even added final /-n/ to words which did not originally have it. An example is *often*, which in Old English was *oft*: in Middle English the common adverbial ending *-e* was added, to make it *ofte*, and in the fourteenth century the analogical /-n/ was tagged on.

For our example of later Middle English we can take a few lines from Chaucer's *Canterbury Tales*, dating from the late fourteenth century. Chaucer turned his back on the traditional English alliterative style of verse, and used instead French and Italian models. He uses rhyme, in stanzas or couplets, and verse lines with a fixed number of syllables.

In Chaucer's verse, many words have a final *-e* in the spelling. In many cases, but not all, this has to be pronounced, probably as [-ə]. In speech, word-final unstressed *-e* was dead or dying in Chaucer's time, but it continued to be used in poetry. In Chaucer's verse, it is elided (and so not pronounced) if it occurs immediately before a vowel. But remember that in many words with initial *h* in the spelling, the *h* was not pronounced, so that in fact the word began with a vowel. This applied to many French loan-words, such as *harlot*, *hazard*, *heritage*, *host*, and *humble*. These had already lost their initial [h-] before they were borrowed into English, and the modern pronunciations are due to the spelling and to Latin influence. Moreover, in the thirteenth century, word-initial /h-/ had been lost in unstressed words in English, so that words like *hit* 'it' and *hire* 'her' developed double forms, a strong form with initial /h-/ and a weak form without it; word-final *-e* would be elided before the weak form, but not before the strong. As a further complication, there were a considerable number of words where the final *-e* in the spelling was purely orthographical, and was never pronounced: this is certainly the case, for example, with the pronoun-determiners *hire* 'her', *hise* 'his', *oure* 'our', and *youre* 'your'. In the following passage, which is in ten-syllable rhymed couplets, I have put a dot over *e* in cases where I think it should be pronounced.

The passage is an excerpt from the delightful animal fable, 'The Nun's Priest's Tale'. Chauntecleer, the cock, has disturbed his favourite wife, Pertelote, by groaning in his sleep, and explains to her that he has had a nightmare:

> Me mette / how that I roméd vp and doun
> With Inne oure yeerd / wheer as I saugh a beest
> Was lyk an hound / and wolde han maad areest
> Vp on my body / and han had me deed
> His colour / was bitwixé yelow and reed
> And tippéd was his tayl / and bothe hise eeris
> With blak / vnlyk the remenant of hise heeris
> His snowté smal / with glowynge eyén tweyé
> Yet of his look / for feere almost I deyé
> This causéd me / my gronyng doutélees
> Avoy quod she / fy on yow hertélees
> Allas quod she / for by that god abouè
> Now han ye lost / myn herte and al my louè
> I kan nat loue a Coward / by my feith
> For certes / what so any woman seith
> We alle desiren / if it myghté bee
> To han housbondés / hardy wise and free
> And secree / and no Nygard ne no fool
> Ne hym / þat is agast of euery tool
> Ne noon auantour / by that god abouè
> How dorste ye seyn for shame / vn to youre louè

That any thyng myghte makė yow aferd
Haue ye no mannės herte / and han a berd

This is not too difficult to understand, but there are things in it which may mislead a modern reader, so we had better have a modern version:

> 'I dreamt that I was strolling up and down in our yard, where I saw an animal [which] was like a dog, and [which] wished to seize my body and to kill me. Its colour was between yellow and red, and its tail and both its ears were tipped with black, unlike the rest of its hairs; its muzzle (was) slender, with two glowing eyes; I still almost die of fear at its look. This caused me my groaning, undoubtedly.' 'Really!' she said, 'Fie on you, spiritless. Alas,' she said, 'for, by God above, now have you lost my heart and all my love. I cannot love a coward, by my faith. For assuredly, whatever any woman may say, we all wish, if possible, to have husbands that are brave, wise, and generous, and discreet, and no miser and no fool, nor one that is frightened of every weapon, nor a boaster. By God above, how did you dare, for shame, to say to your love that anything could make you frightened? Do you lack the courage of a man, and have a beard?'

For the modern reader, the tricky things here are familiar-looking words which have changed slightly in meaning since Chaucer's time, like *smal* 'narrow, slender' and *tool* 'weapon'. But it is not difficult with a little practice to acquire a reasonable facility in reading Chaucer.

Unlike the Peterborough scribe, the scribe here often uses double letters to indicate a long vowel, as in *maad* and *eeris*. In some such words the vowel has since been shortened, for example, *deed* 'dead' and *look* 'look', but in Chaucer we must pronounce it long: [dɛːd], [loːk]. The passage contains one example of thorn, but none of eth, the normal spelling being *th* (for example, *that*). There are no examples of either wynn or yogh, the scribe instead using *w* (as in *wolde*) and either *gh* (as in *mighte*) or *y* (as in *yeerd*).

In vocabulary, the striking thing about the passage, compared with the Peterborough one, is the large number of French loan-words, such as *areest*, *beest*, *caused*, *colour*, and *feith*. Several of them are words relating to moral qualities, especially the kind which would be discussed in courtly circles, such as *avauntour*, *coward*, *hardy*, *secree*. The passage contains fewer Scandinavian loan-words: *bothe*, *deye* 'die' and *housbondes* (already recorded in late Old English), and possibly *nygard* and *tipped*. Scandinavian influence may also have reinforced the Northern English pronunciation of the adjective and preposition *lyk* 'like', which in Southern English would probably have had final [-tʃ].

Chauntecleer and Pertelote are a courtly pair of birds, and address one another by the polite pronouns *ye* and *you*, not by the familiar *thou* and *thee*. Chaucer consistently maintains the distinction between nominative *ye* and accusative *you* ('fy on yow', but 'Now han ye lost'). Notice, too, that *ye* still takes a plural verb (*han*), even though used as a polite singular.

A personal pronoun which we have not met in any earlier passage, but which is normal in Chaucer, is *she*. The origin of this word is disputed. The OE form was *hēo*, and forms like *she* are not found until the twelfth century, the earliest recorded example being *scæ* in the Peterborough Chronicle under the year 1140. It seems that *she* arose in the East Midlands and spread from there, becoming the normal form in literary English by the middle of the fourteenth century, though forms like *heo* and *hue* persisted in the South and the South-West Midlands until the mid-fifteenth century. The northern variant *sho* is recorded from the thirteenth century onwards. It is possible that both *she* and *sho* developed from OE *hēo*, but it seems more likely that they are descended from the feminine of the OE definite article, *sēo*, and a Mercian variant of this, *sīe*. By a stress-change, the falling diphthongs in these words could become rising diphthongs, leading to such forms as [sjoː] and [sjeː], and by a common kind of assimilation these could become [ʃoː] and [ʃeː]. The idea that such a stress-change was possible is supported by our word *choose*, which is descended from OE *cēosan*. The OE word would regularly lead to present-day *cheese*, and forms of this kind are found throughout the ME period, while *choose* probably resulted from a change of the diphthong *ēo* to [joː]. Whatever its origin, the form *she* probably spread so successfully because it provided a clear distinction between 'he' and 'she'.

The passage has the southern plural form *eyen* 'eyes', but also the non-southern plural *eeris* 'ears' (where Old English had *ēaran*), an example of the gradual displacement of the *-en* plural ending by *-es* spreading from the North. The form *tweye* is from the OE masculine *twēgen* (whence also our *twain*); the form *two*, which is also found in Chaucer, is from the OE feminine *twā*. In the verbs, there is an infinitive ending *-n* ('wolde han maad', 'How dorste ye seyn'). There is also a present-plural ending *-(e)n* ('Now han ye lost', 'We alle desiren'). The third-person present singular ending is regularly *-(e)th* ('any woman seith'). This inflection was normal in the South all through the Middle English period, and we regularly find forms like *he saith* or *he sayeth, he walketh*, and so on. The forms with *-(e)s* ('he says', 'he walkes', etc.) spread from the North, and were not predominant in the standard literary language until the later sixteenth century. There are no examples of continuous tenses in the passage: Chauntecleer says 'I *romed* vp and doun', where today it would be more natural to say 'I *was strolling* up and down'. Perfect tenses, on the other hand, are common in Chaucer, as in 'Now han ye lost myn herte'. The opening words of the passage, *me mette*, have been translated 'I dreamed'. Literally, however, they mean something like '(it) dreamed to me', *me* being a dative. Such impersonal constructions are not uncommon in Old and Middle English, giving expressions like *him hungreth* 'he is hungry' and *mē lyst rǣdan* 'it is pleasing to me to read' (that is, 'I like to read'). They were rare by the sixteenth century, but one survival is *methinks*, from OE *mē þync(e)þ* 'it seems to me'.

The syntax of the passage is clearly much more modern than that of the Peterborough passage. There are no examples of S-O-V word-order, and the predominant pattern is S-V, with just one example of the auxiliary preceding the subject when the clause begins with an adverb ('Now han ye lost myn herte'). Striking, however, is the complete absence from the passage of auxiliary *do*, as is normal in Chaucer. Moreover, a relative pronoun is omitted in *a beest Was lyk an hound* 'an animal which was like a dog'. The missing relative is the subject of the relative clause, and in present-day English it is impossible to omit it in such a case.

Middle Scots

The earliest substantial records of the Scots literary language date from the second half of the fourteenth century, the first really big work being John Barbour's long narrative poem *The Bruce* (c. 1375). Thereafter, however, there is a well-documented literary tradition, culminating in the poetry of Robert Henryson and William Dunbar in the late fifteenth and early sixteenth centuries. As in the South, spelling was somewhat variable, but Scots had certain distinctive spelling-conventions of its own. For example, in spellings like *ai*, *ei*, and *oi*, the *i* is inserted to show that the vowel is long, not that it is a diphthong: so the spellings *haim* 'home', *grein* 'green', and *rois* 'rose (the flower)' represented [ha:m] (later [hɛ:m]), [gre:n] (later [gri:n]), and [ro:z]. The spelling *ch* corresponded to southern *gh* (*nicht* 'night'), and *quh-* to southern *wh-* (*quhen* 'when'). In phonology, we have already seen that OE *ā* became northern [a:] (later [ɛ:]), whereas south of the Humber it became [ɔ:]: Scots *haim*, *bain*, *sair*, compared with southern *home*, *bone*, *sore*. OE *ō*, which in the South became ME [o:], in the North became the front rounded vowel [y:], spelt *u* or *ui* (as in *fud* or *fuid* 'food'). In the North, final unstressed *-e* was lost very early, and in consequence short vowels were retained in many words which in the South underwent lengthening. In the North, OE *macan* 'to make' had already lost its final *-n* in Late Old English; this gave Early Middle English *make*, and the final *-e* was lost before the lengthening of vowels in open syllables of two-syllable words, so that the word appears as northern *mak* or *mek*, with a short vowel.

Distinctive Scots grammatical features include the use of *-it* for the ending of the past tense and past participle of weak verbs (*closit* 'closed'); the use of *-and* for the present participle (*dansand* 'dancing'), where elsewhere the ending is *-ende* or *-inde*; and the use of the inflection *-is* for noun plurals (*knychtis* 'knights'), for noun genitives (*the moderis breist* 'the mother's breast'), for the third-person singular present of verbs (*he takis* 'he takes'), and for the present plural of verbs (*makaris . . . playis heir ther pageant* 'poets play here their pageant').

In vocabulary, one striking thing is the paucity of loan-words from Gaelic. There are numerous French loans, for Scotland maintained close relations with France, and also Scandinavian loans, but most of these are also found south of the border.

As an example of Middle Scots, we can look at a brief extract from Robert Henryson's 'Morall Fabillis of Esope the Phrygian', written in the second half of the fifteenth century: two stanzas from 'The Taill of Schir Chantecleir and the Foxe':

> This wylie tod, quhen that the lark couth sing,
> Full sair hungrie vnto the toun him drest,
> Qhuair Chantecleir, in to the gray dawing,
> Werie for nicht, wes flowen fra his nest.
> Lowrence this saw, and in his mynd he kest
> The ieperdies, the wayis, and the wyle,
> Be quhat menis he micht this cok begyle.
>
> Dissimuland in to countenance and cheir,
> On kneis fell, and simuland thus he said:
> 'Gude morne, my maister, gentill Chantecleir!'
> With that the cok start backwart in ane braid.
> 'Schir, be my saull, 3e neid not be effraid,
> Nor 3it for me to start nor fle abak;
> I come bot heir seruice to 3ow to mak.'

This wily fox, when the lark sang, quite bitterly hungry betook himself to the village, where Chantecleer, weary of night, had flown from his nest at the grey dawn. Lawrence [the fox] saw this, and pondered in his mind the tricks, the methods, and the stratagem, by what means he might beguile this cock. Dissimulating in countenance and manner, he fell on his knees, and feigning thus said: 'Good morning, my master, noble Chantecleer!'. At that the cock at once started backward, 'Sir, by my soul, you do not need to be afraid, nor to jump or start back because of me; I only come here to do you service.'

The auxiliary *couth*, literally 'could', is used to form the past tense, rather like later 'do': *couth sing* means 'did sing', 'sang'. The phrase *wes flowen* 'had flown' illustrates the continued use of auxiliary *be* to form the perfect tense with verbs of motion. The word *fra* 'from' is from Old Norse *frā*, the corresponding OE word being *fram*. The southern form of *fra* is *fro*, which survives in the expression 'to and fro'.

During the sixteenth century, Scots was increasingly influenced by the southern language. One reason for this was the prestige of the English poets, such as Chaucer, Gower, and Lydgate. Another was the influence of biblical translations: the Reformation was marked by a whole series of such translations in England, but not in Scotland. The Geneva Bible of 1560, with its Calvinistic marginal comments, was especially influential. By the later sixteenth century, books in the southern language were being printed in Scotland. And when in 1603 James VI of Scotland became James I of England, southern influence increased, for London became the centre from which patronage radiated, for Englishmen and Scots alike. The Scots literary language became increasingly permeated by southern forms, and by the end of the seventeenth century had practically ceased to exist. The distinguished eighteenth-century Scots thinkers and men of letters, David Hume, Adam Smith, and William Robertson, were all born in Scotland, and educated at Scottish schools and universities, but all three wrote in the southern literary language, not in Scots.

This does not mean that people in Scotland stopped speaking Scots, but simply that in writing they adopted the conventions of the South. But since the southern literary language was based on a dialect extremely different from Scots, there was quite a discrepancy for a Scot between the spoken and the written language. This, combined with Scots national feeling, led to the creation of a Scots dialect literature, which attempts in its spellings and its grammar to represent actual Scottish speech. The father of the Scots dialect movement was Allan Ramsay (1686–1758), and its most famous figure was Robert Burns (1759–96). This literary movement continues today, but having a dialect literature of this kind is not the same as having a standard literary language: when Middle Scots was a standard literary language, all written transactions (if not in Latin) were carried out in it. But since the eighteenth century this has not been so: there have been works of literature in Scots, but the history-books and the contracts and the chemistry text-books have been written in what is essentially the southern literary language, though with a few specifically Scottish variations.

8 Early Modern English

The late Middle Ages had seen the triumph of the English language over French in England, and the establishment once more of a standard form of written English. This did not mean, however, that English was now entirely without a rival: Latin still had great prestige as the language of international learning, and it was a long time before English replaced it in all fields. Under the influence of the humanists, the grammar-school syllabus was centred on classical Latin from the early sixteenth century onwards: pupils learned the Latin language, and studied Latin literature, history, and rhetoric. In the universities, Latin was the medium of instruction. Even the natural scientists, the proponents of the New Philosophy, often wrote in Latin. The philosopher of the new science, Francis Bacon, wrote his *Advancement of Learning* (1605) in English, but the book that he intended as his major contribution to scientific method, the *Novum Organum* (1620), was in Latin. And the three greatest scientific works published by Englishmen between 1600 and 1700 were all in Latin: Gilbert's book on magnetism (1600), Harvey's on the circulation of the blood (1628), and Newton's *Principia* (1689), which propounded the theory of gravitation and the laws of motion. Even in Newton's time, however, Latin was falling into disuse, and his *Opticks* (1704) was in English.

English versus Latin

In the defeat of Latin and the final establishment of English as the sole literary medium in England, a considerable part was played by the religious disputes that raged from the fifteenth to the seventeenth century. During the Reformation, people engaged in controversy wanted to be read by as large a public as possible. Many of the people attracted by Protestantism were of humble origins, and lacked a classical education; this meant that controversial books and pamphlets tended to be written in English. When Sir Thomas More wrote for the entertainment of the learned men of Europe, as in the *Utopia* (1516), he wrote in Latin, but when he was drawn into the domestic religious argument against the Reformers he wrote books and pamphlets in English. Milton, similarly, over a century later, wrote defences of the English republic which were intended for the learned men of Europe, and these were in Latin; but the bulk of his controversial prose (on episcopacy, divorce, the freedom of the press, and so on) was intended to have an immediate impact on English politics, and was written in English. The translation of the Bible into English, moreover, and the changeover from Latin to English in church services, raised the prestige of English. The more extreme Protestants, indeed, regarded Latin as a 'Popish' language, designed to keep ordinary people in ignorance and to maintain the power of priests.

Another factor in favour of English was the increase in national feeling which accompanied the rise of the modern nation-state in the fifteenth and sixteenth centuries. The medieval feeling that a person was a part of Christendom was replaced by the modern feeling that a person is English or French or Italian. This national feeling led to a greater interest and pride in the national languages, while the language of international Christendom, Latin, slowly fell into the background. Nationalism led to conscious efforts to create a vernacular literature to vie with that of Greece and Rome, and both Spenser's *Faerie Queene* (1590) and Milton's *Paradise Lost* (1667) were conscious attempts to do for English what Homer and Virgil had done for Greek and Latin.

A third factor in favour of English was the rise of social and occupational groups which had little or no Latin, but which were eager to read and to learn, and wanted books in English. Such were many of the practical men of sixteenth- and seventeenth-century England – skilled craftsmen, instrument makers, explorers, navigators, soldiers – often from the citizen or yeomen classes. A gentleman-scientist like Gilbert wrote in Latin, but there were plenty of Elizabethan treatises on practical subjects like navigational instruments, geometry, and warfare, which were written in English for the plain man, and sometimes by him. Here an important part was played by the spread of literacy and the expansion of the reading-public which followed the introduction of printing in the late fifteenth century.

On the other hand there were social groups which fought hard for the retention of Latin, because their professional monopoly depended on excluding ordinary people from the mysteries of their art; physicians appear to have been particularly bitter in their attacks on medical works published in English. This led to fierce controversy about the suitability of English for works of science and scholarship, which raged especially in the second half of the sixteenth century. This controversy was gradually won by the supporters of English, as more and more fields of study were successfully invaded by it.

But, while English was thus establishing its supremacy over Latin, it was at the same time more under its influence than at any other time in its history. The Renaissance was the period of the rediscovery of the classics in Europe. In England there was quite a revival of Greek scholarship, symbolic of which was the foundation of St Paul's School by Dean Colet in 1509. But always it was Latin that was of major importance, and we see the constant influence of Latin literature, Latin rhetorical theories, the Latin language.

Loan-words from Latin

One result of this Latin influence on English was the introduction of a large number of Latin loan-words into the language. We have already seen that the influx of French words in the Middle English period had predisposed English speakers to borrow words from abroad. In Renaissance England this predisposition was given full scope, and there was a flood of Latin loans, the peak period being between about 1580 and 1660. The introduction of loans was encouraged by the large number of translations made from Latin. When English invaded a field of discourse (for example, rhetoric, logic, geometry, classical history, warfare), the first stage usually took the form of translations of standard Latin works; in the second stage, there were original English works deeply indebted to Latin originals; and in the third stage there were entirely independent English works. In this process, there was a strong tendency for writers to invent English technical terms by adapting those of the Latin originals. It must be added, however, that there was also a 'purist' movement (another manifestation of English nationalism) which attacked the use of loan-words, and advocated the coining of new technical terms from native elements. Such a Purist was Ralph Lever, who in a textbook of logic published in 1573 invented such words as *endsay* 'conclusion', *foresays* 'premisses', *saywhat* 'definition', *witcraft* 'logic', and *yeasay* 'affirmation'. It is striking, however, that none of these coinages caught on, and that we use words derived from the Latin expressions that Lever rejected (*affirmation*, *conclusion*, etc.).

The Renaissance loans were not, of course, the first Latin words to be borrowed by English. We have already seen how words like *mint*, *street*, and *wine* were borrowed while the English were still on the continent, and words like *bishop* and *minster* during the OE period. A few Latin words were borrowed, too, into Middle English: they include religious terms, like *Gloria* and *requiem*; words from the law-courts, like *client*, *conviction*, and *memorandum*; medical and scientific words like *dissolve*, *distillation*, *equator*, and *recipe*; and numbers of abstract words, like *conflict*, *dissent*, *imaginary*, and *implication*.

These Latin loans in Old and Middle English are a mere trickle, but in Early Modern English the trickle becomes a river, and by 1600 it is a deluge. Some of the words were taken over bodily in their Latin form, with their Latin spelling, like *genius* (1513) *species* (1551), *cerebellum* (1565), *militia* (1590), *radius* (1597), *torpor* (1607) *specimen* (1610), *squalor* (1621), *apparatus* (1628), *focus* (1644), *tedium* (1662), *lens* (1693), and *antenna* (1698). Not, indeed, that they were always taken over with their original Latin meaning: in Latin, for example, *focus* meant 'hearth, fireplace' (whence French *feu*), while *lens* was the Latin for 'lentil', and was applied to pieces of optical glass because a double-convex lens is shaped like a lentil-seed.

Some of the loans, however, were adapted, and given an English form. For example, the Latin ending *-ātus* is often replaced by *-ate*, as in *desperate*. In some cases the Latin inflection is simply omitted, as in *complex* (Latin *complexus*). This reshaping is often influenced by the form of French words derived from Latin; for example, the Latin ending *-itas* sometimes becomes English *-ity* (as in *immaturity*), and Latin *-entia* and *-antia* can appear as English *-ence*, *-ency* and *-ance*, *-ancy* (as in *transcendence*, *delinquency*, *relevancy*). Indeed, it is sometimes difficult to be sure whether a word has come into English direct from Latin or via French.

These Latin loans tend to be learned words. Some are scientific words, like *equilibrium*, *momentum*, and *vacuum*. Some are mathematical, like *area*, *calculus*, *radius*, and *series*. Some are legal terms, like *affidavit*, *alias*, and *caveat*. Not surprisingly, quite a few have to do with the Liberal Arts (grammar, rhetoric, logic, philosophy, etc.) or with classical civilization. Many of the Latin loans, however, are less specialized, and belong to the general vocabulary – nouns like *relaxation* and *relegation*, adjectives like *offensive* and *relevant*, verbs like *investigate* and *imbue*. There are a few everyday words, like *album*, *circus*, and *miser*, but the vast majority are the kind of words that are introduced into a language through the medium of writing rather than in speech.

Inkhorn terms

The Elizabethan headmaster Richard Mulcaster commented in 1582 on the large number of foreign words being borrowed daily by the English language, 'either of pure necessitie in new matters, or of mere brauerie, to garnish it self withall'. This points to two different motives for the loans: a utilitarian one ('necessity'), because the language needs new words to say new things; and 'mere brauerie', which means 'sheer ostentation'. Because of the prestige of Latin, the use of Latin loan-words was taken by some people to be a sign of education or of social superiority, marking them off from the common herd. Thus arose a lunatic fringe, which used strange and pompous Latinate words out of 'mere brauerie', where perfectly good English expressions already existed. Such pompous words were called 'inkhorn terms', and were frequently ridiculed, as for example by Thomas Wilson in his influential *Arte of Rhetorique* (1553). Absurd affecters of Latinisms are also depicted in the drama, for example Holofernes in Shakespeare's *Love's Labour's Lost* and Crispinus in Ben Jonson's *Poetaster*. To the modern reader, however, some of the 'inkhorn terms' seem quite unexceptionable, having since been fully accepted. The ridiculous words used by Crispinus in *Poetaster* include nice specimens like *furibund* 'furious', *lubrical* 'smooth, slippery, wanton', *oblatrant* 'carping, reviling', and *turgidous* 'swollen, puffed up'; but they also include *defunct, reciprocal, retrograde, spurious,* and *strenuous*. In any case, the attacks on inkhorn terms were not necessarily attacks on Latin loans in general: Wilson admits that some Latin loans are acceptable, and Shakespeare may make fun of Holofernes and his pedantry, but he himself is no purist, and is a great user of new words.

The remodelling of words

Not only did Latin influence bring in new words; it also caused existing words to be reshaped in accordance with their real or supposed Latin etymology. We owe the *b* in our modern spelling of *debt* and *doubt* to Renaissance etymologizing, for the earlier spellings were *dette* and *doute*, which were their forms in Old French; the *b* was inserted through the influence of Latin *debitum* and *dubitāre*. Here the change was merely one of spelling, for the *b* has never been pronounced in English (except by Holofernes); and the same is true of the *p* inserted in *receipt* and the *c* in *indict*. But there are cases where the actual pronunciation of a word was altered under Latin influence. Thus in Middle English we find the words *assaut, aventure, descrive, parfit,* and *verdit,* which in the Renaissance were remodelled under Latin influence to *assault, adventure, describe, perfect,* and *verdict*. An odd survival of ME *aventure* is seen in the phrase 'to draw a bow at a venture' (from I *Kings* xxii.34), where *at a venture* is a misdivision of *at aventure*, meaning 'at random'.

Some of these Renaissance remodellings are based on false etymologies, thus combining pedantry with inadequate scholarship. Such is the case with *advance* and *advantage*, remodelled from ME *avance* and *avantage*. The modern forms obviously arose from the belief that the initial *a-* represented the Latin prefix *ad-*, but in fact both words derive from French *avant*, which comes from Latin *ab ante*. A similar case is the word *admiral*, a reshaping of earlier *amiral*. This word came into English from French, but the French had it from Arabic, where it occurred as the first two words of such titles as *amir al bahr* 'commander of the sea'. In this case the form with *ad-* is found already in Middle English, and conversely *ammiral* is found as late as Milton. The change in this instance may have been encouraged by the resemblance to *admirable*.

Loan-words from other languages

Although Latin was by far the main source of loan-words in the Early Modern period, a number were borrowed from other languages too. The next largest source after Latin was French; the French loans included military words (such as *bayonet*, *feint*), and words from the life-sciences (such as *anatomy*, *muscle*), but also many words from the general vocabulary (for example, *docility*, *entrance*, *invite*). There were a few words from classical Greek, though most of these came via Latin or French. They tended to be learned words, and many of them are technical terms of literary criticism, rhetoric, theology, or the natural sciences; words which were probably borrowed direct from Greek include *anathema*, *cosmos*, *larynx*, and *pathos*.

A few words were borrowed from Italian and Spanish. Part of a young gentleman's education was the grand tour of the continent, and in the sixteenth century there are frequent sarcastic references to the gallant who comes back to England affecting foreign clothes, customs, and morals, and larding his speech with foreign words. The Italian loans include words to do with warfare (*fuse*, *salvo*, *squadron*), with commerce (*argosy*, *artichoke*, *felucca*), and with the arts (*cupola*, *fresco*, *madrigal*, *opera*). Spanish loans, too, are often concerned with commerce or warfare (*anchovy*, *armada*, *cargo*, *sherry*). Since the early European exploration of America was largely carried out by the Spaniards and the Portuguese, many early words for specifically American things came into English via Spanish or Portuguese. From Spanish came *cannibal*, *cockroach*, and *potato*, and from Portuguese *flamingo* and *molasses*, while *mosquito* could have come equally well from either language. The word *cannibal* comes from the Spanish *Canibales*, a variant of *Caribales* or *Caribes*, the name of a people of the southern West Indies.

The only other sizeable source of loan-words in the period was Dutch. The Netherlands had had close commercial contacts with England ever since the Norman Conquest, and many of the words borrowed by English have to do with seafaring and trade. Middle English examples include *deck*, *firkin*, and *skipper*. Sixteenth-century loans include *cambric*, *dock*, *splice*, and *yacht*, while in the seventeenth century we find *brandy*, *cruise*, *keelhaul*, *sloop*, *smack*, and *yawl*. The Dutch were also famous for oil-painting (seventeenth-century *easel*, *sketch*) and for drinking (ME *booze*).

Word-formation

While large numbers of loan-words entered the language in the Early Modern period, especially from Latin, words nevertheless continued to be coined from existing English language-material by traditional methods of word-formation, especially affixation, compounding, and conversion. Indeed, it is probable that more words were produced in this way than were borrowed from foreign languages, though this fact was not noticed by contemporaries, who were obsessed with inkhorn terms. In fact any loan-word entering the language is soon likely to have other words derived from it by the normal native processes of word-formation. For example, in the fourteenth century the adjective *comfortable* was borrowed from French; by the end of the century the adverb *comfortably* had been derived from it, followed by the adjective *uncomfortable* (1592).

By far the commonest method of word-formation in the Early Modern period was affixation, that is, the coining of new words by the use of prefixes and suffixes. Most of the words thus formed were nouns or adjectives, though there were also some adverbs and a few verbs. The two suffixes most frequently used for forming nouns were -*ness* and -*er*, the former being added to adjectives (*bawdiness*, *briskness*) and the latter to verbs (*feeler*, *murmurer*). Adjectives were often formed by the use of -*ed* (*latticed*) or of -*y* (*batty*, *briny*). Adverbs were normally formed from adjectives with the suffix -*ly* (*bawdily*), but occasionally the ending -*wise* is found (*sporting-wise*). The usual suffix for forming verbs was -*ize* (*anathemize*). There were also many prefixes, of which by far the commonest was *un*-, which was used freely with nouns, adjectives, participles, verbs, and adverbs (*uncivility*, *unclimbable*, *unavailing*, *unclasp*, *uncircumspectly*).

A considerable number of words were formed by compounding, that is, the combination of two or more free morphemes. They are nearly all nouns, and the commonest type is Noun+Noun (*sheep-brand*, *waterdock*). There are also a fair number of the type Adjective+Noun (*Frenchwoman*, *freshman*), and of the type Verb+Object (*scrape-penny* 'miser').

The third reasonably common type of word-formation was conversion, the process by which one word is derived from another with no change of form. Three types were especially common: the formation of verbs from nouns (*to bayonet*, *to gossip*, *to invoice*); the formation of nouns from adjectives (*an ancient* 'an old man', *a brisk* 'a fop'); and the formation of nouns from verbs (*an invite*, *a laugh*).

The words formed by affixation, compounding, and conversion are often ordinary everyday words, or words to do with practical affairs like farming, fishing, and handicrafts. By contrast, as we have seen, Latin loan-words tend to be more formal and literary, and often concern specialized fields of discourse like science, medicine, religion, classical culture, and the liberal arts.

Early Modern English grammar

Speakers and writers of Early Modern English often had a choice of forms or of constructions where today we have no choice – for example, in verb-inflections, personal pronouns, relative pronouns, and the formation of negative and interrogative sentences. Some of the grammatical features of the period can be illustrated by an excerpt from Shakespeare's *Henry IV Part 1*, written in about 1597. The text is taken from the Quarto of 1598. After the robbery on Gadshill, Falstaff and Prince Hal have been performing an extempore play in their favourite tavern in Eastcheap, but are interrupted by the arrival of the sheriff:

Hostesse. O Iesu, my Lord, my Lord.

Falst. Heigh, heigh, the Deuil rides vpon a fiddle sticke: whats the matter?

Hostesse. The Sheriffe and al the watch are at the doore, they are come to search the house, shall I let them in?

Falst. Doest thou heare Hal? neuer call a true piece of golde a counterfet, thou art essentially made without seeming so.

Prince. And thou a naturall coward without instinct.

Falst. I deny your Maior, if you will deny the Sheriffe so, if not, let him enter. If I become not a Cart as well as another man, a plague on my bringing vp, I hope I shall as soone bee strangled with a halter as another.

Prince. Go hide thee behind the Arras, the rest walke vp aboue, now my masters for a true face, and good conscience.

Falst. Both which I haue had, but their date is out, and therefore ile hide me.

Enter Sheriffe and the Carrier.

Prince. Now Master Sheriffe, what is your wil with me?

Sher. First pardon me my Lord. A hue and crie hath followed certaine men vnto this house.

Prince. What men?

Sher. One of them is well known my gratious Lorde, a grosse fat man.

Car. As fat as Butter.

Prince. The man I do assure you is not here,
For I my selfe at this time haue emploid him:
And Sheriffe I will ingage my word to thee,
That I will by to morrow dinner time
Send him to answere thee or any man,
For any thing he shall be charg'd withal,
And so let me intreat you leaue the house.

Sher. I will my Lord: there are two gentlemen
Haue in this robbery lost 300 markes.

Prince. It may be so: if he haue robd these men
He shal be answerable, and so farewell.

There the present-plural of the verb has a zero inflection, as today: whereas Chaucer wrote *han* and *desiren*, Shakespeare writes 'two gentlemen *Haue* . . . lost', and this is the normal usage of the time. Occasionally, the *-en* plural ending is used in the sixteenth century as an archaism, notably in the poetry of Spenser, or to indicate rustic speech; now and then a plural *-eth* is found, especially with *hath* and *doth*; and occasionally we find the old northern *-es* plural ending, as in Shakespeare's 'my old bones *akes*' (*The Tempest*). But these are minority usages, and disappear during the seventeenth century.

In the third-person singular, the passage has *-es* ('rides'), but also the *–eth*-morpheme ('hath'). As we have seen, Chaucer regularly uses *-eth*, but during the sixteenth century this is increasingly displaced in the standard language by *-es*, which is the normal form in speech by the end of the century. The *-eth* forms continued to appear in writing, however, especially in formal styles, and of course are found in poetry right up to the twentieth century, long after they had disappeared from speech. Some *-eth* forms persisted longer than others: the contracted forms *doth*, *hath*, and *saith* are common throughout the seventeenth century, and so are words like *judgeth*, *passeth*, and *teacheth*, in which the *-es* ending would constitute a syllable.

However, the passage also contains the third-person singular form *haue* ('if he haue robd these men'), with the base-form of the verb and no inflection. This is an example of the subjunctive. In Early Modern English, the subjunctive is found in the second- and third-person singular present, for example, *he go*, *thou go*, alongside the non-subjunctive forms, *he goes*, *thou goest/goes*. The verb *to be* has more subjunctive forms, such as *I be*, *thou were*, *it were*. The subjunctive is used to signal doubt, hypothesis, or uncertainty, and so is common after such conjunctions as *if* and *though*. There are a few vestiges of the subjunctive today ('if it be so', 'if he were here'), but they sound somewhat literary and formal. By contrast, the use of the subjunctive in Early Modern English was normal even in colloquial styles.

For noun-plurals, the passage uses the *-es*-morpheme (*masters*, *markes*), but also the mutated plural *men*. The *-es* plural was the normal one in Shakespeare's time, and moreover had by then developed the three allomorphs /-s/, /-z/, and /-ɪz/ (or /-əz/), which were distributed as today (as in *cats*, *dogs*, *horses*). In Early

Middle English, the ending was /-əs/, but a series of sound changes in Late Middle English, and a process of grammatical regulation in the 15th and 16th centuries, led to the modern situation.

The adjectives in the passage are invariable, as today, and so is the definite article *the*. In Shakespeare's time, too, the demonstratives *this*/*these* and *that*/*those* were used as today, but alongside them was a demonstrative *yon*, or *yond(er)*, of obscure origin. When used in the basic local sense, *this* implies 'near the speaker', *that* implies 'remote from the speaker', and *yon* implies 'remote from both speaker and hearer'. Moreover, *yon* carries the additional implication 'visible, in sight', and so almost invariably accompanies (or replaces) a pointing gesture, as when, in the first scene of *Hamlet*, Barnardo says 'When yond same Starre that's Westward from the Pole . . .'.

The passage uses the forms *they*, *them*, and *their*, as against Chaucer's *they, hem, hire*. The weak form *'em* is however quite common in the drama. The form *you* is used for both nominative and accusative ('if you wil deny', 'let me intreat you'). By Shakespeare's time, *you* was the normal form, and the original nominative *ye* was a less common variant; both of them could be either nominative or accusative. Alongside *you*, however, the passage also has *thou*. In the plural, only *you* could be used, but in the singular there was a choice between *you* and *thou*. The difference between them was somewhat like the present-day difference between addressing somebody by their first name, 'John', 'Mary' (= 'thou'), and addressing them by their title and surname, 'Mr Jones', 'Mrs Smith' (= 'you'). Children and animals were addressed as *thou*; so were people of a decidedly lower social class, but in this case the higher-class speaker might fluctuate between *thou* and *you*, sometimes being more patronizing, sometimes more complaisant; for the lower-class speaker, however, *you* was compulsory, for it was insulting to say *thou* to somebody of decidedly higher rank. People of the lower classes normally used *thou* to one another. Among the 'polite' classes, *thou* was the emotionally-charged form: it could be used to express intimacy and affection, but also to express anger and contempt. In the scene from which the passage is taken (II.iv), the Prince is addressed as *you* by everybody except Falstaff, and it will be noticed that Falstaff calls him 'Hal', whereas everybody else says 'my Lord': Falstaff is presuming on his intimacy with the Prince. The Prince himself is entitled to say *thou* to anybody else in the scene, because of his rank, but sometimes changes to the politer *you*. It was also normal to use *thou* when addressing the deity, or abstractions, or material objects. During the seventeenth century, *you* gradually supplanted *thou* in the speech of the gentry and the citizenry, and by the end of the century was the normal form; *thou*, however, continued to be used in the literary language, especially in poetry. The lower classes, too, continued to use *thou*, and it survives in some modern dialects in northern and western England.

An innovation of the Early Modern period was the pronoun-determiner *its*. The traditional possessive form of *it* was *his*, and not until the end of the sixteenth century do we encounter *its*. It is very rare in Shakespeare, occurring only in works published late; and it does not occur at all in the King James Bible of 1611, which invariably uses *his*, as in 'if the salt haue lost his sauour, wherewith shall it be salted' (Matthew V.13). But *its* spread very rapidly, and was in common use by the 1620s, presumably because people found it inconvenient to have the same form *his* for the possessive of both *he* and *it*.

In the passage, Falstaff says 'ile hide me', where we say 'I'll hide myself': for the reflexive use, Early Modern English used the ordinary pronouns, not forms with *-self*; these were reserved for the intensive or emphatic use, as in the Prince's 'I my selfe . . haue emploid him'. There are no relative pronouns in the passage, but there is one place where today we should insert one: 'there are two gentlemen [who] Haue in this robbery lost 300 markes'. This is another example like the one in the Chaucer passage, with the zero-relative in subject position. The common relative pronouns in Shakespeare's time were *who*, *which*, and *that*, but their use was not yet restricted as it is today. *Which* was freely used with personal antecedents, as in 'The Mistris which I serue' (*The Tempest*). More rarely, *who* could be used with non-personal antecedents: 'her lips, Who . . . Still blush' (*Romeo and Juliet*). Today, *that* is used almost exclusively in defining relative clauses; in Early Modern English it is commonly used in such clauses, but not infrequently appears in non-defining ones: in Bacon's *Advancement of Learning*, there are examples like the following: 'Midas, that being chosen judge between Apollo . . . and Pan, . . . judged for plenty'. In the course of the seventeenth century, relative *that* became increasingly confined to defining clauses, while relative *who* and relative *which* became increasingly restricted to personal and non-personal antecedents respectively. The present-day position is reached by the end of the century.

The passage contains several examples of the perfect tense formed with *have*, like 'if he haue robd these men'. There is, however, one example of the perfect formed with *be*: 'they are come to search the house'. Perfects with *be* are common with verbs of motion (*come, enter, run*, etc.) and verbs denoting change of state (*become, grow, turn*, etc.). Even with such verbs, however, we also find perfects with *have*, as in *I haue gone ('walked') all night* (Shakespeare, *Cymbeline*). There is a difference between the two types: in perfects with *have*, the concern of the sentence is with the action of the verb as a continuing process; in perfects with *be*, the concern is rather with the situation that has arisen as a result of the action of the verb.

The passage contains no examples of Verb-Subject word-order, only Subject-Verb. In fact V-S order, including V-S-O, was not uncommon in the sixteenth century, especially in sentences which began with such adverbs as *now, so, then, there* and *thus*: in Tyndale's translation of the New Testament (1534) we read 'For so persecuted they the Prophetes'. V-S word-order declined sharply in frequency during the seventeenth century, although it has never completely disappeared.

The dummy auxiliary

The passage differs from present-day usage in one way which is more important than it may appear. Falstaff says 'If I become not', where we should use the auxiliary *do* and say 'If I do not become'. On the other hand, Hal uses an auxiliary *do* where we should omit it: 'I do assure you'. Here *do* is not emphatic, and 'I do assure' is merely a stylistic variant of 'I assure'. The use of *do* was in fact optional: Shakespeare could equally well say 'I know' or 'I do know', 'I know not' or 'I do not know', 'Know you?' or 'Do you know?'. So auxiliary *do* was used in Early Modern English, but its use was not restricted as it is today.

In present-day English, auxiliary *do* is used in much the same way as the other auxiliaries (*be, have, can, could, will*, etc.). They have four key uses: (1) They are used immediately before *not* (or its weak variants *n't* and *'t*) when a sentence is made negative: 'He may not come', 'I can't remember', 'They wouldn't know', 'He isn't coming'; (2) They are used before the subject of a sentence to form questions: 'May John come?', 'Can you remember?', 'Would they know?', 'Is he coming?'. The use of this construction keeps the subject of the sentence in front of the lexical verb, thus preserving an important feature of Modern English word-order; (3) They are used in echo-repetitions: 'John will come, won't he?', 'You can't remember, can you?', 'He isn't coming, is he?'; (4) When stressed, they are used to assert emphatically the truth of the sentence as a whole: 'John *will* come', 'They *wouldn't* know', 'He *is* coming'. This gives a different effect from stressing any other word in the sentence, which produces only a partial contrast. If I say '*John* will come', I mean 'John and not somebody else'; if I say 'John will *come*', I mean 'come but not do something else'; but if I say 'John *will* come' I am underlining my belief in the truth of the whole sentence.

These four ways of using auxiliaries are a central feature of the syntax of present-day English. In the passages of Middle English that we have looked at, we have seen negative sentences of the form 'I ween there ne beeth in all the world countries none that ne holdeth to their own speech' and 'Ne never were martyrs so tortured'. These typical ME methods of negating sentences are no longer possible – we have to use an auxiliary followed by *not*.

The importance of auxiliary *do* in our present-day scheme is that it is the *dummy* auxiliary: it performs the four main functions of an auxiliary, but is empty of meaning. So we use it when we want to ask a question, or negate a sentence, or have an echo-repetition, or achieve sentence-emphasis, but when none of the other auxiliaries has an appropriate meaning: 'Do you know him?', 'We didn't go', 'She likes Mozart, doesn't she?', 'But John *does* live here'. Notice, however, that questions in which the subject of the sentence is an interrogative word like *who* or *what* (so called '*wh*-questions') do not need auxiliary *do*: 'Who lives there?', 'What gave you that idea'. It is significant that, in *wh*-questions, normal S-V word-order is preserved.

The widespread use of *do* as a dummy auxiliary dates from Early Modern times, but the present-day restriction in its use had not been reached in Shakespeare's time. Its origins are disputed, but one plausible theory is that it arose from causative *do*. The use of *do* as an auxiliary of some kind goes back to Old English (although there it is mainly found in close translations from the Latin) and is not uncommon in Middle English. Originally, however, it was not a dummy auxiliary, but had a *causative* sense. Thus we find ME sentences with the structure *He did them build a castle*, which meant 'He caused them to build a castle'. In the South-Western dialects there was a variant of this construction, with nothing corresponding to *them*, as in *a kastelle he did reyse*, meaning 'he caused a castle to be built' (it is in fact a translation of the French *Chastel fet lever*). But sentences of this second type are potentially equivocal. If we say 'He built a castle' there is already a causative element in the meaning of *built*, since we do not necessarily mean that he built it with his own hands. So ME sentences like *He did build a castle* could be identical in meaning with ones like *He built a castle*. Speakers would thus equate *did build* with *built*, and it is only a small step for this equation to be transferred to non-causative contexts. At that point *did* becomes semantically empty, and 'He did build' is merely a stylistic variant of 'He built'.

The development of this non-causative use of *do* took place in the South-Western dialects in the late thirteenth century, and spread from there. At first it was mainly used in poetry, because it was a convenient device for putting a verb into rhyme-position at the end of a line. For example, a fifteenth-century author, in the poem *London Lyckpeny*, writes the line 'Then I hyed me into Est-Chepe', which he rhymes with 'heape'; but elsewhere in the same poem he has the line 'Then vnto London I did me hye', which he rhymes with 'crye'. Here the choice of *hyed* or *did hye* is clearly just a matter of metrical and rhyming convenience. From verse the usage spread to prose, where it is first found about 1400. It spread slowly in the fifteenth century, and rapidly in the sixteenth, and at the same time the old causative use of *do* died out, its place being taken by *make* and *cause*. So, by the sixteenth century, *do* is commonly used as a semantically empty auxiliary, simply as a stylistic variant. The restriction in its use takes place during the seventeenth century: *do* gradually drops out of affirmative declarative sentences (except for the emphatic use), and comes to be used more and more regularly in negative and interrogative ones. The present-day situation is reached by about 1700.

In the fifteenth and earlier sixteenth centuries, the use of auxiliary *do*, in whatever kind of sentence, tends to be the mark of a rather literary style. But from the later sixteenth century onwards, when the process of restriction is under way, it is the non-modern use of *do* which is rather literary, while the modern restricted use is more colloquial: 'I wish' and 'Do you wish?' are more colloquial than 'I do wish' and 'Wish you?'. Different verbs, however, varied in their resistance to the process of restriction, and even in the late seventeenth century it is common to find such expressions as 'I know not', 'if I mistake not', 'Say you so?', and 'What think you?'.

Changes in pronunciation

In pronunciation, great changes took place in the fifteenth and sixteenth centuries, so that Shakespeare's pronunciation differed considerably from Chaucer's, but differed only in small ways from ours. The biggest changes were in the vowel-system, and the main series of changes is often called the Great Vowel Shift. This was a change in the quality of all the long vowels, which began early in the fifteenth century and was not fully completed until late in the seventeenth. The essentials of the Great Vowel Shift are shown in Figure 11. The arrows show the direction of change. All vowels became closer in quality, except for the two which were already as close as they could be. These two became diphthongized, and the dotted arrows show the probable change in position of the starting-point of the diphthongs in question.

The change began early in the fifteenth century with the diphthongization of the two close vowels, *ME ī* and ME *ū*. The other long vowels then moved up into the space thus made

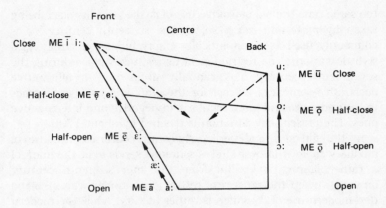

Figure 11   The Great Vowel Shift

available. ME *ū*, often spelt *ou* or *ow* (*house, how*), changed from [u:] to the diphthong [ʊu]. This diphthong gradually became wider, and in Shakespeare's time it was probably [əu], starting from a central position (like the vowel of present-day *go*). During the seventeenth century it reached its present-day quality of [ɑʊ].

When ME *ū* had been diphthongized, ME *ǭ*, used in words like *food*, took its place, moving from [o:] to [u:], where it remained. This had happened by 1500. During the sixteenth and seventeenth centuries, ME *ǫ*, used in words like *boat* and *hope*, moved from [ɔ:] to [o:]. In about 1800, this developed in South-Eastern England into the diphthong [oʊ], which in the early twentieth century became [əʊ].

A similar development occurred with the long front vowels. Early in the fifteenth century, ME *ī* (used in words like *mice* and *fly*) changed from [i:] to the diphthong [ɪi]. This diphthong gradually became wider, and in Shakespeare's time was probably [əi], starting from a central position. During the seventeenth century it became [aɪ], where it has remained. When ME *ī* had been diphthongized, ME *ē* (used in words like *green* and *field*) took its place, moving up from [e:] to [i:], where it remained. This had happened by 1500. During the sixteenth century, ME *ę̄* (used in words like *meat, conceive,* and *complete*) moved from [ɛ:] to [e:]. Throughout the Early Modern period, the vowels descended from

ME ę̄ and ME ę̄ were kept distinct: in Shakespeare's time *see* was [si:], but *sea* was [se:].

During the sixteenth century, ME ā (used in words like *dame* and *bake*) also became closer. It moved from [a:] to [æ:], and then to [ɛ:], which it reached by about 1600. It did not stop at that point, however, but continued to get closer, and in the second half of the seventeenth century it was [e:]. But at that time, ME ę̄ was also [e:], and in the later seventeenth century the two phonemes merged: there is evidence to show that, in the standard language, the same vowel was then used in *sea*, *seize*, *dame*, and *mate*. This is no longer the case today, of course, for in the present-day standard language, it is ME ę̄ and ę̄ that have coalesced, not ME ę̄ and ā: we have the same vowel in *meet* and *meat*, not in *meat* and *mate*. This can be explained if we suppose that there were two different styles of speech, perhaps belonging to two different social groups, and that one of them supplanted the other as the standard form. There is evidence, in fact, that there was a non-standard variant pronunciation going right back to Middle English, in which ę̄ had changed into, or been replaced by, ę̄. In the later seventeenth century the two styles of pronunciation were in competition, and in the eighteenth century the variant pronunciation replaced the other in educated speech. It is likely that this change reflected social changes of the period: the rising middle classes were permeating the gentry, and may have brought some of their pronunciations with them. We still have a few relics of the older style of pronunciation: *break*, *great*, *steak*, and *yea*, as their spelling suggests, all had ME ę̄, and their pronunciation is presumably retained from the style of speech in which ME ę̄ became identical with ME ā. In about 1800, the [e:] from ME ā was diphthongized to the [eɪ] which we use today.

The Great Vowel Shift was asymmetrical, in that there were four long front vowels, but only three long back vowels: in Figure 11, there is nothing in the bottom right hand corner of the vowel-diagram. In fact this space became filled: during the sixteenth century, the ME diphthong *au* (used in words like *cause* and *law*) changed from [aʊ] to the long pure vowel [ɒ:] (like the vowel of present-day *dog*, but lengthened). This later followed the pattern of the Great Vowel Shift by moving closer, to [ɔ:]. Most of the other

ME diphthongs also became pure vowels during the Early Modern period. ME *ai*, in words such as *maid* and *day*, changed from late ME [ai] to early sixteenth-century [ɛi], which by the end of the century had become [ɛ:]. At this stage it merged with ME *ā*, so that in the standard language we have the same vowel in *maid* as in *made*. In some varieties of English, however, the merger did not take place, and many Welsh speakers still distinguish *made* from *maid*. The ME diphthong *ou*, used in words like *soul* and *know*, changed during the Early Modern period from [ɔu] to [ɔ:], at which point it merged with ME *ǭ*, so that we now have the same vowel in *know* as in *boat*. The ME diphthong *iu*, used in words like *new* and *use*, developed in about 1600 from [iʊ] to [ju:]. After certain consonants, however, it simply became [u:], as in *chew*, *June*, and *rude*. In either case, the [u:] merged with ME *ǭ*, so that we have the same vowel in *new*, *rude*, and *rood*. Alone among the diphthongs inherited by Early Modern English, ME *oi*, in such words as *noise* and *royal*, remained unchanged, and its present realization [ɔɪ] is probably very similar to that used by Shakespeare and indeed Chaucer.

In both Middle English and Early Modern English, there was sporadic shortening of long vowels in words of one syllable, especially those ending in a single consonant. There were often long and short variants in circulation side-by-side, one of which has since been standardized. If the shortening took place in the Early Modern period, the spelling shows us that the vowel was originally long, for our spellings, to a great extent, reflect Early Modern pronunciations. The vowels especially prone to shortening were ME *ẹ̄* and ME *ǭ*. When ME *ẹ̄* was shortened, it became [ɛ], as in *breath*, *bread*, *sweat*, *spread*. When ME *ǭ* was shortened it became [ʊ]; if the shortening took place in the sixteenth century, this [ʊ] regularly developed into [ʌ], as in *blood*, *flood*; but if the shortening took place later, the [ʊ] remained, as in *look*, *foot*.

By contrast, there was relatively little change in the short vowels. Round about 1600, ME *a* (used in *hat*, *man*) and ME *e* (used in *bed*, *men*) both became closer: the former moved from [a] to [æ], and the latter from [ɛ] to the rather closer position it has today. The older pronunciations are still heard in much regional English speech. ME *o* (used in *dog*, *fox*) became more open during the seventeenth century, moving from [ɔ] to the almost fully open position [ɒ], where it has remained. There was a more substantial change in ME *u*, which in the course of the Early Modern period split into two distinct phonemes, which have become present-day /ʌ/ (as in *cut*, *son*) and present-day /ʊ/ (as in *pull*, *wolf*). Originally, the phoneme was realized as [ʊ], but in the late sixteenth century it became unrounded in most phonetic contexts, and probably also lowered, giving some kind of [ʌ]. But in some phonetic contexts it remained [ʊ], especially when followed by /l/ or preceded by /w/, /p/, /b/, or /f/, as in *bull, bush, full, put, wolf*. At this stage [ʌ] and [ʊ] were merely contextual variants, allophones of a single phoneme, but during the seventeenth century they became independent phonemes. One way in which this happened is illustrated by the words *luck* and *look*. In *luck*, ME *u* underwent the normal change to [ʌ] in the late sixteenth century. The word *look*, as its spelling suggests, originally had a long vowel, ME ǭ, which regularly became [u:] in Early Modern English, giving the form [lu: k] (still heard in regional English speech); in the seventeenth century, vowel-shortening took place, leading to [lʊk]. But by this time the change of [ʊ] to [ʌ] had already been completed, so that the vowel of [lʊk] did not share in it. At this stage, therefore, there were two words, *luck* and *look*, which were distinguished from one another solely by the difference between /ʌ/ and /ʊ/, which must therefore constitute different phonemes.

Two new consonant phonemes, /ŋ/ and /ʒ], arose during the course of the period. It will be remembered that, in Old English and Middle English, [ŋ] was simply an allophone of the /n/ phoneme, in words like *sink* [sɪŋk] and *sing* [sɪŋg]. But round about 1600 (and earlier in some non-standard varieties of English) word-final [g] was lost after [ŋ], so that *sing* became [sɪŋ]. There were then pairs of words like *sing* and *sin*, distinguished from one another solely by the difference between /n/ and /ŋ/, which therefore constituted separate phonemes. In other positions, [ŋg] was retained, as in the word *finger*; the pronunciation of words like *singing* and *singer* is due to the influence of the base-form *sing*.

The /ʒ/ phoneme arose in the seventeenth century from the group /zj/. In the sixteenth century, *vision* was pronounced ['vɪzjən]. In the middle of the seventeenth century, the group /-zj-/

coalesced into /ʒ/, giving the pronunciation ['vɪʒən]. The group /zj/ could occur only medially, so the new phoneme was restricted to this position. Subsequently, it appeared in word-final position in loans from French, like *rouge* and *garage*.

In some positions, consonants were lost. Until about 1600, initial /k-/ was pronounced in words like *knee* and *knight*, initial /g-/ in words like *gnat*, and initial /w-/ in words like *write*. In Late Middle English or Early Modern English, /w/ was lost before some back rounded vowels (*sword, who*) and at the beginning of unstressed syllables (*answer, conquer*), though in some words it was subsequently restored under the influence of the spelling (*swoon, awkward*). In the sixteenth century, [ç] was still pronounced in words like *night*, which was [nɪçt]. But in some speech-groups, [iç] had become [i:] in late Middle English, so that the word was [ni:t], which became sixteenth-century [nəit], and by about 1600 this pronunciation displaced [nɪçt]. Similarly, [x] was still pronounced in the sixteenth century in words like *though, drought, daughter,* and *rough,* but was lost round about 1600. In some eastern dialects, the [x] did not disappear, but became [f], and some of these forms entered the standard language in the early seventeenth century, leading to the present-day pronunciation of words like *draught* and *rough.*

Table 8.1 gives a summary of the major differences of pronunciation between Middle English and Modern English, by showing the pronunciation of a number of words in Chaucer's time, in Shakespeare's time, and today. The pronunciations are those in conservative standard speech at the times in question. I do not intend to imply, of course, that the pronunciations were necessarily those of Chaucer and Shakespeare themselves.

Some of the earlier pronunciations are still heard in regional speech in Britain: for example, [gɔ:t] is heard in Yorkshire, [hu:s] in the far north of England and in Scotland, [təid] and [həus] in Wales, [ni:t] in many parts of Northern England, and [rɪŋg] in a quadrilateral area whose corners lie roughly at Sheffield, Coventry, Shrewsbury, and Preston (Lancs). Moreover, in much regional speech there is still only one phoneme descended from ME *u,* so that the same vowel is used in *put* and

Table 8.1   *Some major changes in pronunciation since late Middle English*

Chaucer	Shakespeare	Today	Modern Spelling
tiːd	təid	taɪd	tide
greːn	griːn	griːn	green
mɛːt	meːt	miːt	meat
maːk(ə)	mɛːk	meɪk	make
gɔːt	goːt	gəʊt	goat
foːd	fuːd	fuːd	food
huːs	həus	haʊs	house
kʊt	kʊt	kʌt	cut
rɪŋg	rɪŋg	rɪŋ	ring
niçt, niːt	niçt, nəit	naɪt	night
kneː	kniː	niː	knee

in *cut*, though the precise vowel used varies a good deal from place to place.

Strong and weak forms

These phonological changes of Middle English and Early Modern English apply to stressed syllables. In unstressed syllables, the changes were often different: long vowels were shortened, short vowels reduced to /ə/ or /ɪ/, and consonants lost or, in initial or final position, voiced. There are some words, however, which occur sometimes in stressed position and sometimes in unstressed position, for example personal pronouns. Such words therefore develop double forms, which are usually called strong and weak forms. This kind of development has gone on throughout the history of the language, and today there are numerous English words with such alternative forms. If you ask somebody how to pronounce the word spelt *a-n-d*, the answer (unless you have asked a professional linguist) will almost certainly be '/ænd/'. This, however, is just the strong form. More often, in normal speech, we use a weak form, /ənd/, /ən/, or even just /n/.

During the Middle English period, word-initial [h] was lost in unstressed syllables, while word-final [θ], [f], and [s] were voiced to [ð], [v], and [z], and word-initial [θ] was also voiced. The voiced initial consonants of words like *that*, *the*, and *them* go back to ME weak forms, as do the voiced final consonants of *with*, *of*, and *is*. The phonological history of such words can be complicated, however, because it is quite common for a weak form to be restressed and made into a new strong form, from which in due course a fresh weak form can develop. The OE word for 'it' was *hit*, from which arose the weak form *it*. Subsequently this has been restressed and made also into a strong form. In late ME the strong form of the word *you* was [ju:]. This would regularly develop into present-day /jɑʊ/, and indeed in the sixteenth century it is occasionally found rhyming with words like *vow*. In late Middle English, however, there was a weak form [jʊ], and in the sixteenth century this was restressed, and the vowel relengthened to [u:], giving the present-day form.

The fact that many earlier strong forms have disappeared from the language can be illustrated from rhymes. In Shakespeare's time, it is common to find rhymes like *are/spare*, *have/grave*, *is/miss*, *shall/fall*, *was/pass*, and *were/bear*. These were all exact rhymes, depending on old strong forms of *are*, *have*, *is*, *shall*, *was*, and *were*.

9 English in the scientific age

By about 1700, the main changes in pronunciation that made up the Great Vowel Shift were all completed. Third-person forms like *loveth* had disappeared from ordinary educated speech. The pronouns *thou* and *thee* and the corresponding verb-forms like *lovest* had disappeared from standard usage. Auxiliary *do* had come to be used as we use it today. And, all in all, the language differed only slightly from present-day English. This can be seen if we look at a piece of writing from the early eighteenth century. The following is an extract from one of the numbers of *The Spectator* for the year 1711. It was written by Joseph Addison, who was fond of ridiculing the Italian opera, which was then in vogue in London:

> The next Step to our Refinement, was the introducing of *Italian* Actors into our Opera; who sung their Parts in their own Language, at the same Time that our Countrymen perform'd theirs in our native Tongue. The King or Hero of the Play generally spoke in *Italian*, and his Slaves answer'd him in *English*: the Lover frequently made his Court, and gain'd the Heart of his Princess in a Language which she did not understand. One would have thought it very difficult to have carry'd on Dialogues after this Manner, without an Interpreter between the Persons that convers'd together; but this was the State of the *English* Stage for about three Years.
>
> At length the Audience grew tir'd of understanding Half the Opera, and therefore to ease themselves intirely of the Fatigue of Thinking, have so order'd it at Present that the whole Opera is perform'd in an unknown Tongue. We no longer understand the Language of our own Stage; insomuch that I have often been afraid, when I have seen our *Italian* Performers chattering in the Vehemence of Action, that they

have been calling us Names, and abusing us among themselves; but I hope, since we do put such an entire Confidence in them, they will not talk against us before our Faces, though they may do it with the same Safety as if it were behind our Backs. In the mean Time I cannot forbear thinking how naturally an Historian, who writes Two or Three hundred Years hence, and does not know the Taste of his wise Forefathers, will make the following Reflection, *In the Beginning of the Eighteenth Century, the* Italian *Tongue was so well understood in* England, *that Opera's were acted on the publick Stage in that Language.*

If we feel that that piece of writing is very typical of its age, this is largely a matter of tone and style and outlook; there is very little in morphology, syntax, or vocabulary that would not be acceptable in present-day English. The biggest difference is perhaps that Addison writes *sung* where we use *sang*. In Old English, the strong verbs had two different stems in the past tense, as in *ic healp* 'I helped' but *we hulpon* 'we helped', and very often yet another vowel in the past participle, as in *holpen* 'helped'. During Late Middle English, the distinction between the past singular and the past plural disappeared; in some verbs, the singular form was used also for the plural, as in *I rode, we rode*; in others, the plural form was used for the singular, as in *I found, we found*; in yet other verbs, a new past tense was formed from the past participle, as in *I bore, we bore*. By 1500, the distinction between the past singular and the past plural had completely disappeared (except for *was/were*), but there was a good deal of variation in the forms used, and large numbers of new past tenses were formed from the past participle, like *bore* and *got*. By the early eighteenth century, a single past-tense form had been pretty-well standardized for each of the strong verbs. To a great extent these are the same as the ones we use, but there are small differences: there are past tenses like *sung, swum,* and *writ* ('they writ', etc.), and past participles like *arose, ran, shook,* and *spoke* ('he had spoke', etc.). Some of these forms persisted into the nineteenth century.

At one point we should perhaps write *At* rather than *In* ('In the beginning of the Eighteenth Century'), and there is one example of *do* used in an older way ('since we do put'), though this may perhaps be an example of the emphatic use.

The standardization of spelling

Addison's spelling, too, is almost identical with ours. There are minor differences, like *carry'd* and *publick*, and there are small differences in punctuation and the use of capital letters, but essentially the system of orthography is the one we use now. In Middle English and Early Modern English, there had been no standard spelling: spellings varied from writer to writer, and even within the work of one writer. Even proper names were not fixed: Shakespeare, in the three signatures on his will, uses two different spellings of his own surname (*Shakspere* and *Shakspeare*), and other variants of the time include *Shagspere, Shackespere, Shake-speare,* and *Shakespeare.* A powerful force for standardization was the introduction of printing, and by the middle of the sixteenth century, although there was still no standard system, there were quite a number of widely accepted conventions. By the end of the Early Modern period, spelling had become standardized in printed books, though there was still considerable variation in people's private writings.

However, the standard spelling-system which became established by the end of the seventeenth century was already an archaic one, and, broadly speaking, represents the pronunciation of English before the Great Vowel Shift. This explains many of the oddities of present-day English spelling. We still preserve letters in our spelling which represent sounds which long ago ceased to be pronounced, like the *k* and *gh* of *knight,* the *t* in *castle,* the *w* in *wrong.* Distinctions are made in spelling where there is no longer any distinction in pronunciation, as in *meat/meet* and *sea/see.* Conversely, new distinctions have arisen without being recognized in the spelling, so that we use the same letter to represent the vowels of *put* and *putt,* and the same *ng* spelling in *singer* and *finger.* Diphthongs, like the vowel of *mice,* are often represented by a single letter, because the phoneme was a pure vowel in Middle English, and, conversely, modern monophthongs are sometimes represented by digraphs, like the *au* of *author* or the *ou* of *cough.* Superimposed on all this are the effects of Renaissance etymologizing, which accounts for such things as the *b* in *subtle* and the *p* in *receipt.* Such things have introduced considerable inconsistencies into our spelling-system.

One result of these inconsistencies is the prevalence of **spelling-pronunciations**, which arise when a word is given a new pronunciation through the influence of its spelling. This is especially likely to happen when universal education and the wide dissemination of books and newspapers introduce people to words in printed form which they have never heard pronounced in their home environment. Thus the word *schedule* originally began with /s-/, and was commonly spelt *sedule* or *cedul*; the spelling with *sch* dates from the mid-seventeenth century, and has led to the present-day pronunciations, /ʃ-/ in Britain and /sk-/ in the United States. The word *schism* also has an unhistorical spelling: the traditional pronunciation is /sɪzm/, but in recent years the spelling-pronunciation /skɪzm/ has appeared. We have already seen that, under Latin influence, initial *h-* was introduced into the spelling of many words where no /h/ was pronounced – such words as *habit, harmony, hemisphere, herb, heritage, host, humble,* and *humour*; the spelling-pronunciations with /h-/ are not common until the nineteenth century. Spelling pronunciations are encouraged by the commonly held view that the written form of a word is the primary or 'right' one, to which the spoken word should be made to conform; this attitude was long strengthened by the predominance in upper-class English education of classical studies, centred on the written texts of two dead languages. The prestige accorded to the written forms explains the fact that even ordinary everyday words may be given spelling-pronunciations: the influence of the spelling has led, in many people's speech, to the re-introduction of the /t/ in *often* and *waistcoat*, /ð/ in *clothes*, /h/ in *forehead*, /l/ in *Ralph*, and /w/ in *towards*. These consonants had been lost in the traditional standard pronunciations, which would be better represented by such spellings as *offen, weskit, cloze, forrid, Rafe,* and *tords*. In these six words, with the exception of *forehead*, the spelling-pronunciation is now fully accepted in educated speech in England.

Standardization and codification

The standardization of spelling was just one aspect of a more general attempt to regulate the language, an attempt which was especially prominent in the second half of the eighteenth century. From the seventeenth century onwards, there was a growing feeling that English needed to be 'ruled' or 'regulated', as classical Greek and classical Latin were believed to have been. A ruled language is one in which acceptable usage is explicitly laid down, for example by grammars and dictionaries, or by the rulings of an academy. Some people believed that a properly ruled language would also be unchanging. The great classical scholar Richard Bentley observed in 1699 that every language 'is in perpetual motion and alteration', but nevertheless believed that 'it were no difficult contrivance, if the Publick had any regard to it, to make the *English* tongue immutable'. He is perhaps thinking of the possibility of an official body to fix the language, for between about 1650 and 1760 there was quite a strong movement in favour of the establishment of an English academy, on the lines of the *Académie française*. Its functions would be to 'refine' or 'correct' the English language, to lay down correct usage, and perhaps to freeze the language in the desirable state thus attained. This last ambition is delusive: no language which is being used can be prevented from changing. But it is from this period that we inherit the prescriptive attitudes towards language which have been so influential in the last couple of centuries.

Proposals for an academy came to nothing, but the seventeenth century saw the publication of the first grammars and dictionaries of English. The eighteenth century brought the first really comprehensive dictionaries of English, and an enormous number of English grammars, especially in the second half of the century. Whatever the authors of these works may have intended, the dictionaries and grammars were seized on as authorities: they were commonly regarded, not as records of usage, but as prescriptions for correct usage. Moreover, alongside them sprang up a host of handbooks of correct or 'polite' usage, which were entirely prescriptive in intent.

English dictionaries did not exist until the seventeenth century. Before then, there were two-language dictionaries (for example, English-French and Latin-English), but no dictionaries devoted to English alone. The earliest English dictionary, published in 1604, was a dictionary of 'hard words', as were all subsequent ones in that century. Because of the great vocabulary expansion in the later sixteenth century, and the prevalence of 'inkhorn terms', a need was felt for works which would explain the meaning of obscure words. The history of the dictionary in the seventeenth century is mainly one of expansion: Robert Cawdrey's dictionary of 1604 contained about 2,500 words, while that of Elisha Cole in 1676 contained about 25,000. At the same time, the dictionaries included progressively more information, such as etymology, and differences of style or acceptability (elegant words distinguished from vulgar ones, dialect words from general educated usage, archaisms from current words). Not until the eighteenth century, however, did dictionaries attempt to record the ordinary everyday words of the language, the first being *A New English Dictionary* of 1702, perhaps by John Kersey. This was followed by the outstanding dictionaries of Nathan Bailey (1721) and of Samuel Johnson (1755). Johnson's monumental work includes extensive quotations from earlier authors to illustrate word-meanings. These dictionaries helped to stabilize spellings and word-meanings, and inevitably came to be treated as authorities.

Grammars of English also date largely from the seventeenth century. In the sixteenth century, and even later, a book called a *Grammar* was normally a grammar of Latin (just as a grammar school was one where Latin was taught). A couple of short grammars of English appeared in the late sixteenth century. Five were published in the first half of the seventeenth century, and nine in the second half, while in the eighteenth century there was an absolute flood of them. These works were deeply influenced by traditional grammars of Latin. Some grammarians, like John Wallis in his *Grammatica* of 1653, argued strongly that an analysis suitable for the classical languages is not necessarily suitable for English. But in spite of this, the grammarians never escape completely from the Graeco-Latin tradition, and tend merely to re-shuffle traditional material. Moreover, many of them have a strong prescriptionist bent, and in the eighteenth century this bias is reinforced by the large number of handbooks on 'correct' or 'polite' English usage.

These prescriptive works had a quite overt class basis. They were written for the gentry, who represented perhaps ten per cent of the population, and aimed at codifying the usage of the upper classes. There are frequent references to the depraved language of common people, compared to the noble and refined expressions of the gentry. The language of tradespeople in particular comes in for condemnation, shopkeepers' cant being contrasted with the speech of persons of taste and refinement. The prescriptionists also had a regional bias: provincialisms were condemned, and the language of Scots in particular was subject to fierce attack. The exception in this matter was Noah Webster: writing in the period following the American War of Independence, he proclaimed the virtues of American English, claiming that it was the purest and least corrupt form of the language.

The advocates of 'correctness' had no clear criteria for their prescriptions, which in consequence are often confused and contradictory. Sometimes they appealed to logic, as when they condemned multiple negation: this, as we have seen, was normal in the language until the seventeenth century, leading to such sentences as Shakespeare's

I haue one heart, one bosome, and one truth,
And that no woman has, nor neuer none
Shall mistris be of it, saue I alone. (*Twelfth Night*)

The correctors objected to such constructions on the logical ground that two negatives make an affirmative, and for similar reasons they condemned double comparatives and double superlatives, like Shakespeare's 'more nearer' and 'the most vnkindest cut of all'. Another idea behind some prescriptions was that there is an ideal universal grammar, to which the language should be made to conform: originally, language had been divinely instituted, and mirrored actuality perfectly. Since the Tower of Babel, however, it had become much corrupted. In practice, the Universal Grammar to which English was to conform often turned out to be the grammar of Latin: this is seen, for example, in the arguments about the cases of personal pronouns (for example, 'It is me' or 'It is I'?). Some writers, more reasonably, argued from analogies within the language: disputed points of usage could be settled by examining parallels within English. This procedure would tend to regularize the language, but was often undermined by a common belief that large numbers of linguistic distinctions are necessary in order to represent distinctions in the real universe. This belief is behind the insistence that adverbs should be clearly distinguished from adjectives, so that for example the use of *quick* and *exceeding* as adverbs is condemned. Similarly, it was argued that the past tenses and past participles of strong verbs should be distinguished. As we have seen, this differentiation had disappeared in many verbs, and in the early eighteenth century some writers said such things as 'I have wrote' and 'he had chose'. The correctors argued for distinct past participles like *written* and *chosen*. Here, the influence of Latin probably also played a part. Sometimes, an appeal was made to etymology, especially in the matter of word-meanings: the 'correct' meaning of a word was the meaning of some earlier form (English or Latin) from which it was descended. So it was argued that *mutual* must mean 'reciprocal', not 'common', and that *demean* must signify 'behave', not 'debase'. Etymology was also invoked in some disputes about constructions, as when it was argued that 'averse from' is preferable to 'averse to'. Many of the correctors did indeed appeal to custom or usage, but this tended to be mere lip-service: the usage of early eighteenth-century classics like Pope and Addison was often attacked, and there is more than one attack on Johnson's Dictionary for including 'incorrect' usages from earlier authors among its citations.

The various eighteenth-century grammarians and correctors did not, however, always agree with one another. Because of the widely differing criteria appealed to, there were often hot disputes about points of usage. To some extent these may have been caused by the social mobility of the period, and reflect a sense of social insecurity in the disputants. The wealth of the merchant and trading classes led many of them to buy land and attempt to move into the gentry. Money and dress were no longer enough to mark off the gentry from such social aspirants, so that language became increasingly important as a social marker. For the parvenu, the crucial thing is to avoid solecisms, and it is noticeable that the handbooks of usage *pro*scribe more than they *pre*scribe: the main emphasis is on what is to be avoided rather than on what is actually to be said or written.

But even if the correctors often disagreed with one another, they passed on a substantial body of dogma to the nineteenth century, which added to it and passed it on to the twentieth. In the past couple of hundred years, language has become the subject of serious scientific study, and there are now grammars and dictionaries which aim to record and analyse usage, not to prescribe it. But even in our own age there are still handbooks which lay down the traditional rules on such matters as prepositions ('different to/from/than'?), the position in the sentence of *only*, the difference between *may* and *can* and between *shall* and *will*, the cases of pronouns ('Who did you give it to?' or 'To whom did you give it?'?), the splitting of infinitives, the 'correct' meanings of words, and so on.

The verb-system

One of the constructions attacked by some eighteenth-century 'correctors' was the type 'The house is building' (or 'abuilding') and 'The grammar is now printing'. This was condemned on the grounds that an active present participle is incorrectly used in a passive sense. One reason for the persistence of the construction was that sentences like 'The house is being built' were not yet possible. This latter construction in fact arose in the late eighteenth century, and was then itself attacked by some purists.

The reason for the unacceptability in earlier times of 'The house is being built' is that it combines the progressive with the passive. As we have seen, by late ME times there were four main markings of the verb, namely the past, the perfect, the passive, and the progressive. It gradually became possible to combine these markings in various ways in most constructions, and by the Early Modern period most combinations were possible. The sole exception was the combination of the progressive and the passive. So in Shakespeare we find such things as 'my Ladie Hero hath bin falselie accusde' (Perfect + Passive), 'The Iuy which had hid my princely Trunck' (Past + Perfect), 'I haue bin drincking all night' (Perfect + Progressive), 'As if the garment had bin made for me' (Past + Perfect + Passive), and 'both the Princes had bene breathing heere' (Past + Perfect + Progressive). But we never find constructions like 'she is being falsely accused' and 'the garment was being made'. These do not occur until the late eighteenth century.

Since the late eighteenth century, it has been possible to combine any two or three of the four markings. In theory, indeed, it is possible to combine all four, as in 'It had been being eaten': it may not be easy to think of a context where this is required, but it can hardly be argued that the construction is ungrammatical.

The progressive marking signals continuing action over a period ('John was working in the garden') or repeated action over a period ('Smith is scoring a lot of goals this season'), but also implies that the period in question is of limited duration. The fact that the duration is limited explains why we can say 'John was standing on the bank', but not *'London is standing on the Thames': the latter sentence implies that London may at any moment move to some other place, so we have instead to say 'London stands on the Thames'.

The Perfect marking signals what W.F. Twaddell calls 'current relevance': it implies that what is said bears on the immediate situation, or the situation at the time referred to. Some handbooks of English for foreign learners say that the Perfect signals completed action. That this is not so can be seen from such sentences as 'Our family have lived in this house for three hundred years, and intend to go on doing so'. Alternatively, it is sometimes said that the Perfect refers to a nearer past, and the Past tense to a remoter past. But this is also wrong: it's perfectly possible to say 'I've only been there once, about twenty years ago', and to receive the reply 'Oh, I went there this morning'.

If none of the four markings is used, and there is no modal auxiliary, we are left with what is traditionally called the Present Tense of the verb ('I go', 'he goes'). This is not a good name, however, for the so-called Present Tense can refer to the future ('I go to New York next week'), to habitual action ('I go to work every morning'), and even, in colloquial style, to the past ('This chap storms into the pub, bangs on the counter, and says . . .'). It is preferable to call it the *unmarked* form of the verb: since it has none of the four markings, and is not accompanied by a modal auxiliary, it signals nothing but the lexical meaning of the verb in question.

During the whole of the Modern English period, the Perfect and Progressive markings have become increasingly common. In Early Modern English, the unmarked form of the verb is often used in situations where we feel the need for the Perfect or the Progressive. In Shakespeare's *Richard III*, a character says 'Soft, he wakes', where we should say 'Sh! He's waking up', and in *King Lear* a character says 'You spoke not with her since?', where we should say 'You haven't spoken with her since?'.

The Modern English period has also seen a great expansion in the number of phrasal verbs (like *call up* 'telephone'), and prepositional verbs (like *call on* 'visit'). (The difference between the two types is seen if you insert a pronoun object – 'call her up' but 'call on her'.) This is part of the general movement of English from the synthetic towards the analytic. In Old English, the meanings of verbs were commonly extended by the use of prefixes; for example, from *rīdan* 'to ride' were formed *æfterrīdan* 'ride after', *berīdan* 'surround, invest, seize', *forrīdan* 'ride before, intercept', *gerīdan* 'reach or obtain by riding', *oferrīdan* 'cross on horseback, ride across', *ofrīdan* 'overtake by riding', and *oþrīdan* 'ride away'. In Modern English, by contrast, we tend to add an adverb or preposition after the verb. Large numbers of such compound verbs were formed from Late Middle English onwards, and the process still continues, so that we have numerous verbs like *build up* 'advertise', *fall for* 'be captivated by', *put off* 'postpone', *run down* 'disparage', *shrug off* 'treat with indifference', and *start up* 'set (an engine) in motion'. Intransitive verbs are similarly formed from verb-adverb combinations, for example, *butt in* 'intervene, interfere', *ice up* 'become coated with ice', *lose out* 'lose', and *push off* 'depart'. Sometimes a compound verb of this kind is followed by a preposition, and the combination may have a special meaning of its own: *face up to* 'confront', *gang up on* 'combine against', *get away with* 'do with impunity', *meet up with* 'meet, overtake, fall in with', *walk out on* 'abandon'. Another analytic construction which appears to be spreading is the use of verb plus object instead of simple verb, as in *give me a ring* 'ring me', *have a look* 'look', *take a glance at* 'glance at'.

Changes in pronunciation

Figure 12 gives a vowel diagram for the pure vowels of Standard English in about the year 1700. This assumes the style of speech in which ME ę̄ coalesced with ME ā, so that *meat* and *mate* were homophones. As we have seen, this style was supplanted in the first half of the eighteenth century by a style of speech in which ME ę̄ had instead coalesced with ME ẹ̄, so that *meat* and *meet* were homophones.

Apart from this, there have been no really major changes in pronunciation since 1700, though there have been a number of minor ones. Perhaps the most important has been the disappearance of /r/ before consonants and before a pause, at any rate in standard British English. Formerly, the /r/ was always pronounced in words like *barn* and *person* and *father*. But today, in

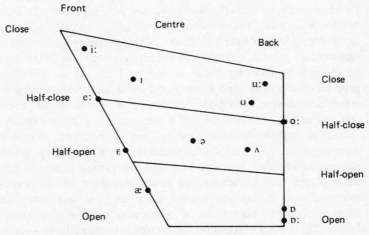

Figure 12   Vowel diagram. The pure vowels of Standard English, c. 1700. Examples: *meet* /miːt/, *bit* /bɪt/, *meat, mate* /meːt/, *bed* /bɛd/, *hat* /hæt/, *bird* /bərd/ *goose* /guːs/, *put* /pʊt/, *boat* /boːt/, *cut* /kʌt/, *cot* /kɒt/, *law* /lɒː/.

RP and indeed in most speech in England, /r/ is never pronounced in words like *barn* and *person*, and is pronounced in words like *father* only if it occurs immediately before a vowel (as in 'father and mother'). The weakening of /r/ before consonants and before a pause had begun by the sixteenth century, but the final disappearance of this /r/ in standard British speech did not take place until the middle of the eighteenth century.

This loss of final and pre-consonantal /r/ did not however take place in all varieties of English. Those varieties in which it was retained are usually called **rhotic**, while varieties in which it was lost are **non-rhotic**. Most North American speech is rhotic, except for some coastal areas in the south-eastern United States and in New England. Both Scots English and Irish English are rhotic, as is the traditional speech of the West Country in England, but Australian, New Zealand, and South African English are all non-rhotic, like RP and most other varieties within England.

Although pre-consonantal and final /r/ has been lost in RP and many other forms of English, it has left its mark on the words where it was formerly pronounced: before disappearing, it caused changes in the vowel which preceded it. In Middle English, *arm* was pronounced [arm], *birch* was [bɪrtʃ], and *here* was [he:r], whereas today they are [ɑ:m], [bɜ:tʃ], and [hɪə]. The /r/ has caused three kinds of change: lengthening, change of quality, and diphthongization. The changes mostly began in Early Modern English, but one of them goes back to ME times, and many of them were not completed until the eighteenth century.

Examples of the lengthening process are *arm*, *bark*, *card*, and *cord*, *horse*, *storm*. These originally had short [a] and [ɔ], which were lengthened in the seventeenth century. The lengthened [a:] was at first just an allophone of /æ/, but after the loss of /r/ it became an independent phoneme, and has developed into present-day /ɑ:/: there was no /ɑ:/ phoneme in Early Modern English. The lengthened [ɔ:] coalesced with the vowel of words like *cause* and *law*, which in Middle English was the diphthong [aʊ], but which became a pure vowel in the course of Early Modern English, and which has developed into the present-day /ɔ:/ phoneme.

In the sixteenth century, words like *herb*, *birth*, and *curse* not only had /r/ pronounced, but also had short vowels identical with those of *bed*, *bid*, and *puss*, their pronunciations being [ɛrb], [bɪrθ], and [kʊrs]. Under the influence of the /r/, all three vowels became [ə], the change taking place in about 1600 for [ɛr] and [ɪr], and forty or fifty years later for [ʊr]. In the later seventeenth century, therefore, the three words were pronounced [ərb], [bərθ], and [kərs]. In the eighteenth century, the [ə] was lengthened to [ə:] and the /r/ lost, giving the pronunciations [ə:b], [bə:θ] and [kə:s]. At this stage, clearly, /ə:/ had become an independent phoneme, and it has developed into the /ɜ:/ phoneme of present-day English. There was no /ɜ:/-type phoneme in Standard English before the eighteenth century. Neither the change of vowel-quality nor the lengthening took place if the /r/ was intervocalic, as can be seen in such words as *merry*, *stirrup*, and *turret*. In some non-standard forms of English, the loss of /r/ took place a good deal earlier, especially before /s/, at a time when the preceding vowel had not yet been modified under the influence of the /r/. This accounts for the words *cuss* and *bust*, which are simply variants of *curse* and *burst*.

Throughout the Modern English period, there have been numerous words with alternative forms, one from ME *er* and the other from ME *ar*. In Late Middle English, *er* became *ar* in pre-consonantal and final position, but this change did not take place in all varieties of speech, even in Standard English, and today we have some forms from one style of speech, some from the other. The outcome in present-day English is /ɜ:/ in one case, as in *certain*, *err*, *herd*, *pert*, and *servant*, but /ɑ:/ in the other, as in *clerk*, *farm*, *harvest*, *marvel*, *sergeant*, *star*. Formerly, two forms often existed side-by-side, as with *servant* and *sarvent*, but in most cases a single form has now been standardized. There are however a few doublets, such as *person* and *parson*, *university* and *varsity*, *perilous* and *parlous*.

When /r/ occurred after a long vowel or a diphthong, an [ə] glide developed between the vowel and the /r/. So *fire* developed from [faɪr] to ['faɪər], and *bower* from [baʊr] to ['baʊər]. When the /r/ was lost in the eighteenth century, the [ə] remained, giving ['faɪə] and ['baʊə]. In some cases the process produced new phonemes, namely the centring diphthongs /ɪə/, /ɛə/, /ʊə/, and /ɔə/, as in *here*, *pear*, *poor*, and *more*, though in most

people's speech the /ɔə/ has since become /ɔ:/, giving the
pronunciation /mɔ:/. After long vowels, /r/ also had a lowering
effect. In the Great Vowel Shift, ME *ā* and ME *ę̄* both moved to
closer positions, but if /r/ followed, this movement was arrested
at [ɛ:]. So *pare* and *pear*, which in the sixteenth century were
[pæ:r] and [pɛ:r], both became [pɛ:r], later [pɛə]. In the case of
[u:], a following /r/ caused lowering, and in many words
sixteenth-century [u:r] became [ɔ:r] by the end of the
seventeenth century. This has developed into present-day [ɔə]
or [ɔ:]. Examples are *coarse, course, court, door, fourth, pour,
sword,* and *whore.* In some styles of speech, however, the
lowering did not occur, and in such cases the [u:r] has developed
into present-day [ʊə], which often exists as a variant
pronunciation alongside [ɔ:], as in *gourd, moor,* and *poor.*

Two other combinative changes of the Modern English period
are worthy of mention: the rounding of vowels after /w/, and the
lengthening of vowels before voiceless fricatives. Originally, as the
spelling suggests, *swan* and *watch* had the same vowel as *ran* and
match, namely ME *a.* In the eighteenth century, the /w/ caused
rounding of the following vowel, which became [ɒ]. The change
did not take place, however, if the vowel was followed by a velar
consonant, as in *quack, quagmire, twang, wag,* and *wax,* which
regularly have present-day /æ/ (though in the case of *quagmire,* a
word not often heard in everyday speech, an analogical
pronunciation with /ɒ/ is now sometimes heard). If the group
[wa] was followed by preconsonantal or final /r/, both rounding
and lengthening took place, leading to present-day /ɔ:/, as in *war*
and *quart.* If the /r/ was intervocalic, the rounding took place but
the lengthening did not, as in *quarrel, warrant.*

Before the voiceless fricatives /f/, /s/, and /θ/, short [æ], from ME
a, became lengthened to [æ:], which later became [a:], and then
[ɑ:]. The lengthened vowel was originally just an allophone of /æ/,
but became part of the /ɑ:/ phoneme once this had arisen in words
like *barn.* The lengthening began in the seventeenth century, and
the lengthened forms became fashionable in the eighteenth.
Examples are *after, castle, bath.* The lengthening did not take place
if the voiceless fricative was immediately followed by a vowel:
compare *pass* with *passage, path* with *mathematics.* Nor did the

change take place in all styles of speech, even in Standard English, and we still have some unlengthened forms, as in *mass* and *ass*. The modern pronunciation of *ass* was probably adopted to avoid an embarrassing homophonic clash with the word *arse*, once that word had lost its pre-consonantal /r/. The lengthened vowel is still heard, however, in the expression 'Silly ass!'. In non-standard speech, the lengthening took place only in the south of England and the South Midlands, and in words like *pass* and *path* the short vowel [a] is still common in regional speech everywhere north of the Wash.

A similar lengthening before voiceless fricatives affected [ɔ], from ME *o*, as in *often, cross, cloth*. The pronunciation of such words with /ɔ:/ was fashionable in the nineteenth century, but the short vowel is now normal, and the other pronunciation sounds old-fashioned.

Another pronunciation which has been the subject of fashion is that of final unstressed *-ing*. In Early Modern English, the normal development was from [-ɪŋg] to [-ɪŋ]. There was, however, a variant style in which it became [-ɪn]. This was not standard usage in Early Modern English, but became fashionable in the eighteenth century, and persisted until the twentieth. In RP, [-ɪn] is now old-fashioned, and [-ɪŋ] normal, but [-ɪn] and [-ən] are common in regional speech.

The influence of scientific writing

The seventeenth century saw the triumph of the scientific outlook in England, and the sciences have had a pervasive influence on the language and the way it has been used in the past three hundred years. As we have seen, Latin gave way to English as the language of science and scholarship. The rise of scientific writing in English helped to establish a simple referential kind of prose as the central kind in Modern English. Other kinds of prose continued to exist, as readers of Carlyle, Ruskin, or Virginia Woolf will be well aware, but a rhetorical or poetical style ceased to be the norm, and what we may call *the plain style* became central, the background against which other kinds of prose were read. The plain style is not of course confined to science, but is found in all kinds of expository writing – history, philosophy, literary criticism, and so on. Nor, unfortunately, do all scientists write in a plain style. But scientific writing, and the scientific attitude in general, played a part in the establishment of this style.

In the later seventeenth century, the influence of science on the way language was used was quite conscious. In 1667 Thomas Sprat wrote a history of the Royal Society, the first scientific society in England and still the most famous. In this book he attacked rhetorical and figurative language, which he said the members of the Royal Society had rejected:

> They have therefore been most rigorous in putting in execution, the only Remedy, that can be found for this *extravagance*: and that has been, a constant Resolution, to reject all the amplifications, digressions, and swellings of style: to return back to the primitive purity, and shortness, when men delivered so many *things*, almost in an equal number of *words*. They have exacted from all their members, a close, naked, natural way of speaking; positive expressions; clear senses; a native easiness; bringing all things as near the Mathematical plainness, as they can: and preferring the language of Artizans, Countrymen, and Merchants, before that of Wits, or Scholars.

Sprat's primitive purity and shortness is a myth: the kind of style he is describing is a highly sophisticated achievement, and not at all primitive. But the passage shows clearly that the scientists had their own ideas about the way language should be used. There is also an interesting contrast with the 'refiners' and 'correctors' of the language, who quite decidedly preferred the language of wits and scholars to that of artisans, countrymen, and merchants.

The scientific vocabulary

The more obvious influence of science on the language, however, has been in the expansion of the scientific vocabulary. Scientists have needed technical terms for an enormous number of things, and it has been estimated that the technical vocabulary of the natural sciences now runs into several *millions* of items. Nobody, obviously, can know more than a small fraction of this vocabulary: most of it must belong to narrowly specialist fields. But there is a considerable scientific vocabulary which is more widely known, and some of the very common words are familiar to the person in the street (like *atom, cell, molecule, nucleus, volt*).

In forming this enormous vocabulary, scientists have drawn on various sources. One device is to take a word already in everyday use and give it a special scientific meaning, which is what the chemists have done with *salt*, the botanists with *fruit* and *pollen* (originally 'fine flour'), the zoologists with *parasite*, the metallurgists with *fatigue*, and the physicists with *current, force, gravity, power, resistance*, and *work*. Another way is to take over words bodily from another language. From Latin have come such words as *abdomen, bacillus, corolla, cortex, equilibrium, formula, genus, quantum, saliva, stamen, tibia*, and *vertebra*. Some words have been lifted from Greek, like *cotyledon, ion, iris, larynx, pyrites*, and *thorax*, but many of these may have come into the language via Latin. A few words have been taken from German, especially in the fields of chemistry and mineralogy, such as *cobalt, paraffin*, and *quartz*. And a few words are derived from the names of modern European scientists, including *amp(ère)* and *coulomb* (French), *gauss* and *ohm* (German), *ångström* (Swedish), and *fermi* and *volt* (Italian). These are all the names of scientific units, and the *farad*, the *kelvin*, and the *watt* are similarly named in honour of Michael Faraday (an Englishman), of William Thomson, Lord Kelvin (born Belfast, educated Glasgow), and of James Watt (a Scot).

But an extremely common way of providing new scientific words is to invent them, using Greek and Latin material. From Greek, for example, are *allelomorph, anode, barometer, cathode, electrolysis, electron, monozygotic, synchrotron*, and *zoology*. From Latin elements are formed such words as *accumulator, atmosphere, habitat, hibernate, invertebrate*, and *transducer*. Some Greek elements have come via Modern Latin, and many scientific words contain both Greek and Latin morphemes, for example *biosphere, haemoglobin, microspecies*. Latin elements are often influenced by the corresponding ones derived from French, as when, in the nineteenth century, the chemical term *valency* was formed from Latin *valentia*. Indeed, in some cases it is difficult to say whether a word is from Latin or from French, as with *epilepsy, tendon, tonsil*. Moreover, such words tend to be international, and are often coined in one language and then spread to others: *chlorophyll* came into English from French in the early nineteenth century, and *vitamin* from German in the early twentieth. The former word is the name of the substance in plants which gives them their green colour, and is made up from the Greek words *chlōrós* 'light green' and *phyllon* 'leaf'. The latter (from German *Vitamine*), was formed from the Latin *vīta* 'life' and the suffix *-amine*, which is itself derived from *ammonia* (Modern Latin) and *-ine* or *-īnus* (French or Latin).

The number of such scientific words formed from classical elements is now enormous. It is sometimes argued that they have the disadvantage of being opaque, that is, that their meaning is not self-evident to a native English speaker. On the other hand, they have the advantage of being intelligible internationally. Moreover, in any specialist field, the research-workers presumably get to know the meanings of the classical elements commonly used there, so that the words are not opaque to them. Indeed, there are Greek elements that are now so commonly used in forming words that their English meaning is understood by most educated people, even if they know no Greek. Such for example are *bio* 'life', *crypto* 'hidden, secret', *graph* 'writing, drawing', *hydro* 'water', *hyper* 'over, above measure', *hypo* 'under', *macro* 'large', *mega* 'large, a million', *micro* 'small, microscopic, one millionth', *mono* 'single', *morph* 'shape, form', *phono* 'voice, sound', *photo* 'light', *pyro* 'fire', *tele* 'distant', and *thermo* 'heat, hot'. Indeed, many of these are used as affixes for forming non-scientific English words, and can be considered an active part of our processes of everyday word-formation.

The great expansion of the scientific vocabulary during the past three hundred years has gone on at an ever-increasing pace. The sixteenth century was especially notable for advances in anatomy, and the great Belgian anatomist Andreas Vesalius had a profound effect on the Elizabethan imagination. From this period, therefore, come many words to do with the human body, like *abdomen*, *skeleton*, *tendon*, and *tibia*, and also a number of names of diseases, like *catarrh*, *epilepsy*, *mumps*, and *smallpox*. In the seventeenth century, too, the new scientific words were predominantly medical and biological (like *lumbago*, *pneumonia*, *tonsil*, *vertebra*), but there were also quite a few new words in chemistry (including *acid*), in physics (including *atmosphere*, *equilibrium*, and *gravity*), and in mathematics (including *logarithm*, *ratio*, and *series*).

In the eighteenth century came an enormous expansion in the vocabulary of the life-sciences, for this was the great age of biological description and classification, as seen in the work of Linnaeus. From this period, therefore, stem many of the descriptive terms of botany and zoology, like *albino*, *anther*, *coleoptera*, *dicotyledon*, *fauna*, *habitat*, *ovate*, and *pinnate*. The great changes in chemical theory in the late eighteenth century also produced many new words, including *hydrogen*, *molecule*, *nitrogen*, and *oxygen*. A major part in the foundation of modern chemistry was played by French scientists, especially Lavoisier, and this is reflected in the fact that these four words all came into English from French. In the nineteenth century, the expansion of the vocabulary became explosive. Many specialized fields were developing rapidly, and most of the new words have never had any circulation outside their own narrow sphere. A few, however, have come into common use, since for one reason or another they impinge on everyday life, so that we all know such words as *accumulator*, *aspidistra*, *cereal*, *conifer*, *hibernate*, *isobar*, *metabolism*, *ozone*, and *pasteurize*.

In our own century the flow has continued, especially in the newer fields like genetics and nuclear physics. Once again, some of the words have got into the language of the non-specialist. Nuclear physics has had a profound effect both in changing our conceptions of the universe and in confronting us with terrifying problems of war and human survival, and most people are familiar with such expressions as *isotope*, *neutron*, and *nuclear reactor*. The word *isotope* also has medical associations, because of the use of radioactive isotopes in some therapies, and other words that bear closely on our health have also obtained a wide circulation, for example *antibiotics*, *penicillin*, *vitamin*. Concern about the environment has led to the wide diffusion of such terms as *biodegradable*, *biosphere*, *ecosphere*, and *the ozone layer*, while other words have obtained general currency because they are connected with widely-used products of technology: *stratosphere* and *supersonic* are commonly linked with airliners, while *nylon* and *transistors* are used in popular consumer goods.

The expansion of the general vocabulary

The expansion of the English vocabulary in the past three hundred years has not been confined to scientific words. As a community changes, there is a constant demand for new words – to express new concepts or new attitudes, to denote new objects or new institutions. In recent centuries our society has become increasingly complex, and the growth of our vocabulary correspondingly great, with many new words in the fields of finance, politics, the arts, fashion, and much else.

In contrast to the Middle English and Early Modern English periods, when enormous numbers of French and Latin loan-words came into the language, the Later Modern period has borrowed relatively few words from other languages, but there has been a trickle of them. Because of the growth of world trade, and Britain's large part in it, we have borrowed words from many distant countries, such as *budgerigar* from Australia, *(tea-)caddy* from Malaya, *ketchup* from China, *raffia* from Madagascar, and *taboo* from Polynesia. In view of the long British occupation of the Indian sub-continent, it is not surprising that a substantial number of words have been borrowed from Indian languages, especially from Hindi, though also from Dravidian languages (*curry*, for example, being a sixteenth-century loan from Tamil). Examples of Indian loans from the Later Modern period include *bangle, cashmere, chutney, dinghy, jungle, pyjamas,* and *shampoo*.

Nearer home, we have continued to borrow words from French, especially ones connected with the arts (*connoisseur, critique, pointillism*), with clothes and fashion (*couture, rouge, suede*), with social life (*élite, etiquette, parvenu*), and more recently with motoring and aviation (*chauffeur, fuselage, garage, hangar, nacelle*). From the Dutch we have taken a few more trading and nautical terms (*gin, taffrail*), from the Italians more words from the arts (*castrato, diva, fiasco, replica, scenario, studio*), and from the Germans a few wartime words (*blitz, ersatz, strafe*). From other languages we borrow words occasionally when there is some special reason, as with Afrikaans *apartheid,* Japanese *kamikaze,* Swedish *moped,* and Russian *sputnik*.

The main ways of expanding the general vocabulary in the Later Modern period have, however, been affixation, compounding, and conversion. As in earlier periods, the prefix *un-* has been widely used, as in *unforgiving, unfunny, unfranked,* and *ungag.* The prefix *de-* has been used especially for forming new verbs, like *decarbonize, decontrol,* and *denationalize,* and can also replace another prefix, as when *demote* is coined as the opposite of *promote.* Other active prefixes include *anti-, dis-, inter-, mis-, non-, pre-, pro-,* and *self-.* A common suffix is *-ize,* which is used to form verbs from adjectives (*miniaturize, privatize, tenderize*) and from nouns (*cannibalize, carbonize, vitaminize*). From these in turn can be formed new abstract nouns in *-ization* (*miniaturization,* etc.). Other active suffixes in Later Modern English include *-able, -ee, -er, -ie* or *-y, -ist, -ly,* and *-wise* (often used in American English for forming new adverbs). Most of these affixes are not of native origin: they have not come down to us from Old English, but have been taken over from Greek, Latin, or French. This is of no importance: they are now a part of the English language, and their origins are irrelevant. Indeed, many of them are so familiar to us that we can use them for making spontaneous coinages in speech or writing ('anti-Common-Market', 'pre-Stalin', 're-transcribe', and suchlike).

Compounding, the formation of new words from free morphemes, has also played a considerable part in the Later Modern period, giving us numerous words like *airmail, bandmaster, graveyard, nosedive, offside, oilcloth,* and *pigskin.* We tend to treat such combinations as single words (a) if their meaning cannot be deduced from the sum of their parts, as in words like *air-umbrella* and *offside,* or (b) if they have the stress-pattern of a single word, as with *paperback* and *redbrick.* The importance of stress, and of the accompanying intonation-pattern, can be seen if you compare *the green house* with *the greenhouse*: the former has full stress on both the adjective and the noun, whereas in the latter the compound noun has stress only on the first syllable. And similarly with *a black bird* and *a blackbird.*

There is, however, a grey area between affixation and compounding. When a compound word has become established, it may in time undergo phonetic changes, and what was originally a free morpheme may become an affix. Numerous compounds have been formed with the word *man* as the second element, for example *nobleman* and *postman* from the sixteenth century. Originally, the element *-man* in these two words was probably pronounced [man], exactly like the independent word, but since it was unstressed it underwent phonetic change, and became [-mən]. In more recent times we have coined new words with this ending, such as *airman* and *frogman*, which have always been pronounced ['ɛəmən] and ['frɒgmən]. It could be argued, therefore, that the element [-mən] is now an affix, at any rate in the standard language. In some varieties of English, however, such as that heard in Northern Ireland, words like *postman* and *airman* are given two stresses, and the element *man* retains its full vowel. In such types of English, the words are compounds. In the standard language itself, indeed, some words often retain the full vowel in *-man*, for example *business-man*, a form recorded from the middle of the nineteenth century.

In some cases, the pronunciation of such an element can change so much that it is no longer recognized as identical with the original word. An example is the ending *-ly*, used to form such adjectives as *bodily*, *kingly*, and *lovely*. This goes back to an OE ending *-līc*, which was originally identical with the independent OE word *līc* 'form, shape, body', and with the same element in OE *gelīc* 'similar, equal, having the same form as'. In the unstressed form of *līc* the final consonant was lost, while in the stressed form it became [k] in the north of England and [tʃ] in the south. The southern form survives in the word *lychgate*, so called because it was the roofed gate leading into the churchyard under which the body was placed while the funeral procession awaited the arrival of the clergyman. The northern form survives in the word *like*, preposition, adjective, and noun. Phonetic change and dialect-variation have obscured for us the relationship between *-ly*, *lych*, and *like*, which were originally the same word. And in Modern English *-ly* is a suffix, not the second half of a compound word: it is an example of the way in which a suffix can develop out of a full word. Now that we no longer feel any relationship between *-ly* and *like*, we can use the latter for forming a new series of compound words. Beside the word *lively*,

222 The English language

which goes back to OE *līflīc*, we have the more recent formation *lifelike*, which consists of what are, historically speaking, exactly the same two elements.

Over a long period, the stressed element of a compound may also change in pronunciation, so that the origin of the word becomes obscured (though our conservative spellings often remind us of it). Examples are *breakfast* (break + fast), *garlic* (gore 'spear' + leek), *holiday* (holy + day), *sheriff* (shire + reeve), *tadpole* (toad + poll 'head'), and *woman* (wife + man). The first element of *garlic* is from OE *gār* 'spear', which in Middle English came to be used for anything shaped like a spear-head, such as a triangular piece of land or the front section of a woman's skirt. The word survives as the dress-making term *gore* 'a gusset'. To the modern reader, the OE compound *wīfmann* 'woman' may seem surprising. But in Old English the word *mann* was not confined to male persons, but simply meant 'a human being', irrespective of sex or age. Most of the phonetic changes which have taken place in these words consist in the shortening of a vowel, either because it was unstressed (as in the -*līc* of *garlic*), or because it occurred before a group of consonants (*tadpole*), or because it occurred in the first syllable of a three-syllable word (*holiday*). Final consonants may also be lost, and in *woman* there has been vowel-rounding under the influence of /w/, though in the plural form *women* this was obviously inhibited by the front vowel of the following syllable.

A process which has been extremely productive in the Modern English period is that of conversion, the derivation of one word from another without any change of form. The word *market*, borrowed from Norman French in the twelfth century, was originally only a noun, as when we say 'A market is held there every Saturday'. Since the seventeenth century, however, it has also been possible to use *market* as a verb, as when we say 'ICI will market this product'. This kind of change is very rare in Old English, but is easy in Modern English, because of the loss of so many of our inflections. There is nothing in the word *market*, taken in isolation, to show what grammatical class it belongs to, whereas the Latin word *mercātus* (from which it is ultimately derived) shows immediately by its ending that it is not a verb (the related Latin verb being *mercārī* 'to trade'). In Old English, similarly, the ending of a word often proclaims its grammatical status, and related words are formed by affixation rather than by conversion. Thus there is an OE noun *dōm* 'law, judgment' and a related verb *dēman* (from earlier **dōmjan*), which have become Modern English *doom* and *deem*. But since the fifteenth century there has also been a verb *to doom*, formed from the noun. Conversely, in the seventeenth century a noun *deem* was formed from the verb (as when Shakespeare's Cressida says 'what wicked deeme is this?'), though this is now obsolete. The word *black*, on the other hand, was originally only an adjective (OE *blæc*), but in Middle English came to be used also as a noun and a verb, so that today we can 'wear black', and 'black our shoes'.

The process of conversion has been highly productive in Later Modern English, and especially in the past century. Examples of verbs formed from nouns are *to audition*, *to garage*, *to headline*, *to pinpoint*, and *to service*. New compound nouns are often formed by conversion from a verb phrase: from the verb *to hand out* has been formed the noun *a handout*, and similarly with *blackout*, *build-up*, *knowhow*, *set-up*, and *walkout*. In these cases the verb phrase usually has double stress (*to hánd oút*) while the noun has single stress (*a hándout*).

Affixation, compounding, and conversion are the major sources of the great expansion of the vocabulary in the Later Modern period, but there are also a number of minor ways in which words have been acquired. One is the process of *shortening*. Most often, this is done by cutting off the end of a word, as when *cabriolet* is shortened to *cab*, and *photograph* to *photo*. Sometimes the end of a whole phrase is cut off, as when *permanent wave* is shortened to *perm*. There may be successive phases of shortening: *public house* was shortened to *public* and then to *pub*, while *taximeter cab* became *taxi-cab* and then *taxi*. Occasionally it is the beginning of the word that is cut off, as when *acute* and *omnibus* become *cute* and *bus*. Other examples of shortening include *bra* (brassière), *nylons* (nylon stockings), *plane* (aeroplane), *prefab* (prefabricated house), *telly* (television), and *van* (caravan).

A few new words are made by *blending*, that is, by combining part of one word with part of another: *brunch* (breakfast and lunch), *motel* (motor hotel), *smog* (smoke and fog), *subtopia* (suburban utopia). Such blends are sometimes called 'portmanteau words'.

Another minor source is illustrated by the word *bikini*, which is taken from the name of a Pacific atoll formerly used for atombomb tests. More often the names of people are made into common nouns. Sometimes the proper noun is combined with a suffix, as in the verb *to pasteurize* (from the name of the French scientist Louis Pasteur). Sometimes a pet-name is taken, as with *bobby* 'policeman', from the name of Sir Robert Peel (whence also came the slang word *peeler*). But often the proper name is taken over unchanged and used as a common noun, as with *cardigan*, *diesel*, *doily*, *mackintosh*, and *sandwich* (from the fourth Earl of Sandwich, who was reluctant to leave the gaming-table even to eat). An example from an earlier age is *derrick*, from the name of an early seventeenth century hangman. A few proprietary tradenames have also been made into common nouns, like *biro* (from the name of its Hungarian inventor), *primus* (stove), and *thermos* (flask).

Yet another source of words is *back-formation*. An example of this is the verb *to sidle*, which was formed in the seventeenth century from the adverb *sideling*, which meant 'sideways, obliquely'. In a sentence like 'He came sideling down the road', *sideling* could obviously be apprehended as the present participle of a (non-existent) verb *to sidle*, and as a consequence this verb was then invented. Similarly, the verb *to beg* was a ME back-formation from the noun *beggar*, which was probably derived from the Old French *begard*. In this case, the *-ar* of *beggar* has been identified with the *-er* suffix by which agent-nouns are formed from verbs (*drinker* from *to drink*, etc.), and the verb *to beg* then invented by analogy with such forms. More recent examples of back-formation are the nineteenth century verbs *to enthuse* and *to reminisce* (from *enthusiasm* and *reminiscence*), and, in our own age, the verbs *to liaise* (from *liaison*) and *to televise* (from *television*). Probably we should also count as back-formations such verbs as *to baby-sit*, *to bird-watch*, and *to mass-produce*, since they appear to be derived from the compound nouns *baby-sitter*, *bird-watcher*, and *mass production*.

Another means by which words come into the standard language is by borrowing from regional dialects or from the language of specialized groups within the speech-community. Such borrowings are called *internal loans*. An internal loan is not a new word, of course, but it is a new acquisition as far as the *general* vocabulary of the language is concerned. The Industrial Revolution, centred on Northern England and the West Midlands, brought some regional words into wider circulation. On a British railway, for example, a gradient is never a *hill*, but is often a *bank* (from northern dialect), and the extra engines used to help push a heavy train up the gradient are *banking-engines*. The word *bogie* (on railway rolling-stock) is also northern, *flange* is of obscure origin, but has probably come into the standard language from regional dialect, and *trolley* was originally a Suffolk word.

The flow of northerners, and especially Scots, to London in the past few centuries no doubt helps to explain the presence in the standard language of such Northern English or Scots words as *bard, bonny, bracken, cairn, canny, eerie, glen, kipper, rowan, scone,* and *tarn*. Some of these are not native English words, but are loans from Scandinavian (like *rowan* and *tarn*) or from Gaelic (like *bard* and *glen*), but they have entered the standard language via regional dialect, and so are internal loans as far as their immediate provenance is concerned. The adoption of Scots words has been facilitated by our knowledge of Scots literature, especially no doubt by the former popularity of Sir Walter Scott.

Words also creep into the standard language from lower-class speech and from the argot of occupational groups: *gadget* is first heard of as sailors' slang in the late nineteenth century, *scrounge* has regional dialect origins but was popularized as army slang in the two World Wars, *spiv* came from the language of race-course gangs, *square* in the sense of 'conventional, old-fashioned' has come in from jazzmen's slang, and *wangle* is first recorded as printers' slang. Such words may at first be eschewed by standard speakers, but can in time attain respectability. Many words which were once considered 'low' or 'vulgar' are now fully accepted. They include such perfectly normal words as *banter, coax, flimsy, flippant, fun, sham,* and *snob,* all of which were frowned on in the eighteenth century.

As a result of the growth of the vocabulary by all these methods, we now have an enormous number of words in English. The great *Oxford English Dictionary*, originally published in parts between 1884 and 1928, ran to ten large volumes in the edition of 1933, followed by a four-volume *Supplement* 1972–86. The second edition of 1989, which contains all the earlier material plus about five thousand new items, runs to twenty volumes. It excludes all narrowly technical words, but nevertheless contains over 290,000 entries. The number of words dealt with far exceeds this, since many entries contain, in addition to the head-word, numerous examples of compounds and phrases derived from it. Besides giving an exhaustive list of meanings, with dated examples, for each word the dictionary gives information on its modern pronunciation, its etymology, its place in the stylistic register (for example, colloquial), the field of discourse it belongs to, and the spellings recorded in different centuries. We are fortunate in having this magnificent historical dictionary of English, and it is the first work of reference to turn to when you want to know anything about the origins and history of an English word.

The loss of words

Besides acquiring new words, we have lost some of the old ones. In the passages of Old English that we have looked at, there are words that have not survived into the modern language, like *swēg* 'noise' and *werod* 'crowd, band'. There are many reasons for the loss of words. There is the obvious one that the word is no longer needed: for everyday purposes we no longer need the words for the various parts of a suit of armour (*cuisse*, *greave*, etc.), or for outdated concepts like *phlogiston* or *fee-penny*, though such expressions may survive in historical contexts. Another reason is the danger of confusion when phonetic change causes two words to become homophones. The words *queen* and *quean* 'woman, shameless woman, harlot' originally had different pronunciations: in Old English the first was *cwēn* while the second was *cwene*, and they were still distinct in Shakespeare's time, *queen* being [kwiːn] and *quean* [kweːn]. But when their pronunciations became identical, in the eighteenth century, there was an obvious danger of ambiguity, and it is not surprising that one of them has fallen out of everyday use.

Another possible reason is that phonetic change makes a word too short to be distinctive, and speakers replace it by a longer word, which gives a bigger margin of safety. This may be one of the reasons for the loss of the OE word for 'river'. This word, cognate with Latin *aqua* and Gothic *ahwa*, was Prehistoric OE **ahu*, which by normal sound laws became **eahu* and then OE *ēa*, which was monosyllabic. This would give a Modern English word **ea*, but this has not survived (except in Lancashire dialect, where it means 'canal'), and instead we use *stream* (also from Old English) or *river* (borrowed from French in the thirteenth century). On the other hand, the fact that a word is reduced to a single phoneme does not necessarily mean that it will disappear: the French word descended from Latin *aqua* is *eau* 'water', and monosyllabic Scandinavian words cognate with OE *ēa* have also survived, for example, Swedish *å* 'stream'. So, other factors must also have been at work in English, including the availability of possible replacements for *ea*, and the cultural prestige of French words.

In fact, it is often difficult to say exactly what has caused one word to die out and another to survive. The prestige of French loan-words in Middle English was not always enough to ensure the replacement of a native word by a loan. The French loans *cete* and *orguil* are recorded in Middle English, but did not succeed in replacing the words *whale* (from OE *hwæl*) and *pride* (from Late OE *prȳde*). The word *noise* presumably had advantages which enabled it to oust *swēg*, but it is difficult to pinpoint them. And, in general, the causes of the death of a word are complex, and often obscure.

Change of meaning

When scientists adopted such words as *pollen*, *salt*, and *work* as part of their specialized vocabulary, they in effect gave the words new meanings. But less conscious changes of word-meaning are going on in the language all the time, so that in later Modern English numerous words have meanings different from those of earlier times. We have already come across several examples, like sixteenth century *living* meaning 'income', fourteenth century *largely* meaning 'liberally', and OE *æcer* meaning 'field'. In these three cases, the earlier meaning has been lost, but it is quite common for new meanings to co-exist in a word with the earlier one, so that a word can in time come to have numerous meanings, a phenomenon often called **polysemy**.

An example of polysemy is the English word *horn*. Its original meaning was 'one of a pair of pointed projections on the heads of oxen, sheep, goats, etc.', but as early as the OE period it was extended to mean 'one of these used as a musical instrument'. Later, similar instruments were made of other materials, such as brass, but they were still called horns. Later still, the word became used for other kinds of noise-producing instruments, like those on motor-cars. There is little danger of confusion from the co-existence of these different meanings, because they all occur in characteristic contexts: 'She plays the horn in the local orchestra', 'He jammed on the brakes and sounded his horn', 'Let's take the bull by the horns'. And the word has more meanings yet. Besides meaning a wind-instrument, it can mean a person who plays such an instrument: 'for several years she was first horn in the Hallé'. Besides referring to the projections on the heads of mammals, it has been used since the fourteenth century for those on the heads of insects and snails, and for the tufts of feathers on the heads of birds; it is the snail usage that has given us the phrase 'to draw in your horns'. Since the sixteenth century the word has also been used as the name of the material that animals' horns are made of ('a figurine carved in horn'). And there are yet other meanings like 'drinking vessel', and the horns of a bow or of the moon or of a dilemma. Indeed, the OED entry for the word has no fewer than thirty main headings. From the brief dated quotations given for each meaning, you can get some idea of the way in which the various meanings have evolved.

The first new meaning to appear in the word *horn* was 'kind of musical instrument'. This obviously arose by a shift in the speaker's and hearer's centre of interest when the word was used – from animals and their weapons to the fact that a noise could be produced from the thing. Many changes of meaning are of this kind: a shift takes place in the focus of interest, in the aspect of the situation which is given prominence, though the precise mechanism of change can vary. A striking example is the word *bead*. The word originally meant 'prayer'. The meaning 'small pierced ball for threading on a string' arose in the fourteenth century from the medieval habit of counting one's prayers on a rosary: *to tell your beads* meant 'to count your prayers', but what an onlooker actually *saw* when people were 'telling their beads' was the movement of the small balls on the rosary. Hence the word *beads* came to be apprehended as referring to those balls, and the modern meaning arose.

Another example is the adjective *fair* (OE *fæger*). It originally meant 'fit, suitable' (the meaning of the cognate Gothic *fagrs*), but in Old English it had come to mean 'pleasant, joyous, agreeable, beautiful'. When used of conduct, it must often have been used in situations in which 'pleasant conduct' meant 'conduct free from bias, fraud, or injustice', so that *fair* came to mean 'equitable, just'. This meaning is recorded from the fourteenth century, and remains one of its chief ones. In the sense of 'beautiful', *fair* is often used of human beings, and especially women, from Old English times onwards. But for various historical reasons (including the fact that peasants got sunburnt while aristocrats didn't), the upper-class ideal of beauty in medieval and early modern England was a blonde one: hair and complexion had to be light in colour. Consequently, a beautiful woman was also a blonde one, and *fair* came to mean 'light in colour', a meaning first recorded in the mid-sixteenth century. The co-existence of the meanings 'beautiful' and 'blonde' is demonstrated by the Shakespeare sonnet (Number 127) in which he asserts paradoxically that his love is fair although she is dark. But the existence side-by-side of these two different meanings, which would obviously occur in similar contexts, offers too much possibility of ambiguity, and the meaning 'beautiful' dropped out of everyday use; since the seventeenth century the usage has been a literary one, found mainly in poetry, and today it survives only in a few consciously archaic (and often jocular) phrases like 'a fair lady' and 'the fair sex'. On the other hand, there is little danger of conflict between the meanings 'equitable' and 'blonde', because the context usually shows whether we are talking about conduct or appearance.

Somewhat similar is the way in which words denoting occupation or social rank often develop meanings referring to the moral qualities (real or supposed) of people in that station. When the word *gentle* was borrowed from French in the thirteenth century, it was used primarily to refer to social rank, and meant 'well-born, of good family'. The meanings 'courteous, generous', and later 'mild, merciful', arose because these were the qualities conventionally attributed to people of that class. Of course, we know that not all gentlemen were gentle, but the idealized picture that a ruling class has of itself may be more influential than the actual facts. The influence of the dominant social class in these matters is shown by the rather different history of the word *villain*: from meaning 'peasant', this came to mean 'scoundrel, criminal'. In this case, plainly, it is the gentleman's view of the peasant that has determined the change of meaning, not the peasant's view of himself. Other examples of words of this kind are *boor* (originally 'peasant, countryman'), *churl* (originally 'man of low rank'), and *bourgeois* (originally 'freeman of a city, citizen').

These words illustrate a common kind of change, the gaining or losing of connotations of approval or of disapproval. Words which formerly had the implication of disapproval, but have since lost it, are (with typical ME or Early Modern English meanings) *precise* 'excessively scrupulous, puritanical', *shrewd* 'malicious, hurtful, cunning', and *sophisticated* 'adulterated, lacking in naturalness'. Words which have lost former implications of approval include *artificial* 'skilfully made, artistic' and *curious* 'careful, fastidious, skilful, exquisitely made'. The group where it is particularly easy to find examples is the one where the implication of disapproval is gained. An example is *lewd* (OE *lǣwede*). This originally meant 'lay, not in holy orders, not clerical', but because the clergy had a monopoly of learning, it came in the thirteenth century to mean 'unlearned, unlettered', and hence in the fourteenth century 'typical of the lower classes, vulgar', and therefore 'ignorant, ill-mannered', and finally 'unprincipled, wicked'. The modern meaning, 'lascivious, unchaste', is a specialization of this last meaning, and is also recorded from the later fourteenth century.

Sometimes a change of meaning is triggered by the *form* of a word: one word is confused with another that it resembles in some way, or its meaning is affected by the meanings (or supposed meanings) of its constituent parts. In Early Modern English, *obnoxious* often had the meaning of its Latin original, 'liable to harm or punishment, exposed to injury'. Its modern meaning, 'offensive, objectionable', is due to the influence of the word *noxious*. A rather different kind of formal influence is illustrated by the adjective *fast*, from OE *fæst*. Today this has two main meanings: (1) 'firmly fixed' (*make a boat fast with a painter*), and (2) 'swift, rapid' (*a fast train*). The first meaning was the original one, and in Old English we find such phrases, as *fæst hūs* 'a firm house', *mid fæstum gelēafan* 'with firm faith', and *fæst innoþ* 'constipated bowels'. In the second half of the fourteenth century we suddenly find alongside this meaning the new one of 'swift, rapid', in phrases like *a fast fleeing*, with no intermediate meanings to form a bridge. The explanation is that the adjective *fast* was influenced by the related adverb *fast* (OE *fæste*, ME *faste*). Like the adjective, the adverb at first had a passive kind of meaning, 'firmly, securely'. When, however, it was used with verbs like *hold*, it could easily acquire a more active sense, 'strongly, energetically, vigorously', because in order to hold a thing securely you often have to exert effort. Next it was used with verbs like *beat*, *fight*, *strike*, in which it could only have an active meaning, 'strongly, vigorously, violently'. Among other verbs of vigorous action, it was used with *run* and *ride*. But to run strongly or vigorously usually means to run *quickly*, and in the second half of the thirteenth century the word acquired this meaning. This becomes clear round about 1300, when *faste* begins to be used with verbs not denoting motion, like *eat*, *fail*, and *sell*. Once the adverb had acquired the meaning 'rapidly', it was not long before the adjective *fast* acquired the parallel meaning 'rapid'. This is an example of analogy, for adjective-adverb pairs usually have related meanings.

There are various other kinds of meaning-change. The reference of a word may be narrowed, as when *starve* (OE *steorfan*) changed from 'die' to 'die of hunger'. Or it may be widened, which often happens when a word moves from a specialist field into the general vocabulary: in chess, *gambit* is a technical term meaning 'an opening in which White offers a pawn sacrifice', but outside chess it means simply 'opening move'. Some changes of meaning are caused by euphemism: words for things which are unpleasant or which are hedged about with taboos (death, sex, defecation) are often replaced by a euphemism, but very soon this simply becomes one of the words for the thing in question, and will need to be replaced by yet another euphemism. There is also rapid turnover of words like *awful, dismal, dreadful, horrid, monstrous,* and so on. Because of the human need to exaggerate for effect, such words rapidly lose their intensity, and have to be replaced by others. Some new meanings begin as figurative expressions: originally, a speaker referring to the *foot* of a hill or the *mouth* of a river was using a metaphor, but by constant use these have ceased to be metaphorical, and are simply two common meanings of the nouns in question. Language is full of dead metaphors of this kind, especially for abstract things, and new figurative meanings constantly arise: examples from our own time include *blanket* 'comprehensive, all-embracing', *bottleneck* (in a production-line or transport system), *ceiling* 'upper limit', *headache* 'problem', and *package*. Some changes of meaning are due to a change in world-view from one age to another: when you read medieval or renaissance texts, you have to beware of words like *choler, grace, nature, sphere,* and *vegetable,* behind which lurk whole systems of thought.

Public school English

Inside England, as we have seen, one form of the language, basically an East Midland dialect, became accepted as a literary standard in the late Middle Ages, and with this went a prestige-accent based on that of the court in Westminster. This does not mean that dialect differences disappeared in England: Standard English was the language of a small minority. Most speakers used a non-standard form of the language, and in each area there was a speech-hierarchy corresponding to the class-hierarchy, differing from Standard English not only in accent but also in grammar and vocabulary. The higher the socio-economic level of the speakers, the nearer their speech was likely to be to Standard English, though the degree of formality of the situation also influenced the level of speech used. Even among the upper classes, Standard

English was not universal: in the plays and novels of the seventeenth and eighteenth centuries we often meet country gentlemen who are represented as using a regional variety of the language. But in the last couple of centuries there has been a strong tendency for the English upper and upper-middle classes to adopt a uniform style of speech. One of the causes of this has been the influence of the great public schools, which have dominated the education of the English gentry at least since the time of Arnold of Rugby in the early Victorian age. This 'public school' English is a variant of the standard South-Eastern language, but has ceased to be a regional dialect and has become a class dialect, spoken by members of the English gentry whatever part of the country they come from. Its distinctive accent constitutes 'Received Pronunciation', and it also has a number of lexical preferences. It has had great prestige, and has been influential all over the world, though the prestige has fallen a good deal during the past half-century, even within England.

10 English as a world language

Today, when English is one of the major world-languages, it requires an effort of the imagination to realize that this is a relatively recent thing – that Shakespeare, for example, wrote for a speech-community of only a few millions, whose language was not much valued elsewhere in Europe and was unknown to the rest of the world. Shakespeare's language was pretty-well confined to England and southern Scotland, not yet having penetrated very much into Ireland or even Wales, let alone into the world beyond. In the first place, the great expansion in the number of English speakers was due to the growth of population in England itself. At the Norman Conquest, the population of England was perhaps a million and a half. During the Middle Ages it grew to perhaps four or five million, but then was held down by recurrent plagues, and was still under five million in 1600. It was approaching six million in 1700, and nine million in 1800. Then, with the Industrial Revolution in full flow, the population expanded rapidly to seventeen million in 1850, and over thirty million by 1900.

At the same time, English penetrated more and more into the rest of the British Isles at the expense of Celtic languages, though it is only during the last two centuries that it has become the main language of Wales, Ireland, and the Scottish Highlands. In 1805, William Wordsworth wrote a poem in which he listens to the singing of a 'solitary Highland Lass', and is moved to ask 'Will no one tell me what she sings?'. He cannot understand her, of course, because she is singing in Gaelic, and there is nobody at hand who is able to interpret. The spread of English was encouraged by deliberate government policy. For example, after the 1745

Jacobite rebellion, many schools were established in the Scottish Highlands, but the medium of instruction was English, Gaelic being forbidden. In Ireland, Brian Friel's play *Translations* (1980) provides a brilliant imaginative recreation of the workings of British colonial linguistic policy in a nineteenth century Irish-speaking community in County Donegal.

However, English has become a world language because of its wide diffusion *outside* the British Isles, to all continents of the world, by trade, colonization, and conquest. The process began with English settlements in North America in the seventeenth and eighteenth centuries. English settlements in the West Indies also began in the seventeenth century, in competition with Spanish, French, and Dutch colonizers. For a couple of centuries there was intermittent warfare between these four powers for domination of the Caribbean, and by the early nineteenth century Britain had firm control of a number of the islands, including Antigua, Barbados, Jamaica, St Kitts, and Trinidad and Tobago. British domination of the Indian subcontinent dates from the second half of the eighteenth century: the East India Company was founded in 1600, and British trading-posts established from the seventeenth century onwards, but it was only from the 1770s that British rule was firmly established. British settlement in Australia began slightly later, after the American War of Independence. The expansion of British influence and power continued at an even greater rate during the nineteenth century. Early in the century, the British displaced the Dutch as the dominant power in South Africa, and during the first half of the century British rule was also established in Singapore, British Guiana, New Zealand, and Hong Kong. The second half of the century was marked by 'the scramble for Africa', in which colonial powers (Belgium, Britain, France, Germany, Portugal) competed for possessions in the African continent. As a result, British rule was established in regions of West Africa (including what is now Nigeria), East Africa (including what are now Kenya and Tanzania), and Southern Africa (including what is now Zimbabwe).

In all these areas, British English has been influential, while in the Philippines and Puerto Rico, both taken by the United States from Spain at the end of the nineteenth century, the American form of English has dominated. And it is perhaps above all the great growth of population in the United States, assisted by massive immigration in the nineteenth and twentieth centuries, that has given English its present standing in the world. In 1788, when the first American census was held, there were about four million people in the United States, most of them of British origin. By 1830, the population was nearly thirteen million; by 1850 it was twenty-three million, and had overtaken that of England; and then it shot ahead – to fifty million by 1880, seventy-six million by 1900, and a hundred and fifty million by 1950. And it is surely American political and economic power, even more than the diffusion of English through the former British colonies and dominions, that accounts for the dominant position of English in the world today. For many years, the United States authorities had an explicit linguistic policy, which insisted on the primacy of the English language: immigrants who wished to obtain United States citizenship had to pass an examination in competence in the English language. A by-product of this system was Leo Rosten's comic masterpiece *The Education of Hyman Kaplan* (1937).

This world-wide expansion of English means that it is now one of the most widely spoken languages in the world, with well over four hundred million native speakers, and roughly the same number who speak it as a second language. The method of its spread, however, also means that there are now many varieties of English, and that it is used for many different purposes in varying social contexts. In North America, Australia, and New Zealand, there was dense settlement by English-language speakers, who outnumbered the original inhabitants (Amerindians, Australian Aborigines, Maoris), and also dominated them politically and economically. The native languages, consequently, had hardly any influence on the language of the settlers. In South Africa, on the other hand, the English-speaking community is small: the vast majority of the population speak a Bantu language such as Zulu or Xhosa, and even the speakers of Afrikaans (a form of Dutch) outnumber English-speakers by about three to one. In spite of this, South African English has undergone relatively little influence from the other languages of the country, presumably because of the long period of British domination and the consequent cultural prestige of English. Relatively unaltered varieties of English also survive in Zimbabwe, where English-speakers form a very small minority, and in the Falkland Islands, which are entirely English-speaking.

In Australia, New Zealand, and South Africa there is very little regional variation in the language. There are social variations: in Australia, some speakers use a 'broader' accent, that is, one that is remoter from RP, and use more local Australian words in their vocabulary, but similar variations are found all over the country. In the United States, on the other hand, there is greater dialect differentiation. The original English-speaking settlers on the East coast developed dialectal differences, and as the frontier was pushed westwards these dialects expanded too, so that there are fairly well marked dialect bands. At the same time, however, they influenced one another, and became more mixed, so that in the West the differences are less sharp than on the Atlantic coast. It is usual to recognize three main dialect areas, the Northern, the Midland, and the Southern. What is often called General American includes parts of all three dialect areas, but excludes the non-rhotic areas, that is, those where final and pre-consonantal /r/ is not pronounced (the coastal South-East, and coastal areas of New England). Canadian English is different again, though much closer to General American than to British English.

The English of the old 'White Commonwealth' and of the United States has remained relatively close to standard British English, and has been the principal language of the countries in question. Elsewhere, the linguistic situation can be extremely different. In those islands of the West Indies which were part of the British Empire, a variety of English became the first language of the population. This language was, however, much influenced by the original languages of the inhabitants, which included both West African and Indian languages. In consequence, there is often a whole spectrum of English in a West Indian country, ranging from an educated standard form which does not differ very greatly from standard British English to forms where the substrate languages have had a profound influence.

In many other areas, English has become a second language, used alongside one or more local languages for public purposes, and often for communication between different language-groups in the community. India, for example, has a population of around seven hundred million, and over two hundred different languages. English is one of the official languages, alongside Hindi and fourteen recognized regional languages, and is widely used as a language of administration and commerce. In former British colonies in sub-Saharan Africa, English usually plays a similar role, whether it is recognized as an official language or not. In Nigeria, the most populous of Black African countries, there are three main languages (Yoruba, Igbo, Hausa), and over four hundred local ones, but English is also an official language, and plays a major role in government and administration. It is also used as a language of wider communication, at any rate among the higher socio-economic groups.

A distinction is usually made between English as a second language and English as a foreign language. A German or a Norwegian learning English learns it as a foreign language: it will not be used for communicating with other Germans or Norwegians, but only with foreigners. Moreover, there is no native tradition of English-speaking in Germany or Norway, and the learner will usually be taught either standard British English or standard American English. But an Indian learns English as a second language: he will expect to use it for communication with other Indians, and will hear it used in the speech-community as a matter of course. Moreover, an Indian will most often learn a local variety of the language, taught by an Indian who speaks that variety.

The distinction between second language and foreign language is not, however, a sharp one, and there are cases, like Indonesia, where classification is disputable. Moreover, there is a considerable amount of variation in the roles played by second languages, for example in education, in the fields of discourse used, and in the giving of prestige or power. In India, the medium of instruction in the schools was changed from English to the regional languages after Independence, and subsequently there has been a gradual process of Indianization of the universities, which at one time were all English-medium. In Nigeria, primary-schools are being built which teach in the local languages, but the secondary schools and the universities are still predominantly English-medium. In Singapore there are four official languages, Chinese (Mandarin), English, Malay, and Tamil. At one time, Chinese was the principal medium of education, but, despite independence (1965), English-medium education has spread until it is now almost universal, while Chinese, Malay, and Tamil are taught as second languages.

The kind of discourse for which English is used varies a good deal. In some communities where it is a second language, including Hong Kong, Indonesia, and many African countries, it is used primarily in the public domain – in administration, business, science-education, and the media. But in some places, including India and Singapore, it is also used in the personal domain – within the family, and among friends. When Hong Kong was still a British colony, Chinese (Cantonese) and English had equal status as official languages, but their fields were sharply divided: English was used in the legal system, in English-medium education, in the upper reaches of commerce and industry, and in the media, but everyday discourse within the Chinese community was carried on in Cantonese, and the use of English for this purpose was disliked. English, it has been said, was the language of power, while Cantonese was the language of solidarity and an expression of ethnicity. In general, English was formal, while Cantonese was intimate. Now that the British have departed, and Hong Kong has been united with the Chinese mainland, English is no longer the language of power, but will probably remain an important second language, especially in view of Hong Kong's world-wide trading activities.

The various forms of English when used as a second language differ in a number of ways from standard British or American English, often because of the influence of the speakers' first language. There are, however, English-based languages which depart even more radically from the standard types, namely pidgins and creoles. A pidgin is an auxiliary language used in the first place for the purposes of trade between groups that have no common language. It thus arises when two or more languages are in contact, and is a simplified form of the dominant one, with influence from the other(s). This restricted type of pidgin may, however, be extended to cover other fields of discourse, and eventually be capable of fulfilling all language-functions. This is especially likely to happen in a multi-lingual area, where the pidgin can perform a useful function as a lingua franca. It may even become an official language: Papua New Guinea's pidgin, called Tok Pisin, is formally acknowledged in the country's constitution. Some pidgins die out because the need for them passes, but others spread and gain wide currency, and there are numerous pidgins in the world today, many of them (though not all) based on European languages, including English. There are many English-based pidgins, especially in the coastal regions of West Africa and on the coasts and islands of South-East Asia.

It sometimes happens that a pidgin becomes the first language of a group. The language is then called a *creole*. There are English-based creoles in the Caribbean, for example in Barbados and Jamaica, on the North coast of South America (Guyana, Surinam), and even in the United States: the creole called Gullah is spoken by about a quarter of a million people living along the South-Eastern coastal areas of the USA. It is possible, too, that Black English, the speech of the majority of black Americans, is descended from a creole. Creoles have also been brought to Britain since the Second World War by immigrants from the West Indies, and local varieties have developed, such as London Jamaican. Creoles probably developed in the Caribbean because of the mixing of populations caused by the slave-trade. The slavers herded together speakers of many different West African languages. At the ports of embarkation, and on the slave-ships, the captives probably communicated with one another in some kind of West African pidgin, which in the Caribbean plantations developed into creoles.

Pidgins and creoles often co-exist with standard varieties of the donor language, and the different forms are then likely to influence one another. In Jamaica, for example, an English-based creole exists alongside Jamaican Standard English, and their mutual influence during the past three centuries has led to a whole spectrum of usage, a 'post-creole continuum'. Speakers often vary their speech according to the social context and the effect they wish to have, moving towards the Standard ('acrolectal') end or towards the Creole ('basilectal') end of the continuum. There is a tendency for more educated speakers and those of higher socio-economic groups to use the standard end of the spectrum, but this is not invariably the case, since there are countervailing forces: creole expressions can be used to proclaim ethnic identity or membership of an in-group, or to suggest informality and sincerity, and are also often used for humour and in songs.

In West Africa, similarly, pidgins exist alongside West African Standard English, and switching from standard to pidgin, or inserting pidgin expressions into standard speech, can have social motivation. This code-mixing or code-switching is depicted in the novels of Chinua Achebe. In *A Man of the People* (1966), the charismatic demagogue Nanga does not normally use his first language, but speaks either English or pidgin. He uses English for formal occasions, and adjusts his accent in accordance with his hearer. He uses pidgin to address lower-class characters (a chauffeur, a cook), and when he is being jocular with his friends and colleagues, or when he wants to project his image as a 'man of the people'. Mrs Nanga, however, never speaks English, but only her local language (represented in the text by English), with a sprinkling of English words interspersed. Odili, the schoolteacher-narrator, uses all three languages: he uses pidgin to talk to a girl-friend who speaks a different local language, to address lower-class characters, and in informal conversation with friends, often jocular.

The development of so many varieties of English has produced problems and controversies about the language, especially in former British colonies which have become independent during the last half-century. During British colonial rule, Standard British English was imposed on such countries as the language of administration, and local departures from it were stigmatized as errors. With Independence, there have been disputes in many such countries as to whether English should be retained as an official language at all, and, if it is retained, whether attempts should be made to teach Standard British English or whether the local variety of English should be adopted as a standard. Various factors have played a part in these arguments – including nationalist feeling, attachment to traditional culture, desire for advances in science and technology, and the conflicting needs for local and for international communication – but there are many cross-currents. In India, after Independence, there was a movement in the Hindi-speaking North in favour of making Hindi the main official language of the country, but this was opposed by many people in the South who spoke Dravidian languages: having Hindi as the main language would give obvious economic and political advantages to northerners, and many southerners therefore favoured the retention of English. In some former ex-colonies, a mastery of English was the privilege of a dominant élite, who therefore supported its retention, while more radical and democratic forces argued for its replacement by one or more local languages. Many of the controversies, inevitably, have been fought out in the field of educational policy. They still go on, but there seems, at the moment, to be a trend in many countries towards continuing to accept English as an official or semi-official language, while recognizing the local variety of English as a standard. Interestingly, some of the most compelling literature in the English language during the last fifty years has come from ex-colonial areas where these arguments have gone on – for example, in East Africa the poetry of Okot p'Bitek and the novels of Ngugi wa Thiong'o, in West Africa the plays and poetry of Wole Soyinka and the novels of Chinua Achebe.

Given the numerous varieties of English in the world today, it is obviously impossible to do more than give a few examples of the differences between them. These can be considered under the headings of Phonology, Grammar, and Vocabulary. Pidgins and creoles, however, will be considered separately, since they are so different from the standard varieties of English.

Phonology

Different varieties of English can differ phonologically in three main ways. First, their phonological systems can differ: for example, the inventory of phonemes may be different. Secondly, the realizations of the same phoneme can be different, that is, be pronounced differently. Thirdly, the distribution of phonemes can differ, that is, different phonemes may be selected for the pronunciation of a given word. To this can be added differences of stress and intonation.

Phonology: North America

The English of North America was separated from British English rather early, and has a somewhat different system. To some extent this results from the fact that most North American speech is rhotic, that is, /r/ is pronounced before a consonant or a pause, whereas in RP it is not pronounced in these positions. Not all North American English is rhotic: in the USA, the speech of the coastal South, of eastern New England, and of New York City is to a considerable extent non-rhotic. The speech of the vast majority of Americans and Canadians, however, is rhotic, and one consequence of this is that the centring diphthongs /ɪə/, /ɛə/, and /ʊə/ do not exist in their system. For an RP speaker, the words *here*, *scarce*, and *poor* are /hɪə/, /skɛəs/, and /pʊə/, but in General American they are /hɪr/, /skɛrs/, and /pʊr/. American speakers may indeed use a vowel such as [ʊə] as an allophone before /r/, giving a pronunciation [pʊər], but their inventory of phonemes contains no /ʊə/. In addition, RP has two phonemes, /ɒ/ and /ɑ:/, where General American has only one, namely /ɑ/: so *dog* and *father* are RP /dɒg/, /ˈfɑ:ðə/, but General American /dɑg/, /ˈfɑðər/. There are, however, regional variations in America, with slightly different inventories of vowel-phonemes in different areas. For example, for some speakers there is no distinction between /ɑ/ and /ɔ/, so that the same vowel (usually [ɑ] or [ɒ]) is used in *cot* and in *caught*. This is characteristic of much speech in the North-West of the USA, and also in Canada. The consonant systems of RP and North American English are identical.

North American English also differs from RP in the realization of many phonemes, especially vowels. In General American, as we have seen, differences of vowel-length play a smaller part than in RP, and length-marks are not normally used in phonemic transcriptions. A difference in consonant-realization concerns /t/ and /d/. When /t/ is intervocalic, in words like *pretty* and *letter*,

244 The English Language

Americans usually make the /t/ with a single rapid tap of the tongue, and frequently also voice it, so that to British ears it sounds like /d/. Many Americans also produce intervocalic /d/ with a single rapid tap, and if they voice their /t/ it does indeed become identical with their /d/, so that *latter* and *ladder* are homophones. The tap realization can also be used when a sonorant consonant rather than a vowel precedes the /t/ or /d/, as in *dirty* (where most Americans pronounce the *r*) and *kinder*. It is also used when the following vowel is at the beginning of the next word, in phrases like *get it*.

Canadian English closely resembles American English in pronunciation, but there is one distinctive difference of vowel-realization. The phonemes /aɪ/ and /aʊ/ have the allophones [əi] and [əʊ] when they occur before a voiceless consonant. So while a Canadian pronounces *ride* and *loud* as [raɪd] and [laʊd], *write* and *lout* by contrast are [rəit] and [ləʊt]. Another feature of Canadian English concerns the lateral consonant /l/. In RP, there are two main allophones of /l/. 'Clear [l]' has a front kind of vowel resonance, and is used before vowels and before /j/, as in *look* and *million*. Elsewhere, as in *old* and *mill*, RP uses 'dark [l]', which has a back kind of vowel resonance, the tongue being raised towards the position used for [ʊ]. Canadian English, on the other hand, uses 'dark [l]' in all positions. American English has both clear and dark allophones, but their distribution differs from that of RP, since in General American 'dark [l]' is used in intervocalic position, in words like *Billy* and *yellow*.

The third kind of phonological difference, that of distribution in individual lexical items, often results from regular sound-laws: a sound-law may operate in one variety of English, but not in another, because the two varieties had already branched off from one another before the sound-law operated. An example is the distribution of the phonemes /æ/ and /ɑː/. In England, the phoneme /ɑː/ arose in the eighteenth century, from three main sources: (1) the lengthening of ME *a* before voiceless fricatives (*staff, ask, bath*). (2) The lengthening of ME *a* before preconsonantal and final /r/, and the subsequent loss of this /r/ (*barn, far*). (3) An originally non-standard development of the ME diphthong *au* (*aunt, dance, example*). This third group consists mainly of ME loans from French, in which ME *a* before nasals became ME *au* in some varieties of English, but remained *a* in others. In the eighteenth century, some forms in which the *au* had developed into [a:] entered the standard language.

American English branched off from British English too early to be affected by the lengthening before voiceless fricatives, so that General American has the same vowel in *ask* as in *hat* (/æsk/, /hæt/), whereas in RP the vowels are different (/ɑːsk/, /hæt/). The same difference between RP and General American is found in the words with variant developments of ME *a* before nasals: so *dance* is RP /dɑːns/ but American /dæns/. The variety of English taken to North America was clearly one in which ME *a* had remained before nasals, and had not changed to *au*. On the other hand, ME *a* was affected by a following /r/ in American English, so that it agrees with RP in having different vowels in *hat* and *far*: RP /hæt/, /fɑː/, General American, /hæt/, /fɑr/.

Phonology: Southern Hemisphere

The phonological systems of Australian, New Zealand, and South African English are virtually the same as that of RP, though in New Zealand there is one phoneme fewer, since /ɪ/ and /ə/ have merged, so that words like *pin* have the same vowel as the first syllable of *about*; the realization of this New Zealand phoneme is a rather close central vowel.

Australian English has the same inventory of phonemes as RP, but nearly all the vowels are realized differently, at any rate in Broad Australian. For example, /æ/ and /e/ are closer than in RP, so that to English ears Australian *pan* sounds like *pen*, and the /ɑː/ phoneme, in words like *park* and *path*, is realized as a front [a:] (as against the more backward [ɑ:] of RP). New Zealand pronunciation is very similar to Australian, but with minor differences: for example, the /ɪ/ phoneme, as in *pin*, is realized in a very retracted position, while the /e/ phoneme, as in *pen*, is very close, almost [ɪ], so that to English ears New Zealand *pen* can sound like *pin*. Some speakers diphthongize the vowel to [ɪə], or even [iə], especially after /j/: the pronunciation of the word *yes* as [jiəs], with a very close vowel and with diphthongization, is a good shibboleth for distinguishing a New Zealander from an Australian. In both Australian and New Zealand pronunciation, the /ɜː/ phoneme, as in *turn*, is realized in a closer and more forward position than in RP, in other words nearer to [eː], and in New Zealand, moreover, it is given lip-rounding, so that it is quite similar to the [øː] heard in such French words as *feu* 'fire'. South African English, like Australian and New Zealand English, has a closer realization than RP for the /æ/ and /e/ vowels, and a fronted and rounded realization of /ɜː/. On the other hand, its realization of the /ɑː/ phoneme, as in *park* and *path*, is a backward [ɑː], as in RP, which in broader South African speech may be rounded to [ɒː]. In broad South African, the /ɪə/ and /ɛə/ phonemes are often realized as the pure vowel [eː], so that *fear* and *fair* are both [feː]. Among the consonants, South Africans tend to realize /r/ as a single tap, rather than as an approximant as in RP, and to produce the voiceless plosives (/p/, /t/, /k/) without aspiration.

Southern Hemisphere English and RP also have some differences in the distribution of phonemes in lexical items, but the differences are less great than those between RP and North American English. In Australia and New Zealand, British settlement did not begin until the end of the eighteenth century, and it is not surprising that Antipodean English agrees with RP in using the /ɑː/ phoneme in words both of the *ask* type and of the *far* type. Most New Zealanders also use /ɑː/ in words like *aunt* and *dance*, but most Australians on the contrary use /æ/.

Final unstressed *-y*, in such words as *city* and *happy*, is /ɪ/ in RP, but in Australia and New Zealand it is /iː/. In unstressed syllables in which the vowel is non-final, RP has a contrast between /ɪ/ and /ə/: *offices* /ˈɒfɪsɪz/ differs from *officers* /ˈɒfɪsəz/. In most Australian speech, however, only /ə/ is used in such positions, so that *offices* and *officers* are homophones, and /ə/ is the vowel of the unstressed syllable in such words as *naked*, *rabbit*, *village*, and *waited*, where RP has /ɪ/. This Australian feature is shared by most New Zealand and South African English. One result of Australian usage is that sometimes Australians make a distinction while RP does not: in RP, the words *taxes* and *taxis* are both /ˈtæksɪz/, whereas in

Australian English the first is /ˈtæksəz/ while the second is /ˈtæksiːz/.

Phonology: West Indies

In the West Indies, the phonological systems of local Standard English vary somewhat from island to island. To some extent this is because some have rhotic speech (such as, Barbados) and some non-rhotic speech (for example, Trinidad), while yet others fluctuate (for example, Jamaica). Even the non-rhotic systems, however, may differ somewhat from RP: in Trinidad, for example, the standard language has only one phoneme corresponding to RP /ɪə/ and /ɛə/, so that *beer* and *bare* are homophones, being pronounced [beə]. Like many other Caribbean varieties, Trinidadian English also lacks a phoneme /ə/: in positions where RP has this unstressed vowel, it uses either [i] or [a]. West Indian English also differs from RP and General American in its intonation patterns, and by a tendency to accent syllables by means of pitch rather than stress.

Phonology: English as a second language.

Varieties of English used as a second language often differ considerably in phonological system from RP and General American. The number of phonemes is often much reduced. In one common form of Nigerian English, for example, there is only one phoneme corresponding to RP /ɪ/ and /iː/, so that *bid* and *bead* are both /bid/; only one corresponding to /æ/ and /ɑː/, so that *hat* and *heart* are both /hat/; only one corresponding to /ɒ/, /ʌ/, and /ɔː/, so that *stock*, *stuck*, and *stork* are all /stɔk/; and only one corresponding to RP /ʊ/ and /uː/, so that *look* and *Luke* are both /luk/. Moreover, there is no /ə/ phoneme, /a/ most often being used instead, so that *singer* is pronounced [ˈsiŋˈga], whereas in RP it is /ˈsɪŋə/. Nor is there a phoneme corresponding to RP /ɜː/, the vowel used often depending on the spelling: *work*, for example, is /wɔk/, a homophone of *walk*. There are perhaps no diphthongs, speakers tending to replace them by a sequence of two vowels: the word *ear*, for example, is [i–a], pronounced as two syllables. Even more striking, perhaps, is that Nigerian English is syllable-timed, not (like RP and General American) stress-timed: in other words, all the syllables in a phrase seemingly occur at equal intervals, not just the stressed syllables. This is indeed one of the major causes of difficulty of comprehension between Nigerian speakers on the one hand and British or American speakers on the other.

Reduction in the number of vowel-phonemes is characteristic of most varieties of African English. Elsewhere, English as a second language tends to be nearer to RP in its phoneme system, though with variations depending on the local language: in India, for example, there is commonly no distinction between /v/ and /w/, and some speakers in addition make no distinction between /dʒ/ and /z/, both being realized as [z]. But, as in Nigeria, a widespread characteristic of English as a second language is the use of syllable-timing instead of stress-timing, usually accompanied by a tendency to mark syllable-accent by pitch rather than stress. Commonly, too, there is no use of intonation for contrastive stress, that is, to pick out a particular word in the sentence for emphasis. This tendency to syllable-timing is commonly found in the English spoken in South Asia, Singapore, and sub-Saharan Africa.

In the varieties of English spoken as a second language, the phonemes have a wide range of different realizations, depending on the first language of the speaker.

As for the distribution of phonemes, there is a tendency to use spelling-pronunciations, and especially to replace unstressed /ɪ/ and /ə/ by other vowels suggested by the spelling. In both Indian English and Nigerian English, suffixes like -*able* and -*ence* are often given full vowels, as are unstressed words like *to* and *of*. There are many differences of stress, and in particular, suffixes such as -*ate* and -*ize* are commonly given the main stress of the word. Often, the stress is moved away from the first syllable, as in the Nigerian pronunciation of *petrol*, stressed on the second syllable, but the opposite process is seen in some Indian pronunciations, such as *defence* and *mistake* with first-syllable stress. Analogy may also operate to cause pronunciation-variants: in Nigeria, the word *maintenance* has become *maintainance*, under the influence of the verb, and is stressed on the second syllable. There is also a tendency in such forms of English for consonant-clusters to be simplified: in Nigeria, final clusters are often reduced, /-st/ for example becoming /-s/ (for example, in *west, passed*), whereas on the contrary the influence of the spelling causes final /-mb/ to be pronounced in words such as *bomb* and *climb*. Many speakers in northern India do not use word-initial /sp/, /st/, or /sk/, instead inserting /ɪ/ or /e/ before the cluster, so that *student* becomes /ɪ'stu:dent/ or /e'stu:dent/, and similarly with *speak* and *school*.

Phonology: stress and intonation

Different varieties of English also differ in patterns of stress and intonation. We have already seen that English as a second language is very often syllable-timed instead of stress-timed, lacks the use of contrastive stress, and tends to use pitch rather than stress to mark syllable-accent, features that are to some extent shared by West Indian English. But there are also differences between the standard stress-timed varieties of the language. RP uses more violent stress contrasts and a wider range of pitch than either North American or Antipodean English, so that to Australian or American ears it may sound over-emotional. It also uses fewer stressed syllables: where an RP speaker gives a word one heavy stress and several weak ones, an American or an Australian often gives it a secondary stress on one of the weak syllables. For example, words ending in *-ary*, like *customary* and *military*, have only one stress in RP, but in North America and Australia are normally given a secondary stress on the *a* of *-ary*, which therefore has a full vowel (whereas in RP it is either /ə/ or is lost completely). In addition, more words in a sentence may be stressed than in RP. An example (given by A.G. Mitchell) is the sentence *Thank you very much*, in which an RP speaker usually stresses only *Thank* and *much*, while an Australian also stresses *very*. The use of more stresses means that an utterance moves more slowly, and Australian speech in particular sounds very slow-moving to RP speakers. Some regional English speech shares in this propensity to stress more syllables, and so also moves more slowly than

RP. For example, in Northern England the word *industry*, which in RP is stressed only on the first syllable, is often also given a stress on the second, while words like *distributive*, which in RP have a single stress on the second syllable, may instead be stressed on the first and the third.

Grammar

There are only minor grammatical differences between the main standard forms of English. For Australian and New Zealand English, the differences from Standard British English are negligible. Perhaps the most notable is the British habit of using a plural verb with singular collective nouns, where Antipodean English insists on a singular verb. With such nouns as *army*, *committee*, *crew*, *government*, and *team*, British English can use either a singular or a plural verb: *The committee is considering the matter* or *The committee are considering the matter*. If the group is being considered as a single entity, the singular is likely to be used (*The army is a voluntary* one), but if attention is focused on the individuals comprising it, the verb is likely to be plural (*The army are above average height*). Antipodean English, however, prefers a singular verb with such nouns, as indeed does American English.

American English differs more from British English, but the differences are minor. Among past tenses of verbs, some American English has the forms *dove*, *fit*, and *snuck* (British *dived*, *fitted*, *sneaked*), and in a number of forms uses /-d/ where British English has /-t/ (for example, *burned*, *learned*, *spelled*, *spilled*). In some verbs of this latter type, British English changes the stem-vowel from /iː/ to /e/ in the past tense, whereas in American English it remains /i/ (such as, *dreamed*, *kneeled*, *leaped*). An American often uses *do have* where a Briton uses *have got* ('Do you have the time?', 'Have you got the time?'). Traditionally, *do have* has also been used in Britain, but has been restricted to certain contexts, especially to refer to habitual action ('Do you have dances in your village-hall?'). In recent years, the more extended American usage has been spreading to the UK. American English has two different past participles for the verb *to get*, namely *got* and *gotten*, where British English has only the first. Formerly, American *I have got* meant 'I have', while *I have gotten* was restricted to 'I have obtained', but in recent years *gotten* has come to be used in a wider range of contexts. An American can use impersonal *one*, and then continue with *his* and *he* ('If one loses his temper, he should apologize'). This sounds odd to the British, who replace *his* and *he* by *one's* and *one* (which also avoids the problem of *his/her* and *he/she*). An American in turn is likely to be surprised by the British use of a plural verb and plural intensive pronoun in sentences like 'The government are considering the matter themselves'. Prepositions, too, are sometimes used differently: a Briton lives *in* Sunset Avenue, whereas an American usually lives *on* it, and a Briton caters *for* people, while an American caters *to* them. There are often also different preferences in the choice of auxiliaries. But, while examples of this kind could be multiplied, they are minor things: in all essentials, British and American grammar are the same.

In the West Indies, where there is a creole-English continuum, there is a tendency for creole grammatical features to occur sporadically even in educated speech, especially when it is informal. Such features include the omission of many inflections (especially the plural and possessive markings of nouns and the third-person singular and past-tense markings of verbs) and the omission of *is* and other parts of the verb *to be*.

In countries where English is a second language, similar differences from British and American grammar are even commoner. A feature frequently found is the sporadic omission of the verb *to be* (for example, in East Africa, Ghana, India, and the Philippines), giving sentences such as *We waiting for the flight*. In some varieties there is sporadic omission of the definite and indefinite article (as in West Africa, Singapore), and of the noun- and verb-inflections (as in Singapore). A number of features are found in both India and Nigeria. These include the use of the progressive verb-tenses where British speakers use unmarked forms ('He is going to his office every morning', 'I am having a cold'), plural forms of nouns which in British English are uncountables (*furnitures*, *litters* 'rubbish'), and the use of *isn't it?* as a universal tag-question ('She is living here, isn't it?', 'We should wait for him, isn't it?'). This last usage, which resembles

French *n'est-ce pas?*, is also common among Welsh speakers, and is obviously economical. Indian English has many differences from British English in its verbal system, such as the choice of different tenses and of different auxiliaries, and the use of Subject-Auxiliary word-order in questions (*Who you have come to see?* 'Who have you come to see?').

Vocabulary

It is perhaps in vocabulary that we see the greatest divergences between the different varieties of English as a first language. Expanding across the vast North American continent, with new flora and fauna and different natural features from those of Europe, building up a new society, with its own political institutions, its own social customs, its own recreations, its various ways of earning a living, the Americans were impelled to adapt old words or invent new ones to meet their many needs. The very names for topographical features evoke a specifically American atmosphere, and words like *bluff*, *creek*, *gulch*, *rapids*, and *swamp* seem as much out of place east of the Atlantic as *coomb*, *fen*, *heath*, and *moor* do west of it. In the southern hemisphere, similarly, the English-speaking communities developed their lexicon to meet the needs of a new society and new environment. Subsequently, many of the new words have been exported to the UK and to other English-speaking countries.

One common way of forming this new vocabulary has been by loans from other languages. In North America, the first contacts of the settlers were with the Amerindians, and a few words were borrowed from them, especially in the seventeenth century. Many of the Indian words were shortened and simplified by the borrowers: *pawcohiccora* was borrowed as *hickory*, and *segankw* became *skunk*. Occasionally, the word was altered to give it English elements with a meaning of their own, as when *wuchak* was borrowed as *woodchuck* (a process known as 'popular etymology'). Like these three words, many of the loans are the names of American flora and fauna, such as *sequoia* and *terrapin* (though the former was originally a Cherokee personal name). Others were for words connected with Amerindian culture, like *totem, wampum,* and *wigwam.* The word *powwow* originally meant 'medicine-man, sorcerer', and passed through a series of meaning-changes before reaching its present one of '(informal) conference, consultation'. Among other words borrowed are some in the sphere of politics, like *caucus* and *Tammany.* Some American place-names and river-names are also Amerindian: *Mississippi* means 'big river', and *Chicago* perhaps means 'place of wild onions'.

Similar loans from local languages are found in the southern hemisphere: for example, Australian *billabong, dingo,* and *woomera* (from aboriginal languages), New Zealand *pakeha* 'white person' and *puckeroo* 'broken, useless' (from Maori), and South African *impi* 'a body of Bantu warriors' (from Zulu).

Since the British were not the only nation engaged in colonization, there were also loans made locally from other European languages, especially in North America. The Americans borrowed several hundred words from the Spaniards, who had very early established permanent settlements in the New World, borrowings being especially common in the South-West of the United States. Many of the loans go back to the seventeenth century, though there are also a large number from the nineteenth. Some of them are topographical, like *canyon* and *sierra,* or words for flora and fauna, like *alfalfa, armadillo,* and *cockroach* (adapted by popular etymology from *cucaracha*). A considerable number come from ranch life, like *bronco, corral, lasso, mustang, ranch,* and *stampede,* with which we can perhaps group words for clothing like *poncho* and *sombrero* (though the latter had already been borrowed into metropolitan English in the sixteenth century with a different meaning, 'oriental umbrella or parasol'). Another interest of the Spanish settlers, mining, is reflected in such loans as *bonanza* and *placer* 'deposit in a stream-bed'. Miscellaneous loans include *filibuster, hombre, pronto, stevedore, vamoose,* and *vigilante.*

In the northern part of North America, there was contact right from the beginning with the French, and a number of words were borrowed from them, especially in the eighteenth century. They again include topographical words, like *prairie* and *rapids,* and flora and fauna, like *pumpkin* and perhaps *gopher.* This last word may be from French *gaufre* 'honeycomb', borrowed as the name of a small rodent because of its honeycomb of burrows. There were also some borrowings from the Dutch settlers in North America, who were centred on New Amsterdam (which in 1644 was taken by the British and became New York). The loans include food names (*cookie, waffle*), miscellaneous words (*boodle, boss, dope, snoop*), and possibly *Yankee*, which may be a diminutive of Dutch *Jan* 'John', and so a patronizing name given by the Dutch to the British settlers in New England. Later, in the nineteenth and twentieth centuries, large numbers of immigrants of many nationalities entered the United States, but their contribution to the American vocabulary is remarkably small, because the languages of the immigrants had low prestige, and they were usually anxious to Americanize themselves as quickly as possible. The largest number of loans are from German, for the German influx in the nineteenth century was massive, and there is still a German-speaking population in the United States. The borrowings include food names like *delicatessen*, educational terms like *semester* and *seminar*, and a number of miscellaneous words like *loafer* and *nix*.

The Australians and New Zealanders lacked any such regular contact with other European languages, but in South Africa there have been borrowings from Afrikaans, the South African form of Dutch. These include *apartheid* 'racial segregation', *dorp* 'small town', *kraal* 'village', and *veld* (earlier *veldt*) 'open country'. This last word is cognate with English *field*, while *kraal* is cognate with *corral*, which we have already encountered as a Spanish loan into American English. The Afrikaans word was a borrowing from Portuguese *corral* and *curral*, and the Spanish and Portuguese words had themselves been borrowed from a Khoisan language of South-West Africa.

Many of the new words, however, are not loans, but have been created by the normal processes of word-formation – affixation, compounding, shortening, back-formation – often with different results in different countries. So there are Australian compounds like *outback*, *stockman*, and *tuckerbox*, and American ones like *bullfrog* and *groundhog*. Some such coinages are for objects peculiar to the new country, but sometimes, inevitably, different words have been coined for the same thing. So while a Briton puts rubbish in the dustbin for collection by the dustman, an American is likely to put trash in the trashcan for collection by the trashman. And whereas a Briton puts petrol in the car and drives on the motorway, an American will put gas in the auto and drive on the freeway. Alternatively, the Briton may travel by tram or by railway, while the American travels by streetcar or by railroad. Moreover, existing English words were sometimes given new meanings in the new environment, like Australian *bush* 'woodland, rural areas', *wattle* 'acacia', and *paddock* (used for any piece of fenced land, whatever its size). In America, similarly, the word *robin* was applied to a bird of the thrush family, and *corn* has been specialized to mean what in Britain is called *maize* (though, under American influence, we eat cornflakes rather than maizeflakes). Occasionally, a word which was lost in England was retained elsewhere, like Australian *fossick* 'rummage, seek around', *larrikin* (at one time 'hooligan', now rather 'a bit of a lad'), and perhaps *wowser* 'fanatical puritan'. In some cases earlier forms of English had alternative words, one of which has been retained in Britain and the other elsewhere. The words *autumn* (a fourteenth century loan from French) and *fall* (*of the leaf*) (recorded from the mid-sixteenth century) both existed in Shakespeare's time with the same meaning, but one is now the normal form in Britain and the other in America.

In the coining of new words and phrases, the Americans in modern times have been more exuberant and uninhibited than the British. After the American Revolution, the Americans broke away from English traditions – linguistic as well as social and political – even more than before and were much less restrained by upper-class ideals of decorum in their treatment of the language. The exuberance and the love of novelty were encouraged by the existence of the ever-moving frontier, which for over two hundred years kept bringing new American communities into existence, and encouraged the pioneer spirit. The frontier spirit is perhaps partly responsible for the American gift for coining lively new phrases, like *flying off the handle* and *barking up the wrong tree*. It may also be responsible for the love of the grandiloquent that turns an undertaker into a *mortician* and a spittoon into a *cuspidor*.

In countries where English is spoken as a second language, new words are often introduced from the local languages, and existing English words and phrases given new meanings. Many such words are found in the countries of the Indian subcontinent. From Hindi, the main language of northern India, have come such words as *dhobi* 'washerman', *dhoti* 'loin-cloth', and *lathi* 'long heavy stick', while from Urdu (now the official language of Pakistan) come *almirah* 'cupboard, cabinet', *jawan* 'soldier', *ryot* 'peasant', *sahib* 'sir, master', and *tank* 'pool, reservoir' (though the first and the last of these Urdu words may themselves have come from Portuguese). New words may be coined from existing English elements, like *co-brother* 'brother-in-law' and *tiffin* 'luncheon' (perhaps from the slang word *tiff* 'to sip'), or formed by conversion, like *extern* 'to banish' (from the noun or adjective). Existing English words may be given new meanings, like *backside* 'at the back of' and *demit* 'to resign', and words or meanings which have gone out of use in the UK may still survive, like *stepney* 'a spare wheel' and *stir* 'public disturbance, demonstration'.

In sub-Saharan Africa, what is striking is not the borrowing or coining of new words, but rather the development of new meanings, the survival of usages which are now old-fashioned in the UK, and the formation of whole new phrases. So, in Nigeria, your Yoruba friend Titi may stop and offer you a lift in her *motor* by saying *Enter!* 'Get in', whereupon you may find it necessary to say to the other passengers *Dress!* 'Move over!'. Titi tells you that she is *very much eager* to introduce you to another Nigerian – *He's bearing Tunji* 'His name is Tunji'. Tunji, she tells you, is *a worker*. You ask whether that simply means that Tunji has a job, and Titi replies *In fact!* 'That's right'. Tunji, she says, is one of those people who *try their possible best* 'do their utmost' in everything. When you get out of the car, you slip and fall on the road, and Titi says *Sorry!* – which is not an apology, but an expression of condolence or sympathy. To help you to recover, she suggests that you might like *a hot drink*, which doesn't mean tea or coffee, but whisky or something similarly spirituous, also known as a [ʃɔt] (a 'short' or a 'shot'). Some months later, when you are back home, Titi sends you a letter, beginning *I am very worried to read from you* 'I'm extremely anxious to hear from you'.

In both the Indian subcontinent and sub-Saharan Africa, there is a tendency among the literate, even in everyday speech, to use rather high-flown language. Latinate words, for example, are often used instead of simpler Anglo-Saxon synonyms. This is probably due, in part, to the influence of English literature: the great Victorian novels once figured large in English-medium higher education.

Pidgins and Creoles

There are numerous pidgins and creoles in the world today, probably well over two hundred. They are based on many different languages, including Swahili, Arabic, Malay, and Japanese, as well as on many European languages. Pidgins and creoles, however, are hybrid language-systems, and the 'donor-language' is not the only source, though it is the dominant one.

A particularly large number are based on English: there are about forty areas where so-called 'English-based' pidgins and creoles are spoken, and in some of these areas several different varieties exist. They fall into two main groups, the Atlantic and the Pacific. The Atlantic varieties include those of the Caribbean, of Guyana, and of West Africa (the Gambia, Sierra Leone, Liberia, Ghana, Nigeria, Cameroon), and the Pacific varieties those of the South Sea islands, of Australia, and of the coasts of South-East Asia.

The distinction between pidgins and creoles is not a sharp one, for sometimes a variety is used by some groups as an auxiliary language and by others as a first language. This is particularly true in West Africa, where the co-existence of more than four hundred different languages means that pidgins are especially useful. Even when used as an auxiliary language, a pidgin can fulfil a wide range of functions: in West Africa, English-based pidgins are used for all normal language functions, alongside Standard English and the local languages, and some speakers use a pidgin more frequently than their native language. In this situation, the pidgin remains under the influence of the standard language, and will tend to evolve towards it. If, however, the pidgin loses contact with the donor-language, as happened with the English-based creoles of Surinam, it may evolve away from it, though perhaps retaining archaic features which have been lost by the donor-language.

In English-based pidgins, the main features taken over into the pidgin are lexical: the new language-system draws on English for vocabulary, but only minimally for phonology, and hardly at all for grammar. Indeed, what is striking is that the various pidgins in the world often resemble one another in structure much more than they resemble the dominant languages from which they are derived. A pidgin tends to preserve the absolutely minimal grammatical structures needed for effective communication, and reduces redundancy to almost nil. One result of this typically pidgin structure is that an English-based pidgin is generally not considered to be a dialect of English, but to be a different language in its own right, though there is an area of overlap: in Jamaica, with its continuum of usage from creole to Standard English, the intermediate varieties ('mesolects') probably *are* to be thought of as dialects of English.

The great simplification of pidgin-creole structures as compared with the donor-language is seen in both phonology and grammar. The number of phonemes is usually reduced: for example, in Jamaican creole many speakers use the same vowel in *block* as in *black* (both [blak]), the same vowel in *beer* as in *bare* (both [biɛr]), the same vowel in *pour* as in *poor* (both [po:r]), the same vowel [a:] in *caught, cross, farm*, and *form*, and the same vowel in both syllables of *matter* (which is ['mata]). Among the consonants, /θ/ and /ð/ are phonemes of a type rare outside English, and in pidgins and creoles they are commonly replaced by /t/ and /d/. Thus in Jamaican creole *thin* is [tɪn] and *father* is ['fa:da]. There is also a tendency to simplify consonant-clusters: in Jamaican creole, the final consonant is dropped from such words as *act, bend*, and *left*. It is also common for /h/ to be lost, even in stressed syllables, so that *health* is [ɛlt].

The morphological system, similarly, is much simplified in pidgins and creoles. Both nouns and verbs commonly have only one form. There is thus no distinction in nouns between singular and plural: in West African pidgin, for example, 'one person' is *wan man*, 'ten persons' *ten man*, and 'many persons' *plenti man*. In verbs, the third-person inflection *-es* is missing, so that the same verb-form is used throughout the present tense: *a kari* or *mi kari* 'I carry', *yu kari* 'you carry', *i kari* 'he/she/it carries', etc. Since the verb has only one form, tenses and aspects are shown either by adverbs or by special particles placed before or after the verb: for example, in West African pidgin, *bin* can be placed before the verb to mark the past tense (*i bin kam* 'he came'), *don* to mark the perfect (*i don kam* 'he has come'), and *go* to mark the future (*i go kam* 'he will come'). There is usually a simplification of the pronoun-system: a single form like *i* is often found for *he*, *she*, and *it*. Often there is a single form for the nominative and accusative of the pronoun and also for the pronoun-determiner: so *wi* may mean 'we', 'us' and 'our', and *dem* may mean 'they', 'them', and 'their'. On the other hand, many pidgins make a pronoun-distinction not found in Standard English, by having separate forms for the second-person singular and second-person plural (just as many Irish speakers distinguish between *you* and *yous*): in West African pidgin, *yu* is 'you (singular)' and *una* or *wuna* 'you (plural)'. Negation is achieved without the use of auxiliary *do*, some much particle as *no* being used instead, as in *wi no sabi* 'we don't know'. Interrogation is also achieved without auxiliary *do* and without change of word-order, simply by intonation: *yu get plet?* 'have you got a plate?'. It will be seen that pidgins are extreme forms of analytic languages: they mostly lack inflections, and rely on free morphemes to indicate grammatical relations. For this reason, word-order is of great importance, and is strictly adhered to.

English-based pidgins and creoles may draw most of their vocabulary from English, but they make changes to it. Words are often used with new meanings, like West African *chop* 'to eat' and *bif* 'animal, meat'. Conversion is common, the same word often being used as noun, verb, and adjective. New compounds are formed: for example, *die* and *man* are combined as *daiman* 'corpse', a form found in both Atlantic and Pacific pidgins. A common device is reduplication or repetition: in Jamaican creole, *smal* means 'small', and *smalsmal* means 'very small'. As could be expected from their origins, all English-based pidgins have a nautical element in their vocabulary, but again with new meanings: for example, from *heave* come forms meaning 'push, lift', from *capsize* forms meaning 'overturn, spill', and in Cameroon is found a word from *man-of-war* meaning 'wasp'. Inevitably, a few words also come into pidgins from the local languages, like West African *akara* 'kind of pancake', from Yoruba. In addition, all English-based pidgins seem to have words derived from Portuguese, especially *saber* 'to know' and *pequeno* 'small, little', the latter often producing a word meaning 'child'. The Portuguese were among the earliest European explorers and colonizers, and it has been suggested that many English-based pidgins were originally Portuguese-based, and were 're-lexified' when English presence and influence replaced Portuguese.

As an example of pidgin, let us look at a short piece of Nigerian pidgin, recorded in Port Harcourt by Dr Loreto Todd in 1985. It is an Igbo speaker's translation of the end of the parable of the Prodigal Son (Luke XV.31–2), and you may find it interesting to compare it with other versions of the same passage which we have looked at earlier (pp. 33–7 above).

> Di papa bin tɔk sei: 'Ma pikin, yu sabi sei yu dei wit mi eni dei eni dei, an ɔl ting wei a gɛtam na yu on. Bɔt i gud mek wi hapi, bikɔs dis yu brɔda bin dɔn dai an i dɔn wikɔp fɔ dai agɛn; i bin dɔn lɔs an wi bin luk i agɛn'.

This is given in a 'semi-phonetic' transcription, often used for this purpose, in which the vowel-symbols are phonetic but the consonant-symbols correspond to English spelling. In the passage, *bin tɔk sei* means 'said', *bin* being the past-tense marker and *sei* a particle which follows verbs of saying and thinking. Then come the two common words derived from Portuguese, *pikin* 'child' and *sabi* 'know', followed by *sei yu dei wit mi* 'that you are with me' (in which *sei* is rather like the conjunction 'that', while *dei* is one of the words corresponding to the verb 'to be'). The phrase *eni dei* means 'every day', and when reduplicated, as here, means 'always'. The word *wei* is a relative, meaning 'who, which, that', but in addition *-am* 'it, him, her, them' is added to the verb *gɛt* 'have', the whole phrase meaning 'everything that I have'. Another word for the verb 'to be' is *na*, and *na yu on* means 'is your own'. No distinction is made between 'you' and 'your', as is also seen in *dis yu brɔda* 'this your brother'. In *bin dɔn dai*, both the past-tense and the perfect-tense markers are used, so that it means 'had died', but the perfect marker alone is used in *i dɔn wikɔp* 'he has returned (woken up)'. The same word is used for *die* and *death*, so that *fɔ dai* means 'from death'. Pidgin tends to use only a small number of prepositions, and the two commonest ones in Nigerian pidgin both occur in the passage, *wit* and *fɔ*.

Standard English

The divergent development that has taken place in the English language as it has spread over the world during the last three hundred years raises the question of Standard English. Does it exist? If so, what is it? We can leave out of account the English-based pidgins and creoles, since these are something *sui generis*, not to be considered as part of the English language. But we are still left with a wide range of varieties of English used as a first or second language.

Fortunately, in the countries where English is a first language, there is a solid core of common usage which makes it possible to talk of 'standard world English'. Regional variations are especially marked in the spoken language, many of them being a matter of accent, and are greatest in informal, slangy, and lower-class speech. But if we examine the more formal uses of language, and especially if we confine ourselves to a formal style of *written* language, the differences become small. In formal writing, the essential structure of the language is practically the same throughout the English-speaking world; the differences in vocabulary are perceptible but not enormous; and the differences in spelling negligible. There is, therefore, a standard *literary* language which is very much the same throughout the English-speaking community, and it is this, if anything, which deserves to be called Standard English.

The situation is different when we consider the use of English as a second language. In such countries as India and Nigeria, a local variety of English is used in writing as well as in speech, and can be considered to constitute a local standard. Whether these varieties of English will remain autonomous and go their own ways, or whether on the other hand they will converge on World Standard English, still remains to be seen.

11 English today and tomorrow

In the English language today we can see both centrifugal and centripetal tendencies. In countries where English is used as a second language, there has been a trend during the past half-century for local standards to become established, and for the language to develop independently of British or American English. If this trend continues, these local varieties may ultimately diverge widely from Standard World English, and become separate languages, just as the various Romance languages evolved from Latin. It is too early to say how likely this is, but it must be a possibility.

On the other hand, the major forms of English as a first language (in Britain, North America, Australia, New Zealand) do not seem to be diverging from one another any longer, and in some respects even seem to be converging, and it is likely that they will continue to constitute a more-or-less unified language as a major medium of international intercourse. The slowing down of the divergent trend has been due to the great development of communications (aircraft, telegraph, telephone) and the rise of mass media (the popular press, the cinema, radio, television). These things have enabled the different regional varieties of English to influence one another, and so reduce their differences. Such influences have been mutual, but at present the major influence is the language of the United States, and this influence penetrates everywhere that English is spoken as a first language. Not only do Americans form by far the largest single body of speakers of English, but also they have a preponderance of economic and political power and prestige. Considerations of this kind play a large part in the influence of a language: Latin became the dominant cultural language of Western Europe, not because it was intrinsically superior to Greek or Arabic or the local languages, but because of the political, military, and administrative achievements of Imperial Rome. Similarly the wealth and power of the United States make her a creditor nation in linguistic matters.

The mutual influence shows itself especially in vocabulary. Many people are surprised to learn that some commonly used words are of American origin (Chapter 10): words like *cockroach*, *loafer*, *stevedore*, and *tornado* are so familiar that we do not think of them as Americanisms, and the same is true, or rapidly becoming true, of more recent importations like *blurb*, *cagey*, *gimmick*, and *rugged* (in the sense of 'robust'). American slang and colloquial words are particularly appealing, like *hassle* 'quarrel, difficulty, fuss', *heist* 'hold-up, robbery', *hype* 'confidence-trick, swindle', *scam* 'ruse, swindle', and *to zap* 'attack suddenly, move quickly'. American influence has always been strong in the entertainments industry, and one reflection of this has been the supplanting of British *producer* by American *director*. In the British professional theatre until fairly recently, the person artistically responsible for the performance of a play was its *producer*, who *produced* the play, while *director* and *to direct* were the corresponding words used for films. But, under American influence, it is now normal for *director* and *to direct* to be used of plays, though the outcome is still called a *production* (and the older usage can still be heard in amateur theatricals). This kind of American lexical influence goes on constantly, but other varieties of English have their own modest exports: from Australia, for example, we have imported *bush telegraph* and *cuppa*.

Dialect mixing

A similar kind of process of convergence is going on inside Britain: the different dialects are being mixed and levelled. In addition to the influence of the mass media, there has been that of universal and compulsory education, dating from the last quarter of the nineteenth century, which has worked against the broader dialect elements, both regional and social. Moreover, the population has been more mobile: the small self-contained community has practically disappeared, there has been continuing migration to the great cities, and in two world wars there has been mixing of men in enormous conscript armies. As a result, the traditional rural dialects of Britain have virtually vanished, and have been replaced by new mixed dialects, based on the great urban centres.

This does not mean, of course, that regional and social differences have disappeared: Manchester speech is still different from London speech, and a Manchester millhand still speaks differently from a Manchester company director. In each region, there is a speech-hierarchy, corresponding fairly closely to socio-economic class. The variations are not just a matter of accent, but also of grammar and vocabulary. The speech of the top of the hierarchy is closest to Standard English in grammar and vocabulary, and to RP in pronunciation. As you go down the hierarchy, the divergences from standard usage become increasingly great. The degree of divergence, however, is also influenced by sex, by age, and by style: women diverge less from the standard than men of the same socio-economic group, and in all groups the divergence is greatest in colloquial and informal style, and smallest in formal situations.

Two very common grammatical features in non-standard speech are the use of past participles as past-tense forms (*I seen him* 'I saw him', *they never done it* 'they didn't do it'), and the use of the same form for adjectives and adverbs (*the lads played real good* 'the boys played really well'). Standard speakers sometimes describe such usages as 'ungrammatical'. This, however, is not a good description. Non-standard speakers have as strict and complete a grammar as standard speakers, but it just happens to be a different one: in their grammar, for example, *seen* and *done* may be the regular past-tense forms of *see* and *do*. Indeed, these usages are extremely economical, and are very much what could be expected from the general development of the language. The fact that they are not now standard is to some extent due to the eighteenth-century prescriptionists, who wanted past participles to be distinguished from past-tense forms, and adverbs from adjectives. One intriguing possibility is that such non-standard usages could become standard: as young people's role-models increasingly become pop-stars and professional footballers, whose speech often comes from the lower socio-economic regions, the stigmatized usage of today may become the accepted usage of tomorrow. But here much depends on general social history, which we can't predict.

In the meantime, we still have in Britain variations of regional and social usage, but the general mixing and levelling effect means that the range of variations has been reduced, and the more idiosyncratic usages are disappearing. And all the varieties are undergoing constant change. In what follows, I shall try to point to some of the changes going on in our own lifetimes, and shall, of necessity, confine myself to the changes taking place in Britain (though many of them no doubt have parallels in the rest of the English-speaking world).

Received pronunciation and regional accents

As we have seen, Received Pronunciation (RP), a non-regional accent based on the speech of the great public schools, has been accepted as a standard inside England for well over a century. Increasingly, however, there has been a tendency for the accent of educated people in South-Eastern England to replace strict RP as the standard: RP has lost some of its prestige, as people educated at public schools have lost their monopoly of power and education. A considerable part has been played by the great post-war expansion of higher education. Today, the majority of university students are not speakers of RP, and it is from them that a large part of the English professional classes are recruited. Most schoolteachers, too, do not use RP, but an educated regional accent, so that the influence of the schools is towards this rather than towards RP.

This is not to say that RP has lost all its magic. It still has prestige, for example in the City, in the higher reaches of the Civil Service, and among officers of the armed forces. Moreover, since it has been so fully described, it is the accent usually taught to foreigners learning British English. But the public schools are no longer felt to have a monopoly of 'correct speech', and the prestige of educated regional speech has risen enormously during the past half-century. Since an educated South-Eastern accent is fairly similar to RP, there is a tendency nowadays for this to be regarded as a standard: it is the accent used, for example, by many radio and television announcers and presenters. On the other hand, there has been a rise in the prestige of *all* regional accents in Britain, and it is probable that we are moving towards the American position, in which it is normal and acceptable for a speaker to use an educated regional accent, and there is no supra-regional class-accent.

There is consequently a tendency in present-day Britain to draw the boundaries of 'acceptable pronunciation', and indeed of 'Standard English' generally, rather wider than formerly, and to take into account the usages of a larger part of the population. Some of the changes that seem to be taking place in the language are therefore more apparent than real: they may be changes in acceptance, rather than actual substantive changes. What formerly existed as a usage in some group, but was considered non-standard, may now come to be accepted as standard, because of the changing definition of 'standard'. It does seem, however, that there are substantive changes going on, in pronunciation, in grammar and in vocabulary.

Changes in vocabulary

The expansion of the vocabulary seems to be going on at a great rate in our time. Many new words continue to be coined from Greek and Latin morphemes for use in science and technology, and some of these get into the general vocabulary, like *cosmonaut* and *stereophonic* (now shortened to *stereo*). Not all new scientific and technical words are coined from Latin and Greek elements. The engineering industries in particular tend to use existing English morphemes, and one common habit is the coining of new compound verbs by back-formation, for example *to case-harden, to centre-drill, to colour-code, to custom-build, to drop-forge, to field-test, to impact-extrude, to instrument-check* and *to self-adjust*.

In the general vocabulary, affixation is still one of the favourite methods of word-formation. Fashionable prefixes in recent years include *audio-* (*audiovisual*), *crypto-* (*cryptocommunist*), *mini-* (*minivan*), and *neo-* (*neoNazi*), but more traditional prefixes also continue to be productive, as in *anti-poll-tax*, *debug*, *non-event*, and *unfunny*. Active suffixes are illustrated by the words *ageism*, *brinkmanship*, *chippie* or *chippy* 'fish-and-chip shop', *circuitry*, *privatize*, *sexist*, and *skateboarder*.

Compounding also continues, especially for the formation of new nouns. The great development of aviation, both civil and military, has led to many compounds beginning with *air-* (*-drop*, *-hostess*, *-mobile*, *-strip*, etc.). The influence of the Women's Lib movement has led to the coining of compounds like *spokesperson*, in which *person* replaces the suffix *-man*. Another popular second element in recent times has been *-centre*. What used to be Employment Exchanges are now called *JobCentres*. A school library often turns into a *resource centre*. A combined radio, CD-player, and tape-recorder is a *music centre*. An elaborately equipped ironing-board is advertised as an *ironing centre*. And I have even seen a church with a large notice outside jokingly proclaiming that it is a GOD CENTRE!

New words are also produced by shortening, like *brill*, from *brilliant*, and *vibes* from *vibrations*. Loans are not a major source of new words, but a few continue to drift in. For example, from French has come *discothèque* (now usually shortened to *disco*), from Mexican Spanish has come *machismo*, and from Swedish the *moped*, while *ombudsman* could equally well be from Swedish, Danish, or Norwegian. The Innuit (Eskimo) languages do not strike one as a likely source of English loans, but in fact the word *anorak* is borrowed from the Eskimos of Greenland.

Change of meaning

One common cause of semantic change in our time appears to be formal influence: the form of a word causes it to be confused with another word, which influences its meaning. An example is the word *format*. This is a technical term of bibliography, referring to the way the sheets of paper are folded in making a book (quarto format, folio format, etc.) – the only meaning recorded in the original edition of the OED. Now, however, people use it to mean 'layout, design' (for example, of a page, a poster), and even more generally to mean 'arrangement, mode of procedure, form': we hear about the format of a lecture-course, a meeting, a conference, a cricket tournament, a symphony. Such a development is common when a word moves out of a specialized field of discourse into the general vocabulary, but it is also probable that *format* has been influenced by another word, namely *form*: for many people, indeed, *format* is now merely a variant of *form*.

Other pairs of words where semantic influence appears to be taking place include *adopt/adapt, amoral/immoral, cautionary/ cautious, differential/difference, diffuse/defuse, fallacious/false, flaunt/ flout, humanitarian/humane, incredulous/incredible, legalistic/legal, masterful/masterly, mitigate/militate, nationalistic/national, perpetrate/perpetuate, prescribe/proscribe, psychiatric/psychological, realistic/real, secretive/secret,* and *sociological/social.* Usually, it is the first word of each pair which takes on the meaning of the second, so that, for example, people say *a masterful ('masterly') sculptor, realistic ('real') progress, psychiatric ('mental') illness,* and *sociological ('social') problems.* Some of these changes are still seen as malapropisms, but others are now commonly accepted.

Among the other changes of meaning in recent times, let me pick out just a few examples. The word *ethnic* frequently occurs in the phrase *ethnic minority,* and is now often used to mean 'having to do with an ethnic minority', as when people speak of *ethnic music.* For some people it has even become a euphemism for 'black'. The noun *exercise* 'practice-operation, task performed as training' is commonly generalized to mean 'operation, task', as in the expression *the object of the exercise* 'the aim or purpose of the task in question'. The usage perhaps arose in military circles, as a deliberate understatement. The adjective *forensic* 'judicial, having to do with the law-courts' often occurs in the expressions *forensic science* and *forensic scientist,* and many people now use it to mean 'scientific' (though always in a judicial context): so *forensic tests* are 'scientific tests carried out to help solve a crime', and a *forensic expert* is 'a scientist who helps police-investigations'. An example of a recent dead metaphor is *question-mark,* used as a synonym for *question*, as when a TV commentator says 'The question-mark now is whether the allies will attack Baghdad'. A recent example of loss of intensity is perhaps the word *obscene*: formerly this was rather a strong word, meaning 'abominable, loathsome', but is now sometimes used as a vague epithet of disapproval, especially in political journalism. Perhaps a similar desire for emphasis is responsible for the popularity of phrases to replace the word *now*: this little monosyllable is often too unemphatic or too laconic for public speakers or journalists, who replace it by such expressions as 'in this day and age', '(as) at the present time', and 'as of now'. This probably has the useful function of increasing the amount of redundancy in the language: as redundancy is lost, by such things as the shortening of words, it can be put back into the system by the expansion of short expressions into longer ones.

It is not only single words that change in meaning: the same thing can happen to whole phrases. Two current examples are the expressions *as far as I'm concerned*, often now used to mean 'in my opinion', and *in terms of*, often used as an omnibus phrase to indicate some unspecified relationship, with some such meaning as 'concerning, with reference to'.

Words which become modish often change in meaning, so keep an eye on such words as *caring, dialogue, dimension, ecological, green, image, interface, profile, scenario*, and *syndrome*. In November 1983, the Conference of Commonwealth Countries called for 'the resumption of a genuine political dialogue between the USA and the USSR'. In a BBC interview on the Conference, the then prime minister, Mrs Margaret Thatcher, commented drily 'We used to call it discussion, now we call it dialogue'.

Changes in pronunciation

In the educated speech of South-Eastern England, the long vowels /iː/ (as in *see*) and /uː/ (as in *too*) are often diphthongized to [ɪi] and [ʊu]. To check your own pronunciation, look into a mirror and say 'ee-ee-ee-ee': if you use a pure vowel your lips and tongue will remain stationary, but if you use a diphthong they will move with each 'ee'. Repeat with 'oo-oo-oo-oo'. Try, too, to *hear* whether or not your vowel is a diphthong. In non-standard speech, these diphthongs often begin at an even opener and more central position, becoming [əi] and [əu].

This change can be seen as a continuation of the Great Vowel Shift: the long close vowels of Middle English, ME ī and ME ū, became diphthongized, and now the vowels that moved up and took their place are being diphthongized in turn. A similar continuation can be seen in the development of the /ɔ:/ phoneme (as in *law*), which is becoming closer in quality. In the Vowel Diagram in Figure 4 (p. 14 above), this phoneme is shown as half-open. Some older speakers use a slightly more open vowel than that, but many younger ones give it a much closer realization, nearer to [o:] (as in French *chose*).

Two changes which are a matter of a change of acceptance are the spread of /ə/ at the expense of /ɪ/ in unstressed syllables, and the use of word-final /-i:/ instead of /-ɪ/. Many speakers, for example, use /ə/ instead of /ɪ/ in the unstressed syllables of *kitchen*, *remain*, *system*, *waitress*, and *women*. Sometimes it replaces other vowels too, for example in words like *boycott* and *sawdust*. The use of /-i:/ in words like *happy* and *city* is common in South-Eastern England, and the vowel is often diphthongized, as it is in other positions. It is probable, however, that these two changes are not actually going on at the present time: the variant pronunciations are quite old ones, and the change is one of acceptability. It is notable that the same pronunciations are common in Australia, and were presumably taken there from southern England in the eighteenth and nineteenth centuries.

A change which does appear to be currently in progress is the redistribution of /ju:/ and /u:/. Words like *new* and *use* had ME *iu*, which was the falling diphthong [iʊ]. Round about 1600, this changed into /ju:/, giving the pronunciations /nju:/, /ju:z/. But in some positions the [iʊ] instead became /u:/, namely after /tʃ/, /dʒ/, /r/, and Consonant + /l/, as in *chew*, *June*, *rude*, *blew*. Later, however, the /ju:/ became /u:/ in other positions, especially after /s/, /l/, and /θ/. This did not happen in all speech-groups, however, and today there are double forms of such words as *suit*, *lute*, and *enthusiasm*. The present trend seems to be for the /u:/-forms to spread at the expense of the /ju:/-forms, so that increasingly *suit* and *lute* are /su:t/, /lu:t/, rather than /sju:t/, /lju:t/. In much regional English speech, and in American English, /u:/ replaced /ju:/ in even more phonetic contexts, and some of these /u:/-forms show signs of entering standard British pronunciation: for example, *resume* is occasionally heard as /rɪˈzu:m/.

Among the consonants, there are two trends affecting /r/, namely the extension of intrusive /r/, and the loss of /r/ in unstressed syllables. Intrusive /r/, heard in expressions like *the idear of it* and *the lawr of the sea*, arises by analogy with words like *father*, which quite regularly have a final /r/ before a vowel, but not before a consonant or a pause. For a long time, intrusive /r/ has been normal in educated speech after /ə/, so that *the idear of it* and *Ghanar and India* are perfectly acceptable. Until relatively recently, however, intrusive /r/ was stigmatized when it occurred after other vowels, so that *the Shahr of Persia* and *the lawr of the sea* were considered vulgar. This now seems to have changed, however, and intrusive /r/ is widespread in educated speech after any vowel. Sometimes the intrusive /r/ goes on to attach itself permanently to the stem of the word, leading to such forms as *drawring board* and *withdrawral*. These are quite common, but probably not yet accepted as standard.

There is a tendency for /r/ to be lost in unstressed syllables. This has long been the case where there are two successive occurrences of /r/, as in *February*, *library*, *temporary*, and *secretary* (the first /r/ being the one that goes). Now, however, in colloquial speech /r/ is often lost in unstressed syllables where there is no other /r/. A TV weather-forecaster has been heard to say /dʒʊənə ˈnaɪt ˈtempətʃəz ˈdʒenəli: . . ./ ('during the night, temperatures generally . . .'). Such pronunciations, indeed, are not universally accepted, but they are perhaps straws in the wind.

Changes are taking place in the way words are stressed. There is a long-term trend in two-syllable words for the stress to be moved from the second syllable to the first: this has happened in living memory in such words as *adult*, *alloy*, *ally*, and *garage*. It is still going on, especially where there are related noun-verb pairs. There are many pairs where the noun has first-syllable stress, and the verb second-syllable stress, and in such cases many speakers now stress the verb also on the first syllable: examples are *annex*, *contest*, *contract*, *escort*, *export*, *import*, *increase*, *progress*, *protest*, and *transfer*. In cases where both the noun and the verb have second-syllable stress, there is a tendency for the noun to be given first-syllable stress, as with *blockade*, *discharge*, *dispute*, *redress*, and *research*; occasionally the verb may also be given first-syllable stress. When the stress is moved on to the first syllable of a verb, it is usually also moved in words derived from it, like *protester*.

In words of more than two syllables, there is an apparent tendency to move the stress from the first to the second syllable, as with *aristocrat*, *communal*, *controversy*, *doctrinal*, *formidable*, *hospitable*, and *pejorative*. The forms with second-syllable stress, however, are not new ones, and here we are dealing with a potential change of acceptance rather than a substantive change. The pronunciations with first-syllable stress are traditional standard ones, and the other forms are permeating from below, as part of the dialect-mixing of our times. The words *cigarette* and *magazine*, on the other hand, are normally pronounced in Britain with the main stress on the final syllable, but nowadays some speakers instead put it on the first, probably as a result of American influence.

Many people have commented in recent years on the common habit among public speakers of putting heavy stress on prepositions: newsreaders often say such things as 'A report ON today's proceedings IN Parliament will be given BY John Smith OF our news-staff'. This is perhaps caused by a desire for clarity and emphasis: something similar is sometimes heard from inexperienced amateur actors, who, in their anxiety to obtain emphasis, tend to stress far too many words. It is also striking that announcers and newsreaders often use 'wrong' contrastive stress. Thus a BBC radio announcer said 'And now, a recital by the young FINNISH guitarist Jukka Sauijiki', giving contrastive stress to the word *Finnish*. This was inappropriate, since no other guitarist had been mentioned or was going to be mentioned. Perhaps such usages, which are extremely common, merely show that the speaker is not thinking about the meaning of what is said, but it is not impossible that changes are taking place in the ways speakers use stress and intonation to give emphasis.

A trend which has been encouraged by the spread of higher education and of foreign travel is the adoption of what can be called 'continental pronunciations'. Words borrowed from other languages soon get assimilated to an English style of pronunciation, either by passing through normal English sound-changes or because of the influence of the spelling. Nowadays, however, such words are often given a 'foreign' kind of pronunciation again. In the traditional pronunciation, the words *armada, Copenhagen, gala,* and *Gaza* had their stressed *a* pronounced /eɪ/, but it is now common for /ɑ:/ to be used instead, and in *armada* this pronunciation is universal. Similarly, *beret, richochet,* and *valet* are now commonly pronounced without their final /t/, *proviso* sometimes has /i:/ instead of /aɪ/, Marlowe's *Dr Faustus* is given the /aʊ/ of the German *Faust* instead of the traditional English /ɔ:/, and *chivalry* is almost universally pronounced with /ʃ/ instead of the traditional /tʃ/. The new pronunciations are not always based on a genuine knowledge of the other language: the word *Raj* was traditionally /rɑːdʒ/, but is now often /rɑːʒ/, a pronunciation which probably owes more to a knowledge of French than to a knowledge of Hindi, while the new pronunciation of *Copenhagen* bears very little resemblance to the Danish.

This 'continental' influence is perhaps reinforced by the 'new' pronunciation of classical Latin, which has continental-style vowels, whereas the 'old' pronunciation had anglicized vowels. Almost any English person today who has learnt Latin will have learnt the 'new' style of pronunciation. This perhaps explains why many people are reluctant to use the traditional pronunciation of those Latin tags which commonly occur in English, like *a priori, quasi,* and *sine die* (traditionally /'eɪ praɪ'ɔːraɪ/, /'kweɪzaɪ/, /'saɪnɪ'daɪiː/). These sound wrong, and people often instead use an approximation to the 'new' Latin pronunciation. This even affects proper names: there is no likelihood that a well-known name like *Julius Caesar* will lose its traditional pronunciation, but Shakespeare's *Coriolanus* is now often pronounced with /ɑ:/ instead of /eɪ/. The same change of vowel is sometimes heard in *apparatus, status,* and *stratum,* and even occasionally in *data.* Besides affecting words which are obviously direct from Latin, the 'new Latin' influence also affects a few words more remotely derived from Latin. Thus the words *deity*, *spontaneity*, and *vehicle* traditionally have their *e* pronounced as /iː/, but nowadays it is often pronounced /eɪ/. The 'new Latin' and 'continental' tendencies must obviously reinforce one another.

Changes in grammar

In grammar we can see the continuation, in small ways, of the long-term historical trend in English from synthetic to analytic, from a system that relies on inflections to one that relies on word-order and grammatical words. An example is the comparison of adjectives, where *more* and *most* are spreading at the expense of the endings *-er* and *-est*. At one time, *-er* and *-est* were used much more widely than today, and in Early Modern English you meet forms like *ancientest*, *famousest*, *patienter*, *perfecter*, and *shamefuller*. In the first half of the twentieth century, adjectives of more than two syllables always had *more* and *most* ('more notorious, most notorious'), while adjectives of one syllable normally had *-er* and *-est* ('ruder, rudest'). Adjectives of two syllables varied, some being compared one way ('more famous, most famous') and some the other ('commoner, commonest'). In this group of two-syllabled adjectives there has been a tendency in recent years for *-er* and *-est* to be replaced by *more* and *most*, and it is now quite normal to say 'more common, most common', and similarly with *cloudy*, *cruel*, *fussy*, *pleasant*, *quiet*, and *simple*. Recently, moreover, *more* and *most* have been spreading to adjectives of one syllable, and it is not at all uncommon to hear expressions like 'John is more keen than Robert' and 'It was more crude than I expected'.

On the whole, noun and verb forms have remained very stable during the Later Modern English period, because of the influence of the standard literary language and of the educational system. One exception is the group of learned nouns borrowed from Greek and Latin complete with their original plural forms (*dogma/ dogmata, formula/formulae, genus/genera, syllabus/syllabi*, etc.). Such words are more and more often given analogical plurals in *-(e)s* (*formulas*, *genuses*, etc.), though sometimes a distinction is made between technical and popular usage: technical *formulae*, popular *formulas.* A slightly different development is seen in nouns which have a learned plural in *-a*, like *bacterium, criterion, datum, medium, phenomenon,* and *stratum.* These words are often used in the plural (we seldom need to talk about one bacterium, for example), and the plural form, lacking the standard English *-es* marking, has been apprehended by many people as a singular. This happened long ago to *data*, which for years has been regularly used by scientists as a singular, but it is now happening to other similar words as well. So now it is quite common to hear or read such expressions as 'the mass media is responsible', 'this criteria', and 'a bacteria'. The decline of the classics in English education has obviously played a part here, but at the same time the change is absolutely in line with the general development of the language: for nearly a thousand years, the whole trend in English noun-plurals has been for the *-(e)s* morpheme to be standardized, an obviously economical development. A parallel case is that of the Italian loan-word *graffiti*. The singular *graffito* is recorded by the OED from 1851, but now that the word has moved out of the specialist archaeological sphere, and is frequently used for modern wall-scribblings (especially in lavatories), the plural *graffiti* has taken over, and is commonly used as a singular. The word is thus going the same way as earlier Italian loans like *macaroni.*

A fairly recent development in England is the tendency for people to use auxiliary *may* instead of *might*. This first struck me in 1968, when an account of a football-match in a 'quality' English newspaper contained the sentence 'Just before half-time, Leeds United may have scored a goal'. This was baffling, since the obvious meaning is 'Leeds United perhaps scored a goal'. Had the reporter perhaps gone away to the bar, and didn't know what had happened? What the writer in fact meant was that they *might* have scored a goal (but had failed to do so). Since then, examples have proliferated, especially (though not exclusively) when the auxiliary is followed by *have* plus past participle. For many of the younger generation, indeed, auxiliary *might* now hardly exists, either *may* or *could* being used instead.

Another change going on among the auxiliaries is that *dare* and *need* are ceasing to be auxiliaries, and are coming more and more to be used as ordinary lexical verbs. Thus it is increasingly normal to say 'Do you need to go?' and 'I don't dare (to) go', rather than 'Need you go?' and 'I dare not go'. In some non-standard speech, the same thing has happened to the auxiliaries *ought to* and *used to*, so that you hear expressions like 'She didn't ought to' and 'He didn't used to'.

A construction which has become normal in recent years is what we can call 'conflated *as*'. If a man has the nickname 'Nobby', we can say 'He is called Nobby', or 'He is known as Nobby'. If these sentences are turned round into subordinate clauses introduced by *as*, the first one becomes 'Nobby, as he is called'. We should therefore expect the second one to become 'Nobby, as he is known as', but in fact the second *as* is invariably omitted, and the phrase comes out as 'Nobby, as he is known'. There is also what might be called 'conflated *and*'. In constructions which appear to require two *and*s, it is not uncommon for the first *and* to be omitted. Recent examples, from 'quality' English newspapers, are the following:

(a) He had a moustache, glasses and was wearing a navy blue pullover.
(b) He jogged, did some exercises and we are hoping he will be fit.

In (a), the co-ordinator has been omitted between the nouns *moustache* and *glasses*. In (b), the change of subject before the third verb would seem to call for a co-ordinator between the verbs *jogged* and *did*. This is an extremely common phenomenon, and is perhaps a sign that there have been changes in people's feeling for clause-structure. If this is so, it may also be connected with a change in people's feeling for sequence of tenses: nowadays it is quite common to find complex sentences where the tense-sequence would have been felt impossible even twenty or thirty years ago.

English tomorrow

It's dangerous to extrapolate or to prophesy, and none of us can guess what the English language will be like in a hundred years time. The changes of recent decades suggest what forces are at work in the language today and the likely shape of things in the next few decades, but the history of the language in the coming century will depend on the history of the community itself.

One of the striking things at the moment is the expansion going on in the vocabulary. If this continues, the change over a century will be comparable to that of such earlier periods as 1300 to 1400 or 1550 to 1650. Another trend is dialect-mixing, with American influence predominant. Unless some global disaster disrupts world communications, this is likely to continue, and the divergent tendencies in the language to be held in check. Inside England, public-school English seems already to have been supplanted by educated South-Eastern usage as a standard, but it is quite possible that other regional varieties of the language will achieve parity of esteem: it is already quite normal for local radio and TV services in the English regions to have announcers and presenters who use the local form of the language. In the British Isles outside England, such regional standards are already well-established. In pronunciation, such trends as the diphthongization of the long close vowels may well continue, and could lead to further changes in the vowel-system. In grammar, the trends of the past thousand years continue in small ways. More substantial changes could be caused by the permeation of the standard language by usages which at present are non-standard. In grammar, for example, past-tense forms like 'I done' might become acceptable, as might the conflation of adjective and adverb forms. In pronunciation, such London habits as the use of the glottal stop (for example, replacing /t/ in words like *butter* and *lot*) and the vocalization of 'dark /l/' (giving pronunciations like [mɪʊk] for 'milk') might enter educated London speech. But whether or not these things happen depends on the social history of the country, which we cannot predict.

What we can be sure of is that the process of change, which we have traced from the early Indo-European records up to modern times, is still going on, and will continue to. It requires an effort of detachment to recognize current change for what it is. We are so thoroughly trained in one form of the language that we are likely to dismiss innovations as mistakes or vulgarisms. On the other hand, if our own elders make similar deprecating noises about *our* use of the language, we probably dismiss them as stuffy old fuddy-duddies. Such conservatism is inevitable, and indeed necessary for the stability of the language, but we need to step outside such attitudes and view the whole speech-community with scientific detachment. We shall then recognize that our behaviour is simply that of one group at one point in time, and that in the next generation the innovations that we deplore may well have become completely respectable, and indeed uniquely right for the users.

Moreover, why not *enjoy* the language that you speak? As speakers of English, we're fortunate in being inside a language of enormous richness and variety: it can be great fun simply to listen to English of many different kinds – from different parts of the world, different social groups, different occupations – and also to enjoy the ways in which the language is changing. In a universe of change, it's natural to long for stability, to want to pin things down and fix them. But it can't be done. The whole of nature is in flux, and so is the whole of human life, and we might as well make the best of the fact. It's not really much good clinging to the bank: we have to push out into the flux and swim.

Notes and suggestions for further reading

1 What is language?

Good general introductions to linguistics are Aitchison 1987, and Atkinson, Kilby, and Roca 1988; Lyons 1968 is still useful. Works of the present century which have been landmarks in the subject include de Saussure 1916, Sapir 1921, Bloomfield 1933, and Chomsky 1957, 1965. The standard work on the phonetics of present-day British English is Gimson 1989; a good introductory work is Roach 1991. Accents of English worldwide: Wells 1982. English intonation: O'Connor and Arnold 1973. Introductions to the structure of English: Hill 1958 and (shorter) Strang 1968. In word-order typology and linguistic universals, the pioneer work was Greenberg 1966; a good introduction is Comrie 1989; Hawkins 1983 and 1988, and Croft 1990 are more advanced. On stress-timing in English poetry, see Barber 1983.

2 The flux of language

Historical and comparative linguistics generally: Hock 1986, Anttila 1989. Linguistic change and its causes: Sturtevant 1961, Martinet 1955, Lehmann 1973, Samuels 1972, Aitchison 1991. History of English: Jespersen 1982, Wyld 1927, McKnight 1968, Baugh 1978, Strang 1970.

3 The Indo-European languages

Indo-European languages: Lockwood 1969, Baldi 1983. For a survey of recent problems in Indo-European linguistics, see Szemerényi 1985. The Indo-European homeland: Schrader 1890, Childe 1926, Gimbutas 1970, Renfrew 1987, Gamkrelidze and Ivanov 1990.

4 The Germanic languages

For Proto-Germanic phonology and morphology see Streitberg 1943 and Prokosch 1939. An introduction to the Scandinavian languages:

Walshe 1965. Lockwood 1976 is a history of the German language, but also contains chapters on Dutch, Afrikaans, and Frisian. On the Germanic languages more generally, Meillet 1917 is still very readable.

5 Old English

Standard works are Stenton 1971 on Anglo-Saxon history, Campbell 1962 on OE grammar and phonology, and Mitchell 1987 on OE syntax. Of the many OE readers, see especially Mitchell and Robinson 1986, which, in addition to annotated texts, contains an excellent introductory section on the language. A good general introduction to OE literature is provided by Godden and Lapidge 1991, while Campbell 1982 is a lavishly illustrated introduction to Anglo-Saxon cultural history more generally. On English place-names see Reaney 1960, Ekwall 1960, Cameron 1977, Smith 1970, and the various county-volumes of the English Place-Name Society. On runes, see Elliott 1989 and Page 1973; a shorter work is Page 1987, in the admirable British Museum series 'Reading the Past'.

6 Norsemen and Normans

For further information on the Vikings see Jones 1984, 1986, and Sawyer 1971, 1982, and on Scandinavian loan-words Björkman 1900–2. On loan-words in English more generally, see Serjeantson 1935. The Edinburgh work on late medieval dialects has been published as McIntosh, Samuels, and Benskin 1986. On the establishment of Standard English, see Leith 1983.

7 Middle English

An introduction to Middle English is provided by Mossé 1952; more elementary is Wardale 1937. For ME phonology see Jordan 1968, 1974. For ME morphology and phonology, Wright and Wright 1928 is still useful; shorter works include Brunner 1963 and Fisiak 1968; Jones 1972 uses a transformational-generative approach. On ME syntax, see Mustanoja 1960. A good ME reader is Burrow and Turville-Petre 1992, which has a useful introduction on the language. On Scots, see Murison 1977, Aitken and McArthur 1979. On the supplanting of Standard Scots by the standard southern language: Devitt 1989.

8 Early Modern English

Works devoted specifically to Early Modern English are Barber 1976 and Görlach 1991. Attitudes to English, and the relationship between English and Latin, are handled by Jones 1953. On the English auxiliaries, see Twaddell 1960, and on the auxiliary *do* Ellegård 1953. The standard work on Early Modern English phonology is Dobson 1968, but this is a work for the specialist; more accessible is Cercignani 1981, but the general reader will do better to rely on the phonology sections of more general works. A good introduction to the historical phonology and morphology of the whole Modern English period is provided by Ekwall 1975. The traditional rural dialects of England were studied by the English Dialect Survey based at the University of Leeds, the results of which were published in a series of volumes from 1962 onwards. A one-volume atlas based on the Survey is provided by Orton, Sanderson, and Widdowson 1978. A useful shorter work is Wakelin 1972.

9 English in the scientific age

A monumental historical grammar and phonology of Modern English is Jespersen 1909–49; shorter works include Wyld 1936, Robertson 1954, and Ekwall 1975. On English spelling see Vallins 1965 and Scragg 1974. For standardization, codification, and prescriptionism see Leonard 1929, Leith 1983, and Milroy and Milroy 1985. On the history of English grammars, Michael 1970, and of English dictionaries, Starnes and Noyes 1946. An admirable brief account of the auxiliaries in present-day English is Twaddell 1960. On the vocabulary of science see Savory 1967 and on vocabulary in general, Sheard 1954. On word-formation in Modern English see Marchand 1969, Adams 1973, Bauer 1983 and on changes of word-meaning in English, Stern 1931 and (introductory) Waldron 1967. For semantics in general see Ullmann 1959, Lyons 1977, Leech 1981.

10 English as a world language

For further reading on American English see Markwardt 1980 and Francis 1958. On Antipodean English see Baker 1945, Mitchell 1947 and Turner 1966. On Jamaican English see Cassidy 1961 and Bailey 1966. Works covering many varieties of English worldwide include Bailey and Görlach 1982, and Cheshire 1991; a useful elementary introduction is Trudgill and Hannah 1982. Wells 1982 is a monumental account of English phonology worldwide. Holm 1988–9 is a substantial survey of pidgins and creoles, while Todd 1990 is an admirable introductory work, expanded in Todd 1984; Romaine 1988 is especially concerned with the theoretical questions raised by pidgins and creoles, and their bearing on the problem of language acquisition and linguistic universals.

11 English today and tomorrow

On changes in English in our own time see Barber 1964, 1985, Foster 1968 and Potter 1969. A comprehensive account of the phonology of present-day English worldwide is given by Wells 1982. A substantial grammar of present-day English is Quirk, Greenbaum, Leech, and Svartvik 1972; a useful shorter version is Greenbaum and Quirk 1990. On language-variation with socio-economic group, with sex, with age, and with style, see Labov 1966 and Trudgill 1983.

Bibliography

1. Primary sources

Bede, the Venerable, *Ecclesiastical History of the English People*, edited by B. Colgrave and R.A.B. Mynors, Oxford: Clarendon Press, 1969

Bible, *The Holy Bible, conteyning the Old Testament, and the New* ('The King James Bible'), London, 1611
  The New English Bible, Oxford: Oxford University Press and Cambridge University Press, 1970

Bond, D.F. (ed.) *The Spectator*, 5 vols., Oxford: Clarendon Press, 1965

Bright, J.W. (ed.), *The Gospel of Saint Luke in West-Saxon*, Boston: D.C. Heath, 1906

Chaucer, G., *The Canterbury Tales. A Facsimile and Transcription of the Hengwrt Manuscript*, edited by Paul G. Ruggiers, Norman: University of Oklahoma Press, and Folkestone: Wm Dawson and Sons, 1978
  The Riverside Chaucer, edited by Larry D. Benson, third edition, Oxford: Oxford University Press, 1988

Dickens, B., and Wilson, R.M. (eds), *Early Middle English Texts*, London: Bowes and Bowes, 1951

Garmonsway, G.N. (ed.), *Ælfric's Colloquy*, second edition, London: Methuen, 1947

Henryson, R., *The Poems*, edited by Denton Fox, Oxford: Clarendon Press, 1981

Higden, Ranulf, *Polychronicon*, edited by C. Babington and J.R. Lumby, 9 vols., London: Longmans, 1865–86

Klaeber, F. (ed.), *Beowulf and the Fight at Finnsburg*, third edition, with supplements, London: D.C. Heath, 1950

Krapp, G.P. and Dobbie, E.V.K. (ed.), *The Anglo-Saxon Poetic Records*, 6 vols. New York: Columbia University Press, 1931–42

Plummer, C., *Two of the Saxon Chronicles Parallel*, 2 vols., Oxford: Clarendon Press: 1892–9

Scragg, D.G. (ed.), *The Battle of Maldon*, Manchester: Manchester University Press, 1981

Shakespeare W., *The History of Henrie the Fourth*, London, 1598

Mr. William Shakespeares Comedies, Histories and Tragedies, London, 1623

Sisam, K. (ed.), *Fourteenth Century Verse and Prose*, Oxford: Clarendon Press, 1921

Sprat, Thomas, *The History of the Royal-Society of London*, London, 1667

Sweet, H. (ed.), *King Alfred's Orosius*, London: Early English Text Society, 1883

Sweet's Anglo-Saxon Reader, revised by Dorothy Whitelock, Oxford: Clarendon Press, 1967

Tacitus, *On Britain and Germany*, translated by H. Mattingly, West Drayton: Penguin Books, 1948

Wright, W.A. (ed.), *The Metrical Chronicle of Robert of Gloucester*, 2 vols., London: H.M. Stationery Office, 1887

Wycliffe, John, *The Holy Bible translated by Wycliffe and his followers*, edited by J. Forshall and F. Madden, 4 vols., Oxford: Oxford University Press, 1850

2. Secondary sources

Adams, V. (1973). *An Introduction to Modern English Word-Formation*, London: Longman

Aitchison, J. (1989). *The Articulate Mammal*, third edition, London: Unwin Hyman/Routledge

(1987). *Linguistics*, third edition, London: Hodder and Stoughton

(1987). *Words in the Mind*, Oxford: Blackwell

(1991). *Language Change: Progress or Decay?*, second edition, Cambridge: Cambridge University Press

Aitken, A.J., and McArthur, T. (1979). *Languages of Scotland*, Edinburgh: Chambers

Anttila, R. (1989). *Historical and Comparative Linguistics*, second edition, Amsterdam: John Benjamins

Atkinson, M., Kilby, D., and Roca, I. (1988). *Foundations of General Linguistics*, second edition, London: Allen and Unwin

Bailey, C-J.N., and Harris, R. (eds.) (1985). *Developmental Mechanisms of Language*, Oxford: Pergamon Press

Bailey, B.L., (1966). *Jamaican Creole Syntax*, Cambridge: Cambridge University Press

Bailey, R.W., and Görlach, M. (1982). *English as a World Language*, Ann

Arbor: Michigan University Press

Baker, S.J. (1945). *The Australian Language*, Sydney: Angus and Robertson

Baldi, P. (1983). *An Introduction to the Indo-European Languages*, Carbondale, Illinois: Southern Illinois University Press

Barber, C. (1964). *Linguistic Change in Present-day English*, Edinburgh: Oliver and Boyd

(1976). *Early Modern English*, London: Deutsch

(1983). *Poetry in English: An Introduction*, London: Macmillan

(1985). 'Linguistic Change in Present-Day English. Some Afterthoughts', in *Papers on Language and Literature*, edited by S. Bäckman and G. Kjellmer (1985). Göteborg: University of Gothenburg, 36–45

Bauer, L. (1983). *English Word Formation*, Cambridge: Cambridge University Press

Baugh, A.C. (1978). *A History of the English Language*, third edition, London: Routledge and Kegan Paul

Björkman, E. (1900–2). *Scandinavian Loan Words in Middle English*, Halle: Niemeyer

Bloomfield, L. (1933). *Language*, New York: Holt, Rinehart and Winston, and London: Allen and Unwin

Bosworth, J., and Toller, T.N. (1898). *An Anglo-Saxon Dictionary*, London: Oxford University Press

Brugmann, K. (1888–95). *Elements of the Comparative Grammar of the Indo-Germanic Languages*, translated by J. Wright, R.S. Conway, and W.H.D. Rouse, 5 vols., London: Kegan Paul

Brunner, K. (1963). *An Outline of Middle English Grammar*, translated by G.K.W. Johnston, Oxford; Blackwell

Burrow, J.A., and Turville-Petre, T. (eds) (1992). *A Book of Middle English*, Oxford: Blackwell

Cameron, K. (1977). *English Place-Names*, third edition, London: Batsford

Campbell, A. (1962). *Old English Grammar*, reprinted with corrections, London: Oxford University Press

Campbell, J. (ed.) (1982). *The Anglo-Saxons*, Oxford: Phaidon

Cardona, G., Hoenigswald, H.M., and Senn, A. (eds) (1970). *Indo-European and Indo-Europeans*, Philadelphia: University of Pennsylvania Press

Cassidy, F.G. (1961). *Jamaica Talk*, London: Macmillan

Cercignani, F. (1981). *Shakespeare's Works and Elizabethan Pronunciation*, Oxford: Clarendon Press

Cheshire, J. (ed.) (1991). *English around the World*, Cambridge: Cambridge University Press

Childe, V.G. (1926). *The Aryans*, London: Kegan Paul, Trench, Trubner

Chomsky, N. (1957). *Syntactic Structures*, The Hague: Mouton
    (1965). *Aspects of the theory of Syntax*, Cambridge, Mass: M.I.T. Press
Chomsky, N., and Halle, M. (1968). *The Sound Pattern of English*, New
    York: Harper and Row
Comrie, B. (1989). *Language Universals and Linguistic Typology*, second
    edition, Oxford: Blackwell
Croft, W. (1990). *Typology and Universals*, Cambridge: Cambridge
    University Press
Crystal, D. (1969). *Prosodic Systems and Intonation in English*, Cambridge:
    Cambridge University Press
Denison, D. (1993). *English Historical Syntax: Verbal Construction*, London:
    Longman
Devitt, A. (1989). *Standardizing Written English*, Cambridge: Cambridge
    University Press
Dobson, E.J. (1968). *English Pronunciation 1500–1700*, 2 vols., second
    edition, Oxford: Clarendon Press
Ekwall, E. (1960). *The Concise Oxford Dictionary of English Place-Names*,
    fourth edition, Oxford: Clarendon Press
    (1975). *A History of Modern English Sounds and Morphology*, translated
    by Allan Ward, Oxford: Blackwell
Ellegård, A. (1953). *The Auxiliary Do*, Stockholm: Almqvist and Wiksell
Elliott, R.W.V. (1989). *Runes. An Introduction*, second edition, Manchester:
    Manchester University Press
Fisiak, J. (1968). *A Short Grammar of Middle English*, London: Oxford
    University Press
Foster, B. (1968). *The Changing English Language*, Harmondsworth,
    Middlesex: Penguin Books
Francis, A.N. (1958). *The Structure of American English*, New York: Ronald
    Press
Gamkrelidze, T.V. and Ivanov, V.V. (1990). 'The Early History of Indo-
    European Languages', in *Scientific American*, March, 82–89
Gimbutas, M. (1970). 'Proto-Indo-European Culture: The Kurgan Culture
    during the Fifth, Fourth, and Third Millennia B.C.'. In Cardona, G.,
    Hoenigswald, H.M., and Senn, A. (eds), 155–97
Gimson, A.C. (1989). *An Introduction to the Pronunciation of English*, fourth
    edition, London: Edward Arnold
Godden, M., and Lapidge, M. (eds)(1991). *The Cambridge Companion to Old
    English Literature*, Cambridge: Cambridge University Press
Görlach, M. (1991). *Introduction to Early Modern English*, Cambridge:
    Cambridge University Press
Greenbaum, S., and Quirk, R. (1990). *A Student's Grammar of the English*

Language, London: Longman

Greenberg, J.H. (1966). 'Some universals of grammar with particular reference to the order of meaningful elements'. In *Universals of Language*, edited by J.H. Greenberg, second edition, Cambridge, Mass: M.I.T. Press

Hawkins, J. (1983). *Word Order Universals*, New York: Academic Press
(ed.) (1988). *Explaining Language Universals*, Oxford: Blackwood

Hill, A.A. (1958). *Introduction to Linguistic Structures*, New York: Harcourt Brace

Hock, H.H. (1986). *Principles of Historical Linguistics*, Berlin: Mouton

Holm, J. (1988–9). *Pidgins and Creoles*, 2 vols., Cambridge: Cambridge University Press

Holmberg, B. (1964). *On the Concept of Standard English and the History of Modern English Pronunciation*, Lund: CWK Gleerup

Holthausen, F. (1934). *Altenglisches etymologisches Wörterbuch*, Heidelberg: Carl Winter

Jespersen, O. (1922). *Language, its Nature, Development, and Origin*, London: Allen and Unwin
(1982). *Growth and Structure of the English Language*, tenth edition, Oxford: Blackwell
(1909–49). *A Modern English Grammar on Historical Principles*, 7 vols., London: Allen and Unwin

Jones, C. (1972). *An Introduction to Middle English*, New York: Holt, Rinehart and Winston

Jones, D. (1962). *The Phoneme: its Nature and Use*, second edition, Cambridge: Heffer

Jones, Gwyn (1984). *A History of the Vikings*, second edition, Oxford: Oxford University Press
(1986). *The Norse Atlantic Saga*, second edition, Oxford: Oxford University Press

Jones, R.F. (1953). *The Triumph of the English Language*, London: Oxford University Press

Jordan, R. (1968). *Handbuch der mittelenglischen Grammatik*, third edition, Heidelberg: Carl Winter
(1974). *Handbook of Middle English Grammar: Phonology*, translated and revised by Eugene J. Crook, The Hague: Mouton

Kurath, H., Kuhn, S.M. and Lewis, R.E. (1952–). *Middle English Dictionary*, 15 vols., Ann Arbor: University of Michigan Press: continuing

Labov, W. (1966). *The Social Stratification of English in New York City*, Washington DC: Center for Applied Linguistics

(1972). *Sociolinguistic Patterns*, Philadelphia: University of Pennsylvania Press

Leech, G. (1981). *Semantics*, second edition, Harmondsworth, Middlesex: Penguin Books

Lehmann, W.P. (1952). *Proto-Indo-European Phonology*, Austin: University of Texas Press

(1973). *Historical Linguistics; an Introduction*, second edition, New York: Holt, Rinehart and Winston

(1974). *Proto-Indo-European Syntax*, Austin: University of Texas Press

Leith, D. (1983). *A Social History of English*, London: Routledge and Kegan Paul

Leonard, S.A. (1929). *The Doctrine of Correctness in English Usage 1700–1800*, New York: Russell

Lieberman, P. (1984). *The Biology and Evolution of Language*, Cambridge, Mass: Harvard University Press

Lockwood, W.B. (1969). *Indo-European Philology*, London: Hutchinson.

(1975). *Languages of the British Isles Past and Present*, London: Deutsch

(1976). *An Informal History of the German Language*, London: Deutsch

Luick, K. (1914–21). *Historische Grammatik der englischen Sprache*, Leipzig: Tauchnitz

Lyons, J. (1968). *Introduction to Theoretical Linguistics*, Cambridge: Cambridge University Press

(1977). *Semantics*, 2 vols., Cambridge: Cambridge University Press

McIntosh, A., Samuels, M.L., and Benskin, M. (1986). *A Linguistic Atlas of Late Mediaeval English*, 4 vols., Aberdeen: Aberdeen University Press

McKnight, G.H. (1968). *The Evolution of the English Language*, New York: Dover Publications.

Marchand, H. (1969). *The Categories and Types of Present-day English Word-formation*, second edition, Munich: C.H. Beck

Marckwardt, A.H. (1980). *American English*, second edition, New York: Oxford University Press

Martinet, A. (1955). *Économie des changements phonétiques*, Berne: Francke Verlag

Meillet, A. (1937). *Introduction a l'étude comparative des langues indo-européennes*, eighth edition, Paris: Hachette

(1917). *Caractères généraux des langues germaniques*, Paris: Hachette.

Michael, I.L. (1970). *Grammatical Categories and the Tradition to 1800*, Cambridge: Cambridge University Press

Milroy, J. and Milroy, L. (1985). *Authority in Language*, London: Routledge and Kegan Paul

Mitchell, A.G. (1947). *The Pronunciation of English in Australia*, Sydney:

Angus and Robertson

Mitchell, B. (1987). *Old English Syntax*, 2 vols, reprinted with corrections, Oxford: Clarendon Press

Mitchell, B. and Robinson, F.C. (1986). *A Guide to Old English*, fourth edition, Oxford: Blackwell

Mossé, F. (1952). *A Handbook of Middle English*, translated by J.A. Walker, Baltimore: John Hopkins Press

Murison, D. (1977). *The Guid Scots Tongue*, Edinburgh: Blackwood

Mustanoja, T.F. (1960). *A Middle English Syntax* Part I, Helsinki: Mémoires de la Société Néophilologique de Helsinki

O'Connor, J.D., and Arnold, G.F. (1973). *Intonation of Colloquial English*, second edition, London: Longman

Odumuh, A.E. (1987). *Nigerian English (NigE)*, Zaria: Ahmadu Bello University Press

Onions, C.T. (1966). *The Oxford Dictionary of English Etymology*, Oxford: Clarendon Press

Orton, H., and Dieth, E. (1962–71). *Survey of English Dialects*, 5 vols., Leeds: Edward Arnold

Orton, H., Sanderson, S., and Widdowson, J. (1978). *The Linguistic Atlas of England*, London: Croom Helm

The Oxford English Dictionary (1989). Second edition, 20 vols., Oxford: Clarendon Press

Page, R.I. (1973). *An Introduction to English Runes*, London: Methuen
  (1987). *Runes*, London: British Museum

Potter, S. (1969). *Changing English*, London: Deutsch

Prokosch, E. (1939). *A Comparative Germanic Grammar*, Philadelphia: Linguistic Society of America, University of Pennsylvania

Quirk, R., Greenbaum, S., Leech, G., and Svartvik, J. (1972). *A Grammar of Contemporary English*, London: Longman
  (1985). *A Comprehensive Grammar of the English Language*, London: Longman

Quirk, R., and Wrenn, C.L. (1957). *An Old English Grammar*, second edition, London: Methuen

Reaney, P.H. (1960). *The Origin of English Place-Names*, London: Routledge and Kegan Paul

Renfrew, C. (1987). *Archaeology and Language, the Puzzle of Indo-European Origins*, London: Jonathan Cape
  (1989). 'Models of Change in Language and Archaeology' in *Transactions of the Philological Society*, Vol. 87 No. 2, 103–55

Roach, P. (1991). *English Phonetics and Phonology*, second edition, Cambridge: Cambridge University Press

Robertson, S. (1954). *The Development of Modern English*, second edition, revised by F.G. Cassidy, New York: Prentice-Hall

Romaine, S. (1988). *Pidgin and Creole Languages*, London: Longman

Ruhlen, M. (1991). *A Guide to the World's Languages, Vol. 1: Classification*, London: Edward Arnold

Samuels, M.L. (1972). *Linguistic Evolution*, Cambridge: Cambridge University Press

Sapir, E. (1921). *Language*, London: Oxford University Press

Saussure, F. de (1916). *Cours de linguistique générale*, Paris: Payot (1960). *Course in General Linguistics*, London: Owen

Savory, T.H. (1967). *The Language of Science*, revised edition, London: Deutsch

Sawyer, P.H. (1971). *The Age of the Vikings*, second edition, London: Arnold

(1982). *Kings and Vikings: Scandinavia and Europe AD 700–1100*, London: Methuen

Schrader, O. (1890). *Prehistoric Antiquities of the Aryan Peoples*, London: Griffin

Scragg, D.G. (1974). *A History of English Spelling*, Manchester: Manchester University Press

Serjeantson, M.S. (1935). *A History of Foreign Words in English*, London: Routledge and Kegan Paul

Sheard, J.A. (1954). *The Words We Use*, London: Deutsch

Smith, A.H. (1970). *The Place-Name Elements*, 2 vols., Cambridge: Cambridge University Press

Starnes, W.T., and Noyes, G.E. (1946). *The English Dictionary from Cawdrey to Johnson*, Chapel Hill: University of North Carolina Press

Stenton, F.M. (1971). *Anglo-Saxon England*, third edition, Oxford: Clarendon Press

Stern, G. (1964). *Meaning and Change of Meaning*, Göteborg: University of Gothenburg, 1931, and Indiana: Indiana University Press

Strang, B.M.H. (1970). *A History of English*, London: Methuen (1968). *Modern English Structure*, second edition, London: Edward Arnold

Stratmann, F.H., and Bradley, H. (1891). *A Middle-English Dictionary*, Oxford: Clarendon Press

Streitberg, W. (1943). *Urgermanische Grammatik*, Heidelberg: Carl Winter

Sturtevant, E.H. (1961). *Linguistic Change*, second edition, Chicago: University of Chicago Press

Szemerényi, O.J.L. (1985). 'Recent Developments in Indo-European Linguistics', in *Transactions of the Philological Society*, 1–71

Todd, L. (1990). *Pidgins and Creoles*, second edition, London: Routledge
(1984). *Modern Englishes*, Oxford: Blackwell
Toller, T.N. (1921). *An Anglo-Saxon Dictionary. Supplement*, Oxford:
Clarendon Press
Traugott, E.C. (1972). *A History of English Syntax*, New York: Holt,
Rinehart and Winston
Trudgill, P. (1983). *Sociolinguistics: an Introduction to Language and Society*,
revised edition, London: Penguin Books
Trudgill, P. (ed.), (1984). *Language in the British Isles*, Cambridge:
Cambridge University Press
Trudgill, P., and Hannah, J. (1982). *International English*, London: Edward
Arnold
Turner, G.W. (1966). *The English Language in Australia and New Zealand*,
London: Longmans, Green and Co
Twaddell, W.F. (1960). *The English Verb Auxiliaries*, Providence Rhode
Island: Brown University Press
Ullman, S. (1959). *The Principles of Semantics*, revised edition, Glasgow:
Jackson
Vallins, G.H. (1965). *Spelling*, revised by D.G. Scragg, London: Deutsch
Visser, F.T. (1963–73). *An Historical Syntax of the English Language*, 3
parts in 5 volumes, Leiden: E.J. Brill
Wakelin, M. (1972). *English Dialects. An Introduction*, London: Athlone
Press
Waldron (1967). *Sense and Sense Development*, London: Deutsch
Walshe, M.O'C. (1965). *Introduction to the Scandinavian Languages*,
London: Deutsch
Wardale, E.E. (1937). *An Introduction to Middle English*, London:
Routledge and Kegan Paul
Wells, J.C. (1982). *Accents of English*, 3 vols., Cambridge: Cambridge
University Press
Wright, J., and Wright, E.M. (1928). *An Elementary Middle English
Grammar*, second edition, London: Oxford University Press
(1925). *Old English Grammar*, third edition, London: Oxford University
Press
Wright, L.B. (1935). *Middle-Class Culture in Elizabethan England*, Chapel
Hill: University of North Carolina Press
Wyld, H.C. (1927). *A Short History of English*, third edition, London: John
Murray
(1936). *A History of Modern Colloquial English*, third edition, Oxford:
Blackwell

Index

Abbreviations: E 'English', EModE 'Early Modern English', LModE 'Later Modern English', lw 'loan-words', ME 'Middle English', OE 'Old English', PG 'Proto-Germanic', PIE 'Proto-Indo-European'.

For technical terms which occur frequently in the book, the Index usually gives just a single reference, to the place where the term is explained.

ablaut, 97–8, 115
Academy, 203
accent, in PG, 92, 96; in PIE 92
accents, *see* pronunciation
Achebe, Chinua, 241, 242
Addison, Joseph, 199–201
adjectives, 20–21, 159–60, 186; comparison of 205, 274; strong declension 89–90; weak declension 89–90
adverbs, 21–2
Ælfric, 122–4
affixation, 20, 120–1, 182–3, 217, 220–3, 254–5, 267
affricate consonants, 8
African languages, 3, 54–5, 237, 257
Afrikaans, 219, 236, 254
agglutinative languages, 28
Albanian, 64, 66, 71
alliterative poetry, 124–6, 150, 167
allophones, 17
allophonic transcription, 17
Altaic languages, 54
American English, 6, 9, 12, 205, 211, 220, 236, 237, **243–5**, 249, **250–1**, **252–5**, 271; dialects, 237; influence of, 48, 262–3, 272, 277
Amerindian languages, 55; lw from, 252–3
analogy, 49–50
analytic languages, 27–8
Anatolian, 66, 71
Angles, 102–4
Anglo-Frisian, 85
Anglo-Norman, 141, 148–9
Anglo-Saxons, 100–4, 134–5
animal communication, 1–2, 25, 26
approximants, 9
Arabic, 52, 53–4, 55, 181, 257, 263
Armenian, 66, 71
Arnold, Thomas, 233
Aryan, *see* Indo-Iranian Languages
assimilation, 43–4
Australian Aboriginal languages, lw from, 219, 253
Australian English, 211, 237, 245–6, 249, 250, 253, 254–5, 263, 270
auxiliaries, 21, 24, 90–1, 117–18, 161–3, 173, 188–91, 275–6

auxiliary 'do', 119, 171, 188–91, 199, 259
Avestan, *see* Old Iranian

back-formation, 224, 254–5, 266
Bacon, Francis, 175, 187–8
Baltic languages, 66, 71
Bantu languages, 54, 236
Barbour, John, 172
Basque, 55
Bede, 102
Bengali, 64
Bentley, Richard, 203
Bible, 33–9, 176; Geneva, 174; King James, 34–5, 123, 124, 187; New English, 33; Greek New Testament, 56; Old English, 36–8; Wycliffite, 35–6
Black English, 240
blending, 223
bound morphemes, 20
breaking, 106, 115–16
Breton, 32, 65–6
Britannic, 65–6
Brugmann, Karl, 93
Burgundian, 85
Burmese, 54
Burns, Robert, 174

Canadian English, 237, 243–4
Caribbean English, 237, 247, 249, 251
case, 37, 88–9, 159–60; of Objects in OE, 118
Catalan, 52
Celtic, 32, 65–6, 69, 71, 234–5; lw in Germanic, 98; lw in OE, 101
Central French, 141, 148–50
centring diphthongs, 12, 212–13
change, linguistic, 32–57; in E, 33–9; mechanisms of, 39–50
changes in pronunciation, 39–48; EModE, 191–8; LModE, 210–14; ME, 153–7; OE, 113–16, 154–5; recent, 269–74, 277
Chaucer, Geoffrey, 133, 142, 145, 149, 150, 159–60, 162, 165, 167–71, 174, 186; versification, 167–8
Childe, V.G., 78
Chinese, 20, 27, 28, 54, 239; lw from 219
Chomsky, Noam, 30–1

Christianity, 106–7; vocabulary of, 122
clause, 23, 24; main, 24; subordinate, 24
cognates, 53
Colet, John, 177
colonization, 235–7, 241–2, 253–4
combinative changes, 61
compounding, 121–2, 182–3, 220–2, 254–5, 267
conjunctions, 21
consonant clusters, 17–18; simplification of, 44, 196, 248–9
consonants, 8–10
continuous tenses, 162–3, 171, 207–9
convergent development, 55–7
conversion, 182–3, 220, 222–3
Coptic, 54
Cornish, 32, 65
creoles, 239–41, 257–61

Danelaw, 128–9, 132, 138, 140, 146
Danish, 61, 81, 84, 267, 273
declensions, 89–90
definite article, 22, 90, 160, 165, 186
demonstratives, 120, 159–60, 186
determiners, 21, 22, 187
dialect literature, 174
dialects, 50–1, 72–3, 187, 263–6; American, 237; ME, 136–40; OE, 56, 104–6
dictionaries, 203–4; OED, 225–6
diphthongs, 6–7, 12
Direct Object, 22
divergent development, 50–53
Dravidian languages, 54, 67, 219, 242
dual number 89, 90
Dunbar, William, 172
Dutch, 61, 81, 85–6; lw in E, 182, 219, 253–4

Early Modern English, 39, **175–98**; grammar, 183–8; lw, 177–82; phonology, 191–8; word-formation, 182–3
East Germanic, 83, 84–5
economy of effort, 43–9
Edward the Confessor, 104, 134
embedding, 24
English as a foreign language, 238–9
English as a second language, 238–9, 247–9, 251–2, 255–7, 261, 262

Eskimo languages, 27, 28, 55, 267
Estonian, 54

Falkland Islands, 237
Faroese, 84
fashion, 41–2
Finnish, 28, 54, 87
Finno-Ugrian, 54, 78
First Sound-Shifting, 93–5
flectional languages, 28
fracture, 106, 115–16
free morphemes, 20
French, 6, 9, 14, 17, 18, 29, 41, 48,
    52–3, 61–2, 140–50, 227, 273;
    lw from, 37, **145–50**, 153,
    167–8, 169–70, 172, 181, 196,
    216–17, 218, 219, 227, 230,
    253, 267; Germanic lw in, 87,
    147, 148
fricative consonants, 8
Friel, Brian, 235
Frisian, 81, 85–6
front mutation, 60–61, 113–15, 121,
    130, 158
functional load, 46–8
functions of language, 26–7
future tense, 161–2

Gaelic, 65–6, 172, 225, 234–5
Gamkrelidze, T.V., 79, 93
Gaulish, 65–6
gender, grammatical, 89, 90, 160
General American, 12, 237, 243–5; *see
    also* American English
gentry, English, 42, 205, 206–7, 230,
    233
German, 9, 14, 35, 38, 58–9, 60–1,
    76, 81, 86, 88–90, 113; lw in E,
    216–17, 254
Germani, 81–3
Germanic languages, 59–61, 67, 71,
    78, **82–99**
gesture, 2, 25–6
Gilbert, William, 175, 177
Gimbutas, Marija, 78–80
glides, *see* diphthongs, semivowels
glottal stop, 8, 277
Gower, John, 174
Gothic, 59–60, 62–3, 84–5, 91, 94–8,
    113, 227, 229
gradation, 97–8, 115

grammar, 20–4; EModE, 34–5, 183–8;
    LModE, 199–200, 207–10,
    250–2, 264–5, 274–6; ME, 36,
    157–71; OE, 37–8, 116–20; PG,
    87–92; PIE, 87–92
grammar books, 203–7
grammar schools, 142–3, 175, 204
grammatical gender, 89, 90, 160
grammatical words, 20–2
Great Vowel Shift, 191–3, 199, 201,
    213, 270
Greek, 32, 34, 56–7, 62–4, 65, 66, 69,
    71, 72, 75, 77, 92, 94–7, 159,
    203, 263; lw in E, 166, 181,
    216–17, 274–5; lw in Germanic,
    122
Grimm's Law, 93–5, 98
Gutnish, 84

Hamitic languages, 53–4, 67
haplology, 44
Harvey, William, 175
Hausa, 54–5, 238
Hawaiian, 14
Hebrew, 53
Hellenic languages *see* Greek
Henryson, Robert, 172, 173–4
Heptarchy, 104
hierarchy in language, 23–4
Higden, Ranulf, 142–3
High German, 85–6
Hindi, 64, 219, 238, 242, 256, 273
Hittite, 66–7, 69, 93
Hong Kong, 239
humanists, 175
Hume, David, 174
Hungarian, 54

Icelandic, 32–3, 84
Igbo, 54, 238
incorporating languages, 28
indefinite article, 166
India, 238–9, 242
Indian English, 248–9, 251–2, 255–6,
    261
Indian languages, 9, 18, 64–5, 67,
    71–2, 219, 237
Indonesia, 238, 239
Indo-European homeland, 67–80
Indo-European languages, 58–80

Indo-Iranian languages, 64–5, 69, 71–2
Industrial Revolution, 225, 234
inflectional languages, 28
inflections, 27, 87–92, 199, 274; EModE, 34, 183–6; LModE, 250, 274–5; ME, 36, 140, 157–60, 165, 171; OE, 37, 116–17
Inglis, 144
inkhorn terms, 179–80, 182, 204
Innuit languages, *see* Eskimo languages
internal loans, 224–5
intonation, 19–20, 220, 272
Iranian languages, 64–5, 71–2
Irish English, 6, 211, 221, 259
isoglosses, 72–3, 137–8
isolating languages, 28
Italian, 14, 32, 41, 52–3, 108; lw in E, 181, 219, 275
Italic languages, 55, 65, 69, 71
i-umlaut, *see* front mutation
Ivanov, V.V., 79, 93

Jamaica, 240–1, 258; *see also* Caribbean English
Japanese, 54, 67, 219, 257
John of Trevisa, 142–3
Johnson, Samuel, 204, 206
Jonson, Ben, 180
Jutes, 102–3

kentum languages, 71–2, 73–4
King Alfred, 104, 119, 121, 128, 138
King Cnut, 104, 130
King Henry III, 141
King Henry IV, 143
King James I, 174
King John, 141
King Stephen, 163
koinē, 56–7
Kurdish, 64
Kurgan culture, 78–80

Langland, William, 145
language families, 50–5
language types, 27–30
Lapp, 54
laryngeal consonants, 93
larynx, 3–4
Late Old English, 39
lateral consonants, 9

Later Modern English, **199–278**, grammar, 199–200, 207–10, 250–2, 264–5, 274–6; phonology, 210–14, 242–50, 269–74; spelling, 201–2; vocabulary, 215–27, 252–7, 266–7, 277
Latin, 22, 28, 29, 31, 32, 48, 51–3, 57, 62–4, 65, 66, 71, 72, 75, 76–7, 88–9, 94–6, 97, 140, 142, 159, 175–81, 203, 205, 214, 222, 227, 230, 253; lw in EModE, 177–81; lw in Germanic, 98–9, 178; lw in LModE, 216–17, 274–5; lw in ME, 166, 178; lw in OE, 122, 178
Lavoisier, Antoine, 218
Lever, Ralph, 178
lexical sets, 22–3
lexical words, 20–2
lexicon, lexis, *see* vocabulary
linguistic change, 32–57; in E, 33–9; mechanisms of, 39–50
linguistic universals, 30–1
Linnaeus, Carolus, 218
lip-rounding, 6
Lithuanian, 64, 66, 71, 94
loan-words, 37, 60, 62; in EModE, 177–82; in Finnish, 87; in French, 87, 147, 148; in LModE, 216, 219; in ME, 128–34, 145–9; in OE, 122; in PG, 98–9; in PIE, 74–5
London English, 144–5, 277
loss of word-final phonemes, 44, 92–3, 157, 165
loss of words, 226–7
Low German, 85–6
Lydgate, John, 174

Malay, 54, 219, 239, 257
Malayo-Polynesian languages, 54, 67
Maori, 253
Martinet, André, 47
meaning, changes of, 48–9, 169, 227–32, 267–9
metathesis, 45
Middle English, 39, **151–74**; dialects, 136–40; French lw in, 145–50, 166, 169–70; loss of final syllables, 93, 157, 165; loss of final /n/, 44, 93, 166–7; morphology, 157–60, 165, 171; phonology, 153–7;

Middle English (*cont'd*)
    spelling, 151–4, 164–5, 167–8,
    169; syntax, 161–3, 165, 171;
    verb-system, 161–3; vocabulary,
    145–50, 166, 169–70
Middle Scots, 138, 144, 172–4
Milton, John, 176, 181
Mitanni, 68
Modern English, 39
Mongol, 54
More, Sir Thomas, 176
morphemes, 20, 23
morphology, 28–9; EModE, 183–6;
    LModE, 199–200, 274–5; ME,
    157–60; OE, 116–18 PG, 87–92
Mulcaster, Richard, 179

nasal consonants, 9
nasal vowels, 4
nationalism, 141, 176, 178, 241–2
negation, 24, 119, 189–91, 205
New English, 39
Newton, Sir Isaac, 175
New Zealand English, 211, 237,
    245–6, 250, 253, 262
Ngugi wa Thiong'o, 242
Niger-Congo languages, 54, 67
Nigeria, 238, 239, 256, 260
Nigerian English, 247–9, 251, 256,
    261
non-rhotic accents, 211, 237, 243
Norman Conquest, 35–7, 62, 111,
    134–50, 151, 234
Norman French, 140, 148–9, 166, 222
North American English, 211, 243–5,
    249, 252–5, 262; *see also*
    American English, Canadian
    English
Northern English, 6, 12, 72–3, 162,
    196, 221, 225, 249–50
North Germanic, 83–4
Norwegian, 61, 81, 84, 267
noun phrase, 23–4; in OE, 120
noun plurals, 49–50, 157–9, 165, 171,
    185–6, 274–5
nouns, 20–1

Object, Direct, 22, 23–4
Okot p'Bitek, 242
Old English, 39, 48, 59–61, 62–4, 75,

    77, 86–92, 94–9, **100–26**;
    dialects, 56, 104–6; morphology,
    37, 116–18; noun plurals, 49–50;
    pronunciation, 107–13; script,
    107–13; sound changes, 113–16,
    154–5; syntax, 118–20;
    vocabulary, 120–2
Old French, 127, 145–50, 147–9
Old High German, 59–60, 86–7, 94, 96
Old Icelandic, 32–3, 84, 86
Old Iranian, 64–5, 71, 72
Old Irish, 66, 71, 96
Old Low Franconian, 86
Old Norse, 59–60, 84, 86, 94, 95, 96,
    113, 127, 130–4, 157
Old Saxon, 85–6, 95
Old Slavonic, 66, 71, 94
Ostrogothic, 85

paganism, 106
Pakistan, 256
palatalization, 110–11, 115
Papuan languages, 55
Pashto, 64
passive, 162–3, 207–8; in OE, 117–18;
    in PG, 91; in Celtic and Italic, 65
perfect tenses, 117–18, 162–3, 171,
    188, 207–9
Persian, 64
personal pronouns, 20–1, 123, 133,
    140, 165, 170, 186–7, 198
Peterborough Chronicle, 163–7, 170
phonemes, 15–18, 23
phonemic transcription, 17
phonetic symbols, 10–13
phonetic transcription, 17
phonology, 2–20, 46–8; EModE,
    191–8; LModE, 210–14, 242–50,
    269–74; ME, 153–7; OE, 107–16;
    PG, 92–8; PIE, 92–8
phrasal verbs, 209–10
phrase, 23
pidgins, 239–41, 257–61
place-names, 61, 101, 128–9
plosive consonants, 8
Polynesian languages, 54, 219
polysemy, 228–30
polysynthetic languages, 28
popular etymology, 252
Portuguese, 52–3, 254, 256, 260; lw
    in E, 181–2

postpositions, 29, 31
predicate, 23–4
prefixes, 20, 27; EModE, 182–3; LModE, 220–2, 267; OE, 120–2, 209
prepositional verbs, 209–10
preposition phrases, 24
prepositions, 21, 161, 272
prescriptiveness, 203–7, 264–5
Present-day English, 262–78
present tense, 208–9
principle of ease, 43–9
printing, 145, 177, 201
progressive tenses, 162–3, 207–9
pronouns, 20–1
pronunciation: American, 243–5; Australian, 211, 245–6, 249; Canadian, 243–4; Caribbean, 247, 249, 258; EModE, 191–8; evidence for, 39; Indian, 248–9; LModE, 210–14; ME, 153–7, 196–7; New Zealand, 211, 245–6; Nigerian, 247–9; OE, 107–13; Received, 6, 9, 10–12, 211, 232–3, 265–6; Scots, 12, 172, 211; South African, 211, 245–6
pronunciation, changes in *see* changes in pronunciation
Proto-Germanic, 81, 83, 84, 87–99; inflections, 87–92; phonology, 92–8; society, 81–3; vocabulary, 98–9
Proto-Indo-European, 67, 87–99; accent, 92; grammar, 87–92; phonology, 92–8; vocabulary, 74–80
Provençal, 52
public school English, 6, 232–3, 265–6, 277
Purism, 178
Pushtu, 64

questions, 24, 119, 189–91

Ramsay, Allan, 174
Received Pronunciation, 6, 9, 10–12, 211, 232–3, 265–6
redundancy, 45, 49, 258, 269
Reformation, the, 174, 175–6
regional speech in Britain, 12, 72–3, 134, 162, 187, 194, 195, 196, 211, 214, 221, 225, 227, 249–50, 263–6, 271, 277
regional variation, 14, 232–3, 263–6
regulation, 203–7
related languages, 51
relative clauses, 24
relative pronouns, 24, 124, 171, 187–8
Renfrew, Colin, 68, 78–9
rhotic accents, 211, 243
rhythm, 18–19
Robert of Gloucester, 135–6, 150
Robertson, William, 174
Romance languages, 52–3, 67
Romanian, 52–3
Romansh, 52
Rosten, Leo, 236
RP *see* Received Pronunciation
runes, 107
Russian, 22, 23, 41, 64, 66, 71, 76, 219

Sanskrit, 62–4, 71, 72, 75, 76–7, 94–5
Sardinian, 52
satem languages, 71–2, 73–4
Saxons, 60, 100, 102–4
Scandinavian languages, 84; lw from, 73, **128–34**, 139 140, 146, 166, 170, 173, 225; place-names from, 128–9
scientific vocabulary, 215–18, 266
scientific writing, 175, 214–15
Scots, 6, 12, 205, 211, 225; *see also* Middle Scots
script: ME, 35, 151–3; OE, 36, 107–13
semantic change, 48–9, 169, 227–32, 267–9
Semitic languages, 53–4, 55, 75, 79
semivowels, 8, 9–10
sentence, 23–4
sentence emphasis, 19, 189–91
Shakespeare, William, 131, 166–7, 180, 183–8, 205, 207–8, 223, 234
shortening, 49, 223, 254–5, 267
Singapore, 239, 248, 251
Sinhalese, 64
Sino-Tibetan languages, 54, 67
slang, 225
Slavonic languages, 66, 67, 71–2
Smith, Adam, 174

social variation, 14, 41–2, 232–3, 240–1, 264–6
sonorant consonants, 8–10
sound laws, 40
sound-system, 46–8; *see also* phonology
South African English, 211, 237, 245–6, 253, 254
Soyinka, Wole, 242
Spanish, 52–3, 254; lw in E, 181–2, 253, 267
speech organs, 2–6
speech–sounds, 2–10, 13–17
spelling pronunciations, 167–8, 196, 202
spellings, 156–7, 222; EModE, 35, 36, 153–4, 240; ME, 35–6, 151–3, 153–4, 164–5, 169; OE, 107–13; Scots, 172; standardization of, 201–2
Spenser, Edmund, 176, 185
Sprat, Thomas, 215
Standard English, 104–6, 134, 144–5, 175, 232–3, 241–2, 261, 265–6
standard languages, 56–7
stop consonants, 8
stress, 18–19, 220, 223, 248–50, 271–2; in French lw, 149; in PG, 92–3, 95–6, 98
stress-timing, 18–19, 247–8, 249
strong forms, 168, 197–8
strong verbs, 91–2, 97, 114, 165, 200
stylistic register, 226, 232, 264
Subject, 22, 23–4
subjunctive: in EModE, 185; in OE, 37, 116–17, 123; in PG, 90–1
subordinate clauses, 24
substratum, 41
suffixes, 20, 27; EModE, 182–3; LModE, 220–2, 267; OE, 120–2
superfamilies, 55
Swahili, 54, 257
Swedish, 22, 23, 44, 58–9, 60, 61, 76, 81, 84, 86, 90, 108, 219, 227, 267
syllables, 7–8, 9
syllable-timing, 18, 247–8, 249
symbols, 25–6
syntax, 22; EModE, 183, 188-91; LModE, 199, 200, 205–9, 275–6; ME, 161–3, 165, 171; OE, 118–20
synthetic languages, 27–8

system in language, 13–24

Tacitus, 81–3, 86, 99, 100, 126
Tamil, 54, 219, 239
Telegu, 54
Thai, 20, 54
Tibetan, 54
Tocharian, 66, 71, 73–4, 75, 76
tone languages, 19–20
tongue-position, 5
Turkish, 22, 27, 28, 29, 54
types of language, 27–30

universals of language, 30–31
Ural-Altaic languages, 54, 67
Urdu, 256

Vandal, 85
velar umlaut, 115–16
Ventris, Michael, 65, 69
verb phrase, 23–4
verbs, 20–1, 207—10; EModE, 184–5; impersonal, 171; ME, 140, 161–3; OE, 117–18; PG, 90–91; strong, 91–2, 97, 114, 165, 200; weak, 91–2, 114
Verner's Law, 95–6, 98, 114
Vesalius, Andreas, 217
Vietnamese, 28
Vikings, 86, 105, 125, 127–8, 134
Visigothic, 85
vocabulary, 22–3, 48–9; EModE, 34, 177–83; LModE, 215–27, 252–7, 266–7, 277; ME, 36, 145–50, 166, 169–70; OE, 37, 120–2; scientific, 215–18, 266
vocal cords, 3–4
vocal organs, 2–6
vocal sounds, 2–10, 13–18
voice, 4
vowel diagram, 5–6, 6–7
vowel lengthening, 154–7, 211–14, 244–5
vowels, 4; long, 6; nasal, 4; short, 6
vowel shortening, 194

Wallis, John, 204
weak forms, 168, 197–8
weak verbs, 91–2, 114, 165

Webster, Noah, 205
Welsh, 9, 22, 29, 32, 41, 64, 65, 66, 71, 75, 94
Welsh English, 41, 194, 196, 251
West African English, 241, 247–9, 251, 256, 261
West African languages, 237, 257
West Germanic, 83, 85–6, 114
West Indies, *see* Caribbean English
West Saxon, 104, 107–8, 132, 136, 151
William the Conqueror, 104, 135
Wilson, Thomas, 180
word-classes, 20–2
word-formation, 20; EModE, 182–3; LModE, 216–17, 220–4, 254–5; OE, 120–22

word-order, 22, 37–8, 274; EModE, 34–5, 188; ME, 161, 165, 171; OE, 37–8, 118–20
word-order typology, 29–30
words, 2, 20–3
word-structure, 17–18, 20
Wordsworth, William, 234

Xhosa, 236

Yoruba, 20, 54, 238, 259

Zimbabwe, 237
Zulu, 54, 236, 253